ADVANCE PRAISE FOR

Bad Girls

"*Bad Girls* rides the cutting edge of new feminist scholarship. This engaging and important volume brings the study of how women are represented in media into the twenty-first century. *Bad Girls* is an indispensable book for rhetorical scholars and others interested in women's issues."

Barry Brummett, University of Texas at Austin

"This courageous book—to write, to publish, to teach—gets down to cases about how embodied subjectivity works and works out in television and film of the postmodern era. Proving the discursive politics that disciplines genders and recuperates transgressors (and the bodies they inhabit), Owen, Stein, and Vande Berg offer accessible readings of texts and the contexts in which they arise. Their unblinking response to the paralyzing force of postfeminism, at once reasoned and impassioned, flings open doors to reconciliation for feminists of all ages and stripes."

Caren Deming, University of Arizona

Bad Girls

FRONTIERS IN POLITICAL COMMUNICATION

Lynda Lee Kaid and Bruce Gronbeck
General Editors

Vol. 6

PETER LANG
New York • Washington, D.C./Baltimore • Bern
Frankfurt am Main • Berlin • Brussels • Vienna • Oxford

A. Susan Owen, Sarah R. Stein,
and Leah R. Vande Berg

Bad Girls

Cultural Politics
and Media Representations
of Transgressive Women

PETER LANG
New York • Washington, D.C./Baltimore • Bern
Frankfurt am Main • Berlin • Brussels • Vienna • Oxford

Library of Congress Cataloging-in-Publication Data

Owen, A. Susan.
Bad girls: cultural politics and media representations of transgressive women /
A. Susan Owen, Sarah R. Stein, Leah R. Vande Berg.
p. cm. — (Frontiers in political communication; v. 6)
Includes bibliographical references and index.
1. Women—United States—Social conditions—21st century.
2. Women in popular culture—United States. 3. Women in motion pictures.
4. Women on television. 5. Feminism—United States. 6. Anti-feminism.
7. Feminist criticism. I. Stein, Sarah R. II. Vande Berg, Leah R. III. Title.
HQ1421.O94   305.420973'090511—dc22   2006100650
ISBN 978-0-8204-6150-2
ISSN 1525-9730

Bibliographic information published by **Die Deutsche Bibliothek**.
Die Deutsche Bibliothek lists this publication in the "Deutsche
Nationalbibliografie"; detailed bibliographic data is available
on the Internet at http://dnb.ddb.de/.

Cover design by Jody Dyer Jasinski

The paper in this book meets the guidelines for permanence and durability
of the Committee on Production Guidelines for Book Longevity
of the Council of Library Resources.

© 2007 Peter Lang Publishing, Inc., New York
29 Broadway, 18th floor, New York, NY 10006
www.peterlang.com

Printed in the United States of America

—for all mothers and daughters.

In Memoriam

Leah Vande Berg 1949–2004

There came a time when we all put on purple hats and hoped for the best. Leah's diagnosis of ovarian cancer did not offer much hope, but she herself possessed an indefatigable spirit whose energy we knew would keep her vital for as long as humanly possible. That spirit manifested itself throughout Leah's life as a powerful force, full of humor, wry insight, intellectual brilliance, and a fierce commitment to evoking from and providing to her students the best that liberal education can offer. Leah's presence lit up conference halls, classrooms, social gatherings, bar lounges, and everywhere in between. She had that rare and most wonderful of combined gifts: mental tenacity and fortitude of heart. Her death leaves the scholarly community of which she was such a devoted member, and the friends and family who loved her and were loved by her, bereft. Leah, you are sorely missed.

Table of Contents

Acknowledgments

We owe a great debt of thanks to Bruce Gronbeck for his incisive remarks that helped move these chapters to needed refinement. We also wish to acknowledge Bruce's positive influence on our intellectual development; he mentored all three of us through our doctoral studies at the University of Iowa. Bruce has always pushed us to think more deeply, write with greater clarity, and to stray with confidence from the beaten path of academic orthodoxy.

We are very grateful to Jody Jasinski for creating the artwork for the book cover. Jody donated her time and talent to this book out of friendship and engagement with the themes in the book. It has been a pleasure and a learning experience to witness the way she renders aesthetic the cultural and political substance of our work.

We thank the professionals at Peter Lang for their support and patience during the development of the book project. There were several delays in finishing the manuscript and we were always accorded additional time and support.

Sarah Stein thanks Vicki Gallagher for her readings of earlier work. She thanks Mary Kay Niehoff for valuable research assistance on women in technology. She also offers her thanks to a North Carolina State University Women and Gender Studies grant that gave her summer support to write. Beverly Lanzetta, Margaret Riordan, Pat Kilcullen, Margo Arrowsmith, Melissa Johnson, Laura Tateosian, and Sally Nyholt provided unflagging friendship, encouragement, and support, without which Sarah couldn't imagine getting this book completed. And finally, Sarah thanks her sister, Rebecca Morgan, and daughter, Lily Oster, who lamented with her when writing felt like slogging through molasses, and rejoiced with her when it flew.

A. Susan Owen thanks Peter C. Ehrenhaus for his generosity and endurance. Peter read and responded to the book manuscript during all phases of development. His feedback and suggestions were instrumental in shaping the book. Susan thanks her department chair, Jim Jasinski, for supporting the book project in a variety of ways. Susan also thanks Margaret Birmingham and Alissa R. Jolly for their invaluable assistance in the preparation of the manuscript. Finally, Susan thanks the University of Puget Sound for a John Lantz senior fellowship which gave her time to work on early phases of the book project.

Susan and Sarah offer their thanks to Heather Hundley for her assistance and support in putting the finishing touches on the book.

Susan and Sarah are grateful for the years of friendship and partnership they had with Leah Vande Berg. The book project was forged from their mutual experiences as mature women working in higher education.

Foreword

The Politics of Representation

Bruce E. Gronbeck

Students of (C)ultural (S)tudies dwell on the boundaries of lived experience and intellectualized critique. They shuttle back and forth between those domains with one eye on the social identities, structures, and interactions occurring within the spheres of collective life, with the other on abstracted notions of power, human understanding, ethics, and critical-cultural assessment. A checkpoint through which they regularly pass goes by the name "representation(s)." Before anything useful can be said about representation and its politicalization, we need to deal with the word itself.

As the noun moved over from French to English in the fifteenth century, *représentation* suggested a sense of presence or appearance, a bearing or air that created a sense of character for an observer.[1] It suggested, in other words, a relationship between some aspect or characteristic of a person and a meaningful image or signified that was left upon a perceiver's mind. The word was inherently relational, even interactive, in articulating what John Locke[2] some two hundred years later would posit as the essence of the problem of human understanding: the devices whereby processes of perception (taking in sense data) were related to processes of reflection (forming sense data into ideas). In all of this, Locke argued that human understanding depended upon a leap—of mind, of faith, of hope. Human beings had to operate as though they knew, at least fairly assumed, that the quality of sense data was high enough and the activities of reflection were disciplined enough to produce "human knowledge" reliable enough to permit people to live their lives without material catastrophe.

But also near the end of the fifteenth century a (now) more common understanding of "representation" appeared: representation understood as a material reproduction of some person or thing in a drawing, painting, sculpted statue, or bas relief. Here was the beginning of Stuart Hall's first notion of representation: "to describe or depict [something], to call it up in the mind by description or portrayal or imagination; to place a likeness of it before us in our mind or in the senses."[3] In this usage, a representation is that which *stands for or in the place of* something else—a photograph standing for the person whose picture has been snapped, a holographic image standing for the person electronically outlined on a photosensitive surface.

Such a representational process is less relational, then, than substitutive. It becomes the foundation of what many—I think erroneously—saw as Locke's understanding of the way in which words represented the external world: a representational theory of meaning, in which verbal language is more or less equivalent (because of its substitutive force) to its referents.[4] A "horse" is a horse, of course. But it is not, because a word such as "horse" not only denotes the animal but also connotes, at least since C.K. Ogden and I.A. Richards[5] drew their triangle of meaning, whatever other ideas or thoughts—evaluations, attitudes, experiences—come to mind when a particular person uses that word. Your "horse" and my "horse" may both reference horses, but (1) a race horse or a draught horse? (2) positively or negatively? (3) dappled or bay? (4) based on experiential memories or picture books? "Standing-for" is a problematic concept.

Furthermore, the material presentation of a something in the standing-for definition creates an additional difficulty: having to specify the status of the material presentational process. If I paint a nice picture of or carefully photograph a horse, someone's going to call it art. And when they do, another type of value will have been added to the representation: the aesthetic overlays an imaginative, a fantastical, set of associations with horseness that positions horses in non-material universes. The Black Stallion, Black Beauty, or the Four Horses of the Apocalypse now are stood in for by "horse," producing what Kant identified as an oscillation between a sign and its referent—the imaginative and material worlds.

A third sixteenth-century understanding of "representation" empowered the word discursively: "The action of placing a fact, etc., before another or others by means of discourse."[6] "To represent" became a speech act wherein some aspect of the world or human conduct is reproduced in words conveying, as the *OED* definition continues, "a particular view or impression of a matter in order to influence opinion or action." The standing-for, in this expanded conception, features an assemblage of signs that begin to add meanings to— Hall's second definition of "representation"[7]—that which is represented. Those additional meanings are present not only because of our experience with horses, but because when horses are placed within discursively reproduced and elaborated discourses, they become much more complex animals. Reading the novel *Seabiscuit* inscribes one's understanding of horses into the worlds of racing and news, the lives of jockeys and owners, and the aesthetics of ambition, struggle, triumph, and transcendent achievement. Here, representation becomes a constitutive process.[8]

Fourth and finally, the word took on what to most of us is a very common meaning in the wake of democratization: "The fact of representing or being represented in a legislative or deliberative assembly."[9] The precise force of such representation was ambiguous right from the eighteenth-century origin of this meaning. When Edmund Burke stood for the Bristol seat in Parliament, he carefully distinguished between representative as messenger and as husbander:

> Parliament is not a congress of ambassadors from different and hostile interests; which interests each must maintain, as an agent and advocate, against other agents and advocates; but parliament is a deliberative assembly of one nation, with one interest, that of the whole; where, not local purposes, not local prejudices, ought to guide, but the general good, resulting from the general reason of the whole.[10]

In this sense of "representative," therefore, we face a tension, even, between the representative as prototypical, the first among a many, and as typical, an average or usual specimen of a many. As with a horse show, is the Best in Breed superior to all others or a collection of characteristics typical of all others? Typification[11] becomes the ambiguated concept in social constructionism and its understanding of representativeness.

While the editors of the *OED* of course were clever enough to include definitions shading the idea of "representation" in other, mostly archaic, directions, these four conceptions of that word provide a web of significations capable of complicating ever so nicely the ideas of the politics of representation that undergird this book. Representation as impression, substitution, discourse, and typification/typical performance—these ideas play here not only singly, as in the *OED*'s enumeration of meanings, but they gambol with each other in a dance that makes the politics of representation a wonderfully complicated set of practices.

Individually, the perspectives provide us with varied political practices: (1) Representation as impression produces notions about politics as masking, as imagaic, as institutional sleights of hand that governors deploy before the governed. So, the "logic of representation" as understood by the likes of Greene[12] mystifies power relationships in hopes of supporting dominant over subordinate (oppositional) readings of discourse, creating "rhetorical fictions" that support powerful figures and institutions. (2) The politics of representation as (material) substitution is seen most crudely in the giant posters of dictators filling public places in totalitarian states or in the mass circulation of the images of American presidents in daily journalistic photo opportunities. A bit more subtly, substitutive vocabularies are employed to shield and insulate the powerful from critique: naming bombs and missiles of destruction "daisy cutters" (shrapnel-laden bombs) or "peacekeepers" (ICBMs capable of delivering ten independently targeted warheads from a single missile); authorizing the search of citizens without court order in the name of the "Patriot Act"; or removing agricultural price supports to operationalize the "Freedom to Farm"

Act.   Rhetorics of representational substitution fill our politics and other cultural practices in struggles over value orientation and motive attribution.

(3) Discursive practices can be deemed representational politics when they are recognizable generically (as a Petrarchan sonnet or a Senecan tragedy) or linguistically (as the language of economics or Foucauldian criticism), and formed around politicized topics—e.g., institutional authority and operations, interpersonal power relations, processes of legitimation and justice. Languages of socially legitimated practices—how one is supposed to carry out one's job in particular locations in a hierarchy—or of superior authority as it is related to subordinate responsibilities are typical political practices illustrating representation within extended discourses. These discourses can take argumentative shapes (reason-giving talks about why one should act in particular ways) or narrative forms (stories about successful and unsuccessful job performances). And, they can run at considerable length, as in inspirational biographies of Jane Addams or Malcolm X, and work powerfully, especially when they satisfy Kenneth Burke's[13] criteria for representative anecdotes: stories that are meant to essentialize, legitimate, and guide social thinking and personal action.

And (4), representations understood as typifications (of either kind) fill political processes. Presidents and generals give Medals of Honor and Purple Hearts to ordinary citizens and soldiers who demonstrated extraordinary—and exemplary—bravery and sacrifice, pointing the way to others in hopes that they, too, will serve the needs of state in times of crisis. Football coaches plaster stickers on helmets of team members who acted in game-winning ways in hopes of inspiring teammates. The western prototype is Everyman, protagonist in the late-medieval morality by the same name who becomes the heroic model for John Bunyan's *Pilgrim's Progress*, Edmund Spencer's *The Faerie Queene*, and Philip Roth's melancholic reinscription of this typification in his recent novel *Everyman*. All of these heroes struggle to exemplify personally and/or socially validated virtue and, in complementary fashion, to regulate or at least redefine their vice, with their performances celebrated (or condemned) in public memory. And all are essentially ambiguous: both one-of-a-kind extraordinary and yet derivative of characteristics we assume all citizens of that type will share and emulate.

What, then, of the politics of representation that will be identified, probed, interpreted, and judged by the authors of this book? The transgressive women who drive the plots of the television shows and films archived in this book engage in multiple politics of representation: Their perceived characters—their bearing, their airs—work ironically, as they transgress social and institutional norms of thought and behavior, and yet because of the cultural milieu within which their stories are told, their transgressions are potentially transformative, at least sometimes within those milieus. Thelma and Louise assuredly transgress the social and legal norms even of the American west, and yet their flight in a 1966 Thunderbird convertible into the Grand Canyon may not transform the fictive (diegetic) universe within which the plot is managed, but produces considerable public dialogue about women's constricted social status and options following the film's 1992 release. The seemingly transgressive extremity of their behavior and discursive practices marks them, wittingly or not, as cultural revolutionaries in a time when the feminist revolution was presumably dying down.

In a more complicated example, the representations of the women of *Sports Night* are politicized in multiple ways: they enter the masculinized world of sports talk, using it to put male subordinates and coworkers in their place; they're represented as desired and desiring females who yet employ logics of representation to command in marvelously powerful ways the broadcast operation at airtime; and, the pair of them are typifications of two forms of female/feminist leadership: the powerful, extraordinary bitch-commander and the more ordinary, competent-but-softer manager. Living in the organizational hierarchy between the African-American Executive Producer and the on-camera and behind-the-scenes staff, *Sport Night*'s producer and associate producer are transgressors in a male world who talk the talk and walk the walk of disruptive, reformative, feminized force. They become representations in both of Hall's senses of that word who, even in their occasional doubts, constitute a potentially utopian professional world.

Yet, the politics of representation would not be complete were not the negative consequences of transgression likewise visible. The at-times self-dissatisfaction of women written into *Sports Night* episodes does not have much bite. In the chapter treating the movie *The Net* and the Fox series *VR5*, however, self-dissatisfaction is driven much deeper as body and mind—as well as mind and soul?—are cloven; the virtual-mental and even virtual-moral worlds may feel liberating, yet the material body can weigh down the most agile of minds and the purest of souls. More than that, the disconnect between daughter and mother marking both vehicles illustrates a fracturing of cultural history, of the transhistorical, intergenerational contacts that can sustain women even in their most distressing situations. The heroines are represented as inhabiting discursively inscribed environments that destroy their selves and herstory, and so the representation of the two of them—one finally reconnected with maternal origin, the other not—comes with clear moral uptakes regarding transgression. Self doubt and anxiety about social-political impotency cast long shadows over the movie and TV series.

Self doubt and anxiety, however, pale before the representations of soldiering women in the chapter dealing with *G.I. Jane, Courage Under Fire,* and *The General's Daughter.* The first of these films leaves its protagonist in a study in ambivalence: strong but vulnerable, able to save but needing rescue by men, always subject to misogyny and sexual contamination by comrade and enemy alike. The second pair of movies gives us their women dead, having paid the ultimate price for their respective transgressions. Overall, we have represented women who've entered and departed from that ultimate domain of masculinity, the brotherhood in arms, no better off than they were before the cry for equal rights and equal opportunity echoed through the halls of Montezuma, the shores of Tripoli, and all of the other gathering places for citizen-warriors.

The emplotment of female transgression in popular stories has provided us triumphs and failures, glories and disgracements, in a series of television and film vehicles from the post-Vietnam period to the end of the twentieth century. As the author-editors of this volume, Susan Owen, Sarah Stein, and Leah Vande Berg smuggle in the notion of cultural transgression at another level as well: Their introduction and epilogue make clear that they themselves as cultural-critics are on a transhistorical mission in this book. The metaphor of the mothership not only enters some of the critical studies comprising the core of the work, where those women who've lost their ties to past gendered struggles are required to re-live them, but it marks the framing of the whole book as well. Owen, Stein, and Vande Berg are writing as soldiers from the period of the Second Wave reaching out to their sisters of the Third Wave. In the celluloid and magnetic-tape dramas of the 1970s, 1980s, and 1990s they explore the representative discourses that should provide today's sisters with concern, warning, and calls to action. They themselves become representations in the fourth sense: they speak the speeches of the Second Wave agitators who, though recontextualized in a seemingly postfeminist world, nonetheless know that the battles over gender in this country are never over, but only episodic.[14]

A victory there, a triumph there—these in no way elide the need for wariness, self-interest and self-defense, and even the inscription of here-and-now gender politics with some of the symbolic markers from the there-and-then. Transgression still comes with personal, social, economic, and, yes, political consequences that must be resisted, as always. The "open letter" that concludes this volume locates and amplifies the voice of public memory even in many, many of the films and television programs of today. The emphasis on "the rhetorical slipperiness of postfeminism, postmodern irony, and ideologically constructed pleasures" (see the epilogue of this book) makes this volume a punch in the gut—exactly what we should expect from Bad Girls.

Peter Lang's "Frontiers in Political Communication" series has a forward-looking trajectory. Yet, several of its volumes—including this one—demonstrate that often we must look backward to see the future. The ambiguities of "representation" make its politics a cacophony of voices speaking across time, place, domain, and interests.

Notes

1 *Oxford English Dictionary*, s.v. "representation."
2 John Locke, *An Essay Concerning Human Understanding*. Ed. P. H. Niddith (1695; rpt. New York: Oxford UP, 1979).
3 Stuart Hall, *Representation: Cultural Representations and Signifying Practices* (Thousand Oaks, CA: Sage, 1997) 16.
4 There certainly is general agreement that Locke posited *ideas* as representatives of the external world, based on a theory of resemblances between human perceptions of primary and secondary qualities of things and humans' ideas about those things. But, he also understood language ("signs" is the word he uses) as representative of ideas-about-the-world, not the world itself. The gap that he saw between signs and the signifieds external to mental operations is still central to semiotics.
5 C.K. Ogden and I.A. Richards, *The Meaning of Meaning: A Study of the Influence of Language Upon Thought and of the Science of Symbolism*. 8th ed. (1923; rpt. New York: Harcourt, Brace & World, 1946) 11.
6 *OED* "representation."
7 Hall 16.
8 *Representations and the Media*. Prod. Sut Jhally. Northampton, MA: Media Education Foundation, 1997.
9 *OED* "representation."
10 Edmund Burke, "Speech to the Electors of Bristol, 3 Nov. 1774." http://press-pubs.uchicago.edu/founders/documents/v1ch13s7.html.
11 Peter L. Berger and Thomas Luckmann, *The Social Construction of Reality: A Treatise on the Sociology of Knowledge* (Garden City, NY: Anchor Books, 1966) passim.
12 Ron W. Greene, "Another Materialist Rhetoric." *Critical Studies in Media Communication* 15.1 (1998) 21–41.
13 Kenneth Burke, *A Grammar of Motives* (1945; rpt. Berkeley, CA: U of California P, 1969).
14 Kevin R. Philips, Ed., *Framing Public Memory* (Tuscaloosa, AL: U of Alabama P, 2004).

Introduction

Why We Write

As we write this introduction, Samuel Alito is being confirmed as a Justice for the Supreme Court of the United States. In this same week, Betty Friedan and Coretta Scott King died. The temporal convergence of these events is coincidental, but the symbolic convergence is not.

Friedan and King were instrumental in leading two of the great human rights movements of the twentieth century. Friedan broke through the myth of female satisfaction with the subordinate and tightly circumscribed roles male power allotted women.[1] King worked with Martin Luther King, Jr. in shaping the civil rights struggle for Black Americans, and then led the movement after his death.[2] In contrast, Alito's documented record reveals a man intent on severely limiting the impact of those hard-fought human rights for women and minorities, while expanding the power of the executive branch of the federal government to undermine legislation that protects privacy, health, and the environment. His commitment to the Reagan-era tactic of calling for jurisprudence by "original intention" means the nation has just gained a Supreme Court justice whose aim is to interpret the Constitution as constructed by the Founding Fathers, when women and people of color had the legal status of chattel.

The three events mark the end of a period in American history that saw the rise of feminism and fall of the feminist movement as a productive force in the public sphere. The rhetoric of postfeminism drives the political and social complacency of women and men who were once attuned to the oppressiveness of discourses of gender. Alito's confirmation can be viewed as the inevitable outcome of the orchestrated right-wing political campaign to reverse both the personal autonomy gained by women over their bodies and the feminist agenda of human and environmental rights, aided by the fracturing of women's collective political power by capitalist culture and postfeminist rhetoric.

Bad Girls: Cultural Politics and Media Representations of Transgressive Women is a study of inter-generational tensions in portrayals of women and public institutions—in careers, governmental service, and interactions with technology. It examines representational practices of film and television stories beginning with post-Vietnam cinema and ending with postfeminisms and contemporary public disputes over women in the military. In each of our narrative studies, women occupy professions not previously portrayed in popular culture and subsequently rarely portrayed again. Using iconic texts and their contexts as its primary focus, the book offers a rhetorical and cultural history of the tensions between remembering and forgetting in representations of the American feminist movement between 1979 and 2005.

Our theoretical and conceptual frameworks proceed from the assumption that Gitlin so cogently summarized, that "commercial culture does not manufacture ideology; it relays and reproduces and processes and packages ideology that is constantly arising both from social elites and from active social groups and movements throughout the society (as well as within media organizations and practices)."[3] It argues that "the hegemony of liberal capitalist society is deeply and essentially conflicted…[and] at the center of liberal capitalist ideology there is a tension between the affirmation of patriarchal authority—currently enshrined in the national security state—and the affirmation of individual worth and self-determination."[4]

In investigating the disciplining of feminist politics through the world of fantasy media, we examine cinematic and television narratives in light of their intersections with cultural history, a history read not as a chronicle but rather as a series of decisive moments. Our overarching premise is that particular historical junctures provide an opportunity for imaginings of different femininities and alternative gendered constructions, imaginings that support both liberatory transformations and re-inscriptions of gendered stereotypes crucial to the maintenance of masculinist hegemony. The widely disseminated popular belief that representational practices and gender politics are no longer significant factors in the ongoing struggle for equality in our country makes this study especially timely.[5] Popular media present those battles as having been won, and gender no longer a constraint in a woman's life, liberty, and pursuit of happiness.[6] In the face of rhetorical appeals for collective amnesia, serving as thinly veiled rationalizations for dismantling legislative and judicial protections for human rights that prove costly and inconvenient for capitalist economies, we offer this book as a critical resistance, as counter-memory.

I Exist, Therefore I Transgress

Our use of "transgressive" to describe the characterizations of women we study dispenses with the traditional definitions of sinful or criminal. We define transgression for women with a more radical inflection; that is, as ontological transgression, where *existence itself* constitutes a transgression against nature or divinity or man himself.

Our exploration of ontological transgression begins by considering the history of cultural conditions in which notions of female transgression were invented and codified. Eve serves as the primordial Christian sign for the culturally inscribed transgressiveness of women. Race slavery in the North American colonies exemplifies the alleged immutable transgressiveness of blackness. In both of these cases, the body itself is read as unforgivably and undeniably different and therefore subject to varying degrees of discipline, surveillance, and exploitation by white, Western men. Biology and God are crafted rhetorically so as to decree an irrefutable social hierarchy. To be born female or black (or both) meant learning that the entitlements of membership in a free society are only selectively available. In that sense, embodied existence as "other" is itself transgressive: I exist, therefore I transgress.

Female and black bodies could, of course, work to redeem themselves to whatever extent permissible. Obedience, silence, invisibility, and uncompensated labor were the historically prescribed paths to white male tolerance and salvation. The fracturing of consciousness that arises from this embodiment leads women to hide in and merge with hegemonic discourses of gender by adopting feminine drag, or living as outliers, relegated to the margins of political and economic channels of change. Black female bodies have borne the burden of two intersecting historical trajectories of oppression, positioning black women and girls ontologically as double-transgressors.

We also explore transgression as a cultural practice. Here, we want to identify three overlapping rhetorical strategies important to the work we do in this book. First, we speak of transgression as willful acts of remembering oppression. Permit us to elaborate. Ontological transgressors necessarily live deeply fractured lives. W.E.B. DuBois described the black experience of Jim Crow apartheid as producing "double consciousness." Second Wave feminists famously said of the women's liberation movement that "the enemy has outposts in our heads."[7] Shirley Chisholm remarked in her pro-ERA speech on May 21, 1969, that though she was "no stranger to race prejudice," she had been "far oftener discriminated against because I am a woman than because I am black." Each of these examples of fractured lives illustrates lived experience with life-long subjugation. In these utterances we see that the *memory* of oppression is vivid, palpable, and hurtful. In a Foucauldian sense, the fracturing is at once painful *and* productive, capable of causing debilitating psychic pain and yet producing willful memory of an oppressive past. We believe that this productive moment of memory is vitally important to the maintenance of a free society and, therefore, vital to feminist politics and the struggle for civil rights.

The second rhetorical strategy of transgression concerns the inheritors of liberation. What happens to the productive (and painful) moment of remembering the oppressive past when generations pass the torch? What happens to memory and memory construction when one generation has little or no lived experience with oppressive conditions of the past? The consequences of mediated constructions of collective amnesia can be seen in mass mediated stories about historical realities that often function as highly compressed metonymies. For example, abortion stories are presented as if feminist history is synonymous with abortion. Labor practices, childcare, domestic violence, and political representation are erased as foundational concerns of feminism. Worse yet, "abortion rights" become the catalyst for political splintering among and between communities of women. Popular media representations of feminist politics fail to construct hardships from the past, thus the possibilities for solidarity in the present and future are lost before they can be imagined. Moreover, we believe that disconnection with the material realities of history supports and is in the service of capitalism. The goals of human rights movements necessarily run contrary to the status quo of profit earning. Fair wages, safe working conditions, equal opportunities, health care, and childcare run contrary to established economic interests, entrenched labor practices, and the entitlements of wealth.

The third rhetorical strategy of transgressive representation we observe is the staging of exploitative symbolic acts as ironic, and, therefore, liberatory texts. In this sense, "transgression" itself has become a site of struggle, appropriated by a tone of smirking irony (discussed in greater detail below) that permeates popular media. Paris Hilton in a black leather bikini washing a car in a burger ad's hollow imitation of *Cool Hand Luke*, and rap lyrics featuring "ho," "bitch," and "nigga," serve as recent examples. Such media artifacts capitalize on the notion that oppressive signifiers of the past have been emptied out by the obliteration of inequitable racial and gendered social barriers. That the Paris Hilton ad is "banned"—though readily available for viewing via the Internet and thus seen by far more than on conventional television—and that the rap songs engender parental restrictions serves to configure these media products as revolutionary for the young. That they are regressive co-optations serving to re-inscribe demeaning sexualized and racialized objectifications useful to the interests of patriarchal rule is overlooked. We view such representational practices as acts of willful ignorance.

Cultural Politics and Media Representations

At the beginning of the twentieth century, all a woman had to do to be transgressive was to try to move into the public sphere. In many ways, that is still all a woman has to do. Women who attempt to enter contemporary political life find themselves subject to ideological wars framing debates such as the impact on the health of the family in homes with working mothers. Sullivan and Turner's analysis of 1993 media coverage of attorney Zoe Baird's confirmation hearings exemplifies how unchanging are the reactions to women's bids for full expression of their potential:

> When Baird's critics relied on the boundary between private and public life to destroy her nomination for Attorney General, she became the symbolic figure who atoned for the sins of women who not only juggle private and public roles, but who also dare to suggest that those roles, and the gender-differentiated notions of caring which underlie them, are not separate.[8]

The public sphere of popular fiction is another place where real political work is done. Producing meaning—by media creators and media audiences—is not, as Stuart Hall reminds us, a politically neutral activity.[9] Take, for example, the racial border crossings in 1965 when the first ever African American actor (Bill Cosby) co-starred in a prime time dramatic series (*I Spy*), and in 1966 when the first interracial kiss occurred (on the bridge of *Star Trek's* Enterprise)—nationwide fictional acts that took the American political and social life "where no one has gone before." *M*A*S*H* and *China Beach* helped recuperate the antihero warrior, *The Mary Tyler Moore Show, Designing Women,* and *Murphy Brown* helped define what being a liberated woman meant in the 1970s, 1980s, and 1990s. Ellen Degeneres played a closeted lesbian who left that closet on a highly rated episode of her eponymous sitcom in 1997, and *Brokeback Mountain* has begun the twenty-first century's mediated negotiations of iconic masculinity and homosexuality. The *Murphy Brown* storylines of the 1990s were particularly effective at blurring the borders of fictional characters and non-fictional social roles. Murphy's pregnancy as an unrepentantly unmarried, single woman brought then Vice President Dan Quayle's worry about the effect her fictional pregnancy would have on the body politic.[10] Quayle's link of a popular television series with the poverty of values responsible for such social anarchy as the then-recent LA riots provides a powerful illustration of the intersection of politics and media.

Historically, the media have played a vitally important political role in disciplining feminist politics. For example, from its inception in 1883 *The Ladies' Home Journal*—known as the "monthly Bible of the American home"—was a significant voice in defining women's political, social, and personal roles. The magazine, which by 1904 had a monthly circulation of one million, acknowledged in its editorial content, fiction, and advertising "women's inarticulate longings for personal autonomy, economic independence, intimacy, sensuality, self-work and social recognition." However, for 40 years—through January 1920—the *Journal's* editorial philosophy persuasively argued that these desires could best be met not by efforts to gain political suffrage but by recognizing that women were "essentially domestic creatures" who could best serve their country not by involvement in the public sphere or by producing goods, but rather by consuming goods and "influencing their husbands and sons."[11]

In the 1940s, with World War II as a catalyst, dramatic changes occurred in the economic outlook for women: "The eruption of hostilities generated an unprecedented demand for new workers, and, in response.... Instead of frowning on women who worked, government and the mass media embarked on an all-out effort to encourage them to enter the labor force."[12] After the war ended, the soldiers returned home to college educations on the GI bill, though women received no comparable reward for their parts in the war effort. As they forced women out of their higher paying wartime jobs in staggering numbers,[13] "the career woman, along with other types of independent women and working women, virtually disappeared from the screen."[14] As Marjorie Rosen explained, "Movies heretofore stressing female strength, now began to distort it.... The two innovations, or rather, important changes in films of the fifties were, paradoxically, contradictory.... We saw on the screen two types of women: the sex symbols and the clean wholesome Mrs. Americas. In between was, with rare exceptions, a great big void."[15]

These examples illustrate what John Hartley has termed "the politics of pictures":

> Neither the public domain nor the public itself can be found in contemporary states; they've literally disappeared. However, both of them are very familiar figures, figures of speech, in which everyone spends quite a bit of time. So while they don't exist as spaces and assemblies, the public realm and the public are still to be found, large as life, in media.... the popular media of the modern period are the public domain, the place where and the means by which the public is created and has its being.... [Thus], it becomes necessary to look at these mediations to discover the state of the contemporary political domain. This entails a new kind of political analysis—not the study of government, nor of constitutional and electoral arrangements, nor of the way a sovereign power executes its will. Instead, it is necessary to ask what institutions and what discourses are engaged in making the mediated representations of the public domain, what the resulting picture of the public looks like, and who speaks for—and to—the public so created.[16]

Admittedly, studies of the politics of media representations are not traditional political science studies, but they are studies of contemporary politics.[17] Indeed, as Hartley has noted, mediated representations "are much more socially pervasive, commonplace components of everyday life than straightforward politics is, or ever has been, for most people. Their public, political aspects are real, and engagement with them is personal and practical...They are...the form in which democracy is diffused and disciplined."[18]

Cultural Ambivalence

So, where does that leave us today? "Cultural ambivalence" is the term we at least provisionally define as a state in which a society as a collectivity faces enduring oppositions that cannot be resolved, cannot be cognitively and emotionally eliminated except through amnesia or suppression, and continue to make demands upon individuals' thoughts and behavior.

In such a time and in many situations, the inevitability and even desirability of difference runs headlong into the impelling urge to unity and even the desirability of sameness. The blindness of justice demands a level of regularity and uniformity that can seem to trample the freedom to be unique. Kenneth Burke's relentless search for a formula to explain the simultaneity of social division and cooperation is with us yet today.[19] *E pluribus unum* has ever been America's enduring problematic: how can we conceive of and then operationalize a oneness out of the many without erring in the direction of either the repressiveness of oneness or the fragmentation and disconnectedness of the many? We see in these struggles over the simultaneous claims of unity versus the demands of individuation the cultural ambivalence of discourses of the economy, politics, sociality, epistemology, and subjectivity.[20]

More intriguingly, then, what are the particular areas of cultural ambivalence in gender relations? That is, what are the arenas of gendered cultural ambivalence wherein those relations are symbolized, performed, and complicated? In the texts we analyze, three dimensions of the politics of difference are critical. First, separate spheres continue to situationally and socially define areas of work and life, at the same time that stories of transgression imagine the blurring and invasion of those spheres. We will see those tensions in the analyses of Chapters Two and Four on fictional women hackers of *The Net* and *VR5*, and real-life women in information economy occupations. Second, material differences are manifest in the ongoing confusion of the construction of gender differences with sexual differences, yet hierarchies established by conventional gendered discourses are challenged and even reversed, redeploying power in the process; such strategies will be evident in Chapter One's analysis of the post-Vietnam narratives, such as *Alien* and *Terminator II*, and Chapter Three's discussion of *Ally McBeal* and *Sex and the City*. Third, symbolic segregation foregrounds differences in male and female language and visuality—argument vs. story-telling, technotalk vs. cultural-talk, male vs. female gaze—in tension with transgressions in the form of argumentative women who appropriate male idioms. Chapter Five's women producers in *Sports Night* and female protagonists in other narratives both reverse the norms of the male gaze (*Sex and the City*) and confront them (*G.I. Jane* in Chapter Six's discussion of women in combat).

In the gendered stories of our times, then, there is no drive to resolution. Sex and gender are binary, as the separate spheres, material differences, and symbolic segregation arenas suggest, yet the binary is both asserted and denied as the stories end in ambivalence: neither hegemony nor resistance prevails. These imaginings, therefore, do not resolve conflicts over gendered relations of power but rather are left open-ended.

For many feminists, at least potentially, these stories are troublesome. They do not address gender relations in such a way that women either "win" or not. The dialectic of twentieth-century feminism that uses cultural critique to free and empower women in what too often appears to be a zero-sum game is not affirmed in these late-twentieth century popular narratives. They do not use dialectical weapons to destroy the gender binary, for it does not die.

Historical Disconnect, Postfeminism, and Smirking Irony

People have asked why we write this book now, expressing surprise that analyses of women's fictional roles could yield anything new to the understanding of current society and of power and control over women's place in it. For these people, South Dakota's resolution to ban *all* abortions for all women and regardless of rape or incest, signed by their governor within weeks of Alito's assignment to the Supreme Court, came as a shock. Not for us. In the face of the cultural ambivalence that forwards alternative discursive possibilities and then too often allows them to be re-bounded by hegemonic inscriptions, we embrace critical memory of the embodied, embattled history of women. We do so to re-ignite change as the foundational objective of the feminist agenda.

A profound disconnect from the historical experience and grating realities of women's lives throughout the globe is descriptive of both the current state of public awareness and an outcome of several discursive strategies. The most obvious of these is readily apparent throughout mass media, in journalism, advertising, and entertainment products. Labeled "free market feminism"[21] or "commodity feminism,"[22] it employs kick-butt portrayals of womanhood in the remake of *Charlie's Angels* (2000) and similar images to reduce feminism to fashion and lifestyle choices. As Manzano states in her critique of the masculinized manipulations of people and sexuality in *Charlie's Angels*,

> It's not just a coincidence that the marketable, media-friendly, Third Wave feminist emphasis on individual action dovetails nicely with our capitalist economy's prescription for success. We live and work in an economy that rewards greed. If you want to succeed in this economy, you have to be selfish. You benefit only at the expense of others. If you can't or won't compete, you won't survive.[23]

The mass-mediated imaginary conflates feminism with emblematic events that never took place, such as bra burning, or strident attitudes generalized from specific contexts and voices.[24] In political arenas, feminism's broad concern with human rights, reproductive health, and ecological welfare is ignored, enabling anti-abortion forces to cast feminism as merely another advocacy group for pro-abortion legislation.

One of the most potent rhetorical forces undermining the feminist agenda surfaces in what is popularly termed postfeminism. To understand how this dimension of historical disconnect came into play requires a look at Second Wave feminism's failings as well as the efficacy of capitalistic culture.

The primary failures of 1970s feminism were those that involved inclusions and distinctions among women, and that worked to *support* difference as well as defend against it. How was this manifest? The Second Wave feminist vanguard was primarily white and middle-class; their belief in the potential of collective sisterhood overrode their recognition of racial and class differences among women. The failure to reach out to women of color and a range of social classes, and to include the particularities of their experience and needs in framing feminist values and political strategies rendered these differences divisive.[25] Further, the challenge of negotiating the tension between negating and embracing difference proved too great. Gendered difference throughout history has been invoked to buttress hierarchical frameworks, and hierarchies always put masculinity on top. To be supportive of the value and importance of differences between men and women seemed to acquiesce to millennia of female subjugation; equality *for* women came to be represented as equality *of* women and men.

Acknowledging the binarisms of essentialism vs. non-essentialism, masculinity vs. femininity, and other polarizations formative of U.S. culture was a necessary stage in the conversations that erupted as Second Wave feminism took shape. Entrenching those binarisms, however, fractured the feminist front and hindered our ability to teach our daughters and students about a range of feminisms. It further impoverished the imaginative range of possibilities that liberated womanhood could entertain. The subsequent generations of young women want to experience and express sexuality without guilt imposed by patriarchal values *or* by feminist anxiety about sexual objectification, to freely explore multiple modes of engaging the social world. The freedom to seek and express spiritual authority, captive for millennia in male-controlled religious structures, is another site of human exploration that Second Wavers rejected for its historical record of oppression. That the Second Wavers could not easily embrace a range of feminisms and ways of engaging with the world because of the hierarchical subtext to all discussion of difference between men and women is understandable; the remarks made by the recently deposed president of Harvard about the innate inferiority of women's capacity to do science is evidence of how powerfully hierarchal definitions of difference still hold force.

But the failure to support more fluid explorations of identity is one aspect of the current generation of young women's propensity to define their political yearnings *against*, rather than *with*, feminism: "I'm not a feminist, but…." In embracing a postmodern read to the texts we study, to admit to fluidity and the possibility of a range of readings, we seek to reverse some of the exclusionary impulses of the past.

A crucial inter-generational difference lies in the embodied experience of Second Wave feminists and today's young women. The Mothership is aging—and the young want a sexier ship. To adopt a technological metaphor, our lived experience does not interface with theirs. Young women have different preoccupations than we had in the sense that the current generation's bodies do not carry as memory what our bodies do. Mothership bodies carry memories that arouse and maintain anxiety—memories of a time before abortion rights and before liberties by Second Wave feminism that are now taken for granted. Such memories are a fabric woven of material realities that are not forgotten—and lead us to say, *Be careful not to forget or lose sight of history. Failure to remember past oppression carries very real dangers.*

We view feminism as transgressive in that it politicizes memory and knowledge construction. The "undoing" of feminism, as Angela McRobbie terms it, appropriates transgression in the service of willful amnesia and playful ignorance.[26] Our earlier reading of Paris Hilton's burger ad aligns with McRobbie's view of postfeminism in popular media culture: First, invoke the specter of feminism through public acts of sexism (feminist objection is good for publicity). Second, pre-empt objection by framing the sexism as irony, as a joke. Third, declare feminism obsolete (unnecessary) or harmful (oppressive). The cultural space of postfeminism offers young female and male consumers, "educated in irony and visually literate,"[27] the option of forgetting a history of oppression and jettisoning the political burdens of feminism as a political movement. For male viewers, "tradition is restored."[28] For female consumers, "what is proposed is a movement beyond feminism, to a more comfortable zone where women are now free to choose," as *consumers*, but not necessarily as political agents.[29]

Postfeminism and its companion "power feminism" are on a continuum of what Carolyn Heilbron describes as the retreat from feminism begun in the late 1970s.[30] Postfeminist rhetoric claims that the war is over and won—essential liberties gained for women by Second Wave feminism give current generation women the power, gleefully, to reclaim demystified femininity. With that reclamation work comes the ability to portray "sexiness" again—but now used to bolster individuation and uphold "choice" as measured by consumer power. Third Wave feminists' inclusive agenda of assuring that women of all races, classes, and sexual orientations, both locally and globally, are the subjects of economic and political struggle can be abandoned and with it a sense of the need for collective empowerment. The Founding Fathers' power model of capitalist culture can be re-embraced, while the lives of the founding mothers of past feminist movements can be thankfully rejected and forgotten, lest the taint of single motherhood, economic impoverishment, and political discontent rub off.

Power feminism carries this rejection a step further. Popular writers such as Katie Roiphe[31] and Naomi Wolf[32] gained significant media attention for extolling the notion that Second Wave feminism promoted models of victimization and passivity for women, characterized as a state of asking for special privileges. Eradicating any means of response to real assaults on women's bodies, minds, and spirits, power feminism eschews any hint of aggressive resistance to structural oppression in order to change institutions and people, in favor of a forward-looking adjustment to hegemonic realities. Its invitation reads, *Don't focus on what has happened* to *me, but what can happen* for *me now.*[33]

What happens to history in power feminism? What is its place? White patriarchy's claim that "history is progress" becomes the answer: *Why look back when you can look ahead?* The willful forgetting implicitly advocated by postfeminism allows contemporary conditions of women's lives to remain politically disconnected from collective action and from their historical precedents. Young women continue to suffer crippling eating disorders encouraged by media-reinforced self-loathing of their bodies; this in turn translates into loss of self-confidence and an inability to envision horizons beyond catching an upwardly mobile husband.[34] In industries such as academia, professional publications feature columns on the struggles of women professors to "juggle" domestic labor and timelines necessitated by childbearing and child-raising with tenure-path career demands put in place by men for male lifestyles.[35] These columnists often write pseudonymously out of fear of reprisals by department chairs and deans.[36] A 2006 news report cites the decline in the number of women entering the workplace.[37] The participation rates in the prime workforce age group of eighteen to fifty-four in 2006 has declined to 75 percent from its peak of 77 percent in 2000, far below the 90 percent participation rate of men. Despite popular press and religious right attempts to portray working mothers' lives as failing to fulfill them or their children's needs, the report shows that in 2003 women spent more time on childcare than did mothers in 1975 when far fewer mothers worked outside the home. They also spent more time on the job, taking the extra hours out of their sleep time. The basis for fewer women entering the workforce is the failure of adequate childcare and of men sharing domestic labor. Women reported wishing to work or return to jobs but being unable to stretch their hours further. A thirty-seven-year-old former computer industry development executive quoted in the report states, "Most of us thought we would work and have kids, at least that was what we were brought up thinking we would do—no problem. But really we were kind of duped."[38] We beg to differ. We were not duped, we were *robbed*.

The rhetoric of postfeminism continues to ignore that women still bear responsibility for the domestic sphere: as one observer states, "the glass ceiling begins at home."[39] Recent news items extol the achievement gap created by women leading men in acquiring and excelling in college,[40] but fail to connect the dots to the failure of that achievement to change the economic picture for those same women, as they continue to earn seventy-eight percent of their male counterparts' wages for equal labor,[41] and occupy only thirty-one percent of the highest earning jobs.[42] Women are often channeled into lower-paying jobs because of ongoing cultural biases against their capabilities and fears of their lesser commitment to the job in light of present or future caretaking responsibilities for children or the elderly.[43] This remains the economic Catch-22: for all the talk of liberated men who would never consider their female mates to be less than their equal, once children enter the picture, women continue to carry the brunt of household responsibilities. Whether they are working outside of the home or have sufficient income to elect to stay at home during child-raising years, the weight of caretaking falls on them, and employers continue to justify discriminatory hiring practices based on evidence of women employees' lack of single-minded focus on the job. Those mothers who do stay at home or work part-time often elect to do so because their pay scale is considerably less than their husbands and quality childcare is prohibitively expensive. For middle- and upper-class women with elite educations, the impact this interval has on their future earning power and job potential can be shockingly negative.[44]

One of the rhetorical strategies by which the ongoing economic subjugation of women is obscured can be observed in the ironic tone of contemporary media representations, a tone that serves the ahistoricism of postfeminism. Embedded in the Teflon slipperiness of irony that undermines feminist political critique—*lighten up, can't you take a joke, we can have it all*—these representations produce discursive slippages into which entrenched masculine hegemony reinstates itself unopposed.

The ironic take on all things cultural is presented as a prophylactic and even a political action against oppressive politics, reactionary religion, and the structural inequities of free-market capitalism on a global scale, yet it primarily targets the young and undermines critical awareness of the seduction of rampant consumerism. The smirk manifests the smarminess of this ironic stance. Smirking irony rationalizes "ambivalent pleasures" such as the sexism, racism, and hetero-normative lyrics of rap, or the *Vanity Fair* cover featuring nude Hollywood actresses ranked for their "sizzle" factor by a male editor-in-chief.[45]

The province of privilege, of vacuity, and of disconnect, smirking irony is aggressively ahistorical. As philosopher Jedediah Purdy states, "From comedians to commercials, viewers are invited to join TV programmers in celebrating just how much more clever they are than TV programmers. Everyone is in on the joke, which is not at anybody's expense, but at the expense of the very idea that anyone would take the whole thing seriously...Irony does not stand alone. It is a way of passing judgment—or placing bets—on what kinds of hope the world will support...[a way one] resists disappointment by refusing to identify strongly with any project, relationship, or aspiration."[46]

The agency gained for productive transgression by the past generation's feminists has now been appropriated by the willful forgetting and disabling irony of postfeminism. The concept of gender as performance[47] contributes to the undermining of feminist political critique. The postfeminist view of discursive slippage as trendy refuses to accept the burden of history that shows that same slippage resulting in male re-domination of arenas once liberated by feminist politics.

The disconnect from historical memory functions as a clear and necessary strategy of patriarchy and capitalism. We're asked to participate in weaving together a tapestry of amnesia: *we'll all just play, and we'll all be in on the joke.* In parallel fashion, gender construction is now immaterial, playful, and therefore no longer oppressive.

But we *remember*. Memory separates us from the current generation; it represents our refusal to subjugate history to capitalist demands. We carry in our bodies the memory of living in a pre-*Roe v. Wade* world, where a cinematic narrative such as *Splendor in the Grass* could be told straight-faced—and *received*—as a cautionary tale about female lives in ruin from premarital sex. We remember a time when women had little control of their bodies and therefore little control of their destinies. We remember the oppressive social conditions that birthed the human rights movement for economic, social, and political opportunities for all women. More to the point, we see that some of those social conditions remain impervious to progressive change. Women still do not represent the body politic in numbers equal to men. Women still earn less than their male peers. Reproductive freedoms for women remain precarious and under siege from the religious right and conservative political forces. And so we write this book as a political invitation to our sisters and brotherly advocates to remember why we re-engaged this fight forty years ago and why it remains a vitally important cause.

Structure of the Book

The popular media texts we examine articulate at transitional junctures underlying concerns over social, political and economic issues of control over borders and bodies. We present case studies that are stories of struggle and of slippage. We look at particular historical moments when the possibilities for feminist consciousness are present, only to be hijacked by popular representations before they could be imagined another way. At the same time, we acknowledge that once the genie is let out of bottle, it's really hard to stuff her back in. Transgressive women, "bad girls," are very popular in contemporary popular narratives. But whose interests do they serve? We pose that question in the first chapter of the book.

At the historic moment of the Vietnam War when heroic masculinity was struggling, it was no longer so hard to imagine different femininities. When feminism burst on the popular scene, the possibilities were great—yet the paucity and narrowness of representations of feminisms sabotaged any real potential for revolution. Rhetorical ambivalence characterizes the underlying tone of these characterizations: an ambivalence arising from the difficulty of getting traction on discursive slippages that undermine focused critique and responsive action. The resulting ambivalence too often facilitates avoidance of the political realities of gender hierarchies in American society.

Our analyses start with the Vietnam War because that is when we learned as feminist women that we had no *place*, that we were not to be the leaders in the cultural revolution. The critical analyses that we offer in this book unfold historically from post-Vietnam era to the present, and examine the narratives within public and political contexts. Chapter One, "Hijacking Feminism in Post-Vietnam Cinema: Tough Women and Tangled Memories," explores through analysis of warrior and action film narratives the political transgressiveness of female bodies and the postfeminist consciousness produced as a result of Vietnam and the crisis of white masculinity. Tracing an historical arc beginning in 1979, the chapter examines the challenge to American political culture and American cinematic traditions posed by survival of the "final girl."[48] Starting with Ridley Scott's *Alien* film series, the analysis demonstrates how Sigourney Weaver's characterization of Ripley (mostly) resisted sexual objectification and romantic heterosexual entanglements, how her body was re-scripted for the *mise-en-scene* of the "action" film genre, and how she drove the narrative forward and resolved its constructed conflicts. The debts other contemporary female heroic characters in television owe to this aesthetic formula for representing female agency are evident in series of the 1990s. In exploring the complexity, possibilities, and constraints of these characterizations of the female heroic, the analysis makes visible the threat posed to patriarchal politics by these characters' transgressive choices and actions. At the same time, the analysis suggests how the interests and histories of women are usurped in the narrative by the interests and histories of fathers and sons.

Chapter Two, "Hacking Women: The Politics of Disconnect," unfolds an historical arc beginning from the "Running Woman" of the "1984" Macintosh commercial[49] through the 1995 theatrical release of *The Net* (starring Sandra Bullock), and the television series *VR5*. The 1995 texts star women as computer hackers, screen imaginings seldom repeated again. The characters' technical proficiency marks a significant border-transgression, at the same time that uneasiness over the impossible alignment of femininity with machines is expressed. In these texts we see how issues relating to sexuality, sociality, and familial identity circumscribe the fictional worlds of women hackers. In particular, these texts align the narrative histories of the women protagonists with absentee mothers, mothers who in both *The Net* and *VR5* are physically present but cognitively and emotionally absent. Mutual relatedness between mothers and daughters cannot be imagined for these empowered, transgressive women. Yet, in presenting the mothers as narrative elements at all, albeit unable to relate to their daughters, these texts buck the general trend in representations of women who long for and obsess over the fathers, expressive of the wish to join the brotherhood and thus the patriarchy, as illustrated in the first chapter.

Chapter Three, "Leaving the Mothership: Postmodernity and Postfeminism in *Ally McBeal* and *Sex and the City*," represents the historical decade of the 1990s. The analysis explores the character of Ally as the quintessential "power feminist"—she has a high-powered law degree, she works for a high-powered legal firm and makes a lot of money, she is confident about her professional credentials and actions, she dresses in a sexually provocative manner, she is resolutely self-focused, and if it were not just for the lack of a boyfriend, she would be the perfect realization of capitalism's commodity feminist. The pleasures of the postmodern visual style combine with the pleasures of postfeminism. The chapter draws comparisons between Ally and the women of *Sex and the City* in order to parse the distinctive political perspectives afforded by comedy vs. humor, and to assess the representation of Third Wave feminism and suggest a possible rapprochement between Second and Third wave feminisms.

Chapter Four, "Designing Women as Consumers…Again—Gender and the Myth of the Level Playing Field in the Information Age," moves away from fictional representations, revealing the cultural context out of which popular texts such as Chapter Two's *The Net* and *VR5* arise. Chapter Four looks at a more generalized media landscape from the 1980s to the present for an overview of the institutional presence of women in computing. The chapter pulls together studies from the past two decades to examine the claims made for the liberatory potential of new technology and its actual effect in women's professional lives. It provides a critique of the *realpolitik* to reveal the ongoing economic and cultural conditions that continue to marginalize women from the driving forces shaping our technological future. Arguing that a fundamental difference in the role of consumer/user vs. producer/expert must be taken into account in analyzing the rhetoric of transformation that pervades talk about the information age, this chapter investigates how women's lack of participation in computing design and technical decision-making undermines the potential of new technologies for political and economic change.

Chapter Five, "Oh, to Be Given a Sporting Chance…: Televisual Representations of Women in the World of Sports News," looks at the short-lived late 1990s series written by Aaron Sorkin, who went on to write and produce the hit *West Wing*. The narrative represents its transgressive central female characters as two highly competent sports news producers. Successfully reproducing the consecrated male gossip known as sports talk, the women of *Sports Night* nevertheless must negotiate the tense narrative balance between their love and mastery of their professions and the technology used in the production of their weekly television show with the ever-present need to recuperate male expertise in technology and media.

In Chapter Six, "It's a Dick Thing: Ambivalent Coding of American Female Soldiers in Gulf War Narratives," we trace an historical arc that begins in 1973, when President Nixon disbanded the military draft, to the moment in 2006 in which a report was made public on the reality of sexual assault on U.S. women soldiers by U.S. male military personnel. In analyzing the films *G.I. Jane*, *Courage Under Fire*, and *The General's Daughter*, we encounter a narrative logic of undecidability in textual and material conditions that deepens the rhetorical ambivalence surrounding the place of women in the military. The unforgivable female body appropriating the talk and invading the locker room in Chapter Five's *Sports Night* here appropriates the walk and enters the most sacrosanct of all masculine strongholds—the trenches.

The concluding epilogue reflects on what has been learned in the cultural wars over feminism, and what must change to recoup the political energies of the next generation of women and men. In doing so, the authors address the young women who are the daughters, nieces, students, and friends of the

Second Wave feminists in "An Open Letter from the Second Wave Mothership."

In sum, the themes of our book are evident in our analyses of the irony and the ahistoricism underlying many of the texts we encounter, and in our concern for the contextualizing material realities of women's lived experience. The discursive slippage of smirking irony preempts urgent claims on our attention from the immediate structural inequities that continue to dim the hopes of women, and from the wider societal and environmental wreckage of unopposed capitalism. Ahistoricism robs women of the crucial inscription of herstory into history; to lose history is not just to lose ground in the intersexual battles of the Second Wave, but to lose place in the very constitution of humanity. And finally, in the best spirit of American pragmatism, we attend to the material, practical needs of and opportunities for women's lives that provide ground and horizon for the representations we consider. People's interactions with media representations are pervasive, personal and practical, and it matters to "ask what institutions and what discourses are engaged in making the mediated representations of the public domain, what the resulting picture of the public looks like, and who speaks for—and to—the public so created."[50]

Notes

[1] Betty Friedan wrote *The Feminine Mystique* in 1963, providing an analysis of the social, political, and economic structures that define women's lives. The book sparked the Second Wave feminist movement, a social revolution that grew out of the radical notion that women and men were equal. In 1966, Friedan helped found the National Organization for Women (NOW), a non-governmental group devoted to political action aimed at reversing the subjugation of women.

[2] Coretta Scott King helped lead the civil rights movement against racial segregation with her husband, Dr. Martin Luther King, Jr. His assassination in 1968 placed her in the leadership role, and she continued as an activist, suffering arrest and threats for the next twenty years. Her active commitment to racial equality begun with the Civil Rights movement brought her national and international recognition.

[3] Todd Gitlin, "Prime Time Ideology: The Hegemonic Process in Television Entertainment," *Television: The Critical View,* ed. Horace Newcomb, 6th ed. (New York: Oxford University Press, 2000) 576.

[4] Gitlin 590.

[5] See, for example, Brian L. Ott, "(Re) Locating Pleasure in Media Studies: Toward an Erotics of Reading," *Communication and Critical/Cultural Studies* 1, no. 2 (2004): 194–212.

[6] See Angela McRobbie, "Post-feminism and Popular Culture," *Feminist Media Studies* 4.3: (2004): 255–264.

[7] Sally Kempton, "Cutting Loose" *Esquire* July 1970: 57.

[8] Patricia A. Sullivan and Lynn H. Turner, "The Zoe Baird Spectacle: Silences, Sins, and Status," *Western Journal of Communication* 63.4 (1999): 425.

[9] Stuart Hall, ed., *Culture, Media, Language: Working Papers In Cultural Studies, 1972–79* (London: Centre for Contemporary Cultural Studies, University of Birmingham, 1980).

[10] See Bonnie Dow, *Prime-Time Feminism: Television, Media Culture, And The Women's Movement Since 1970* (Philadelphia: University of Pennsylvania Press 1996); John Fiske, *Media Matters: Everyday Culture and Political Change* (Minneapolis: University of Minnesota Press, 1994); Lauren Rabinovitz, "Ms-Representation: The Politics of Feminist Sitcoms," *Television, History, and American Culture* (Durham, NC: Duke University Press 1999) 144–167.

[11] Jennifer Scanlon, *Inarticulate Longings: The Ladies' Home Journal, Gender, and the Promises Of Consumer Culture* (New York: Routledge, 1995) 4–7.

[12] William Henry Chafe, *The American Woman; Her Changing Social, Economic, and Political Roles, 1920–1970* (New York: Oxford University Press, 1972) 135–136.

[13] Sheila Tobias & Lisa Anderson, L. (1973, June). "Whatever happened to Rosie the Riveter?" *Ms.*, 92–97.

[14] Betty E Chmaj, "The Changing Image of American Women, 1930–1974," *The Study of American Culture: Contemporary Conflicts* (ed.) L. S. Luedtke (Deland, FL: Everett Edwards, 1977) 140.

[15] Marjorie Rosen, "Goodbye Sweet And Lovely: Movies that Women's Lib Would Like to Burn," *Movie Digest* July 1972.

[16] John Hartley, *The Politics of Pictures: The Creation of the Public in the Age of Popular Media* (London: Routledge, 1992) 1.

[17] See Todd Gitlin, *The Whole World Is Watching: Mass Media In The Making & Unmaking Of The New Left* (Berkeley: University of California Press, 1980); *Inside Prime Time* (New York: Pantheon Books, 1983); *The Twilight of Common Dreams: Why America Is Wracked by Culture Wars* (New York: Henry Holt and Company, 1995).

[18] Hartley 3.

[19] Kenneth Burke, "The Range of Rhetoric." *A Rhetoric of Motives* (Berkeley: U of California Press, 1950) 3–46.

[20] Bruce E. Gronbeck, "The Twentieth-First Century Reconstitution of American Political Culture." John D. Lees Lecture for the American Political Group of the Political Studies Association (UK), (2006). 7 August 2006 http://www.uiowa.edu/commstud/faculty/gronbeck/21st_reconstitution.pdf.

[21] Angie Manzano, *"Charlie's Angels*: Free-Market Feminism," *Off Our Backs* 30.11 (2000). 5 April 2006 http://wwwoffourbacks.org/MorFeat.htm.

[22] Robert Goldman, Deborah Heath, and Sharon Smith, "Commodity Feminism," *Critical Studies in Mass Communication* 8.3 (1991): 333–351.

[23] Manzano 2.

[24] Susan Faludi, *Backlash: The Undeclared War Against American Women* (New York: Crown, 1991).

[25] bell hooks, *Feminism is For Everybody: Passionate Politics* (Cambridge, MA: South End Press, 2000).

[26] McRobbie 259–260.

[27] McRobbie 259.

[28] McRobbie 259.

[29] McRobbie 259.

[30] Carolyn Heilbron, *Reinventing Womanhood* (New York: Norton, 1979).

[31] Katie Roiphe, *The Morning After: Sex, Fear, and Feminism on Campus* (Boston : Little, Brown and Co., 1993).

[32] Naomi Wolf, *Fire With Fire: The New Female Power and How It Will Change the 21st Century* (New York: Random House, 1993).

[33] Sonja Foss and Cindy Griffin join this conversation with their concept of "invitational rhetoric." Women are encouraged to give up combative, argumentative stances in favor of

listening and accepting the positions of others. Moreover, invitational rhetoric encourages a forward-looking perspective that abandons the past as burdensome baggage. See Sonja K. Foss and Cindy L. Griffin, "Beyond Persuasion: A Proposal for an Invitational Rhetoric," *Communication Monograph* 62.1 (1995): 2–19.

[34] Ann Blythe, " Free to Be Me and You at Duke," *News and Observer*, 27 February 2006: 1B.

[35] Lee Tobin McClain, "Mom on Sabbatical," *Chronicle of Higher Education* 2 December 2006: C1.

[36] Liza P. Grey, "Working toward Motherhood," *Chronicle of Higher Education* 17 February 2006: C2.

[37] Eduardo Porter, "Fewer Women Entering Workplace," *News & Observer* 3 March 2006: 3A.

[38] Porter 3A.

[39] Linda Hirshman, "Choice Feminism," *Homeward Bound* (21 November 2005). 15 December 2005 at http://www.prospect.org/web/page.ww?section=root&name=ViewWeb&articleId =10659

[40] Tamar Lewin, "The New Gender Divide: At Colleges, Women Are Leaving Men in the Dust," *The New York Times* 9 July 2006. 9 July 2006 http://www.nytimes.com/2006/07/09/education/09college.html?hp&ex=1152504000&en=1788c6468b950bc6&ei=5094&partner= homepage.

[41] "Gains in Learning, Gaps in Earnings: A Guide to State and National Data" (Washington, D.C.: American Association of University Women, 2005). 9 July 2006 http://www.aauw.org/research/statedata/.

[42] "Women Still Underrepresented Among Highest Earners," *Issues in Labor Statistics* (U.S. Bureau of Labor Statistics, March 2006). 9 July 2006 http://www.bls.gov/bls/whatsnew.htm.

[43] "Questions and Answers on Pay Equity," National Committee on Pay Equity (January 2005). 9 July 2006 http://www.pay-equity.org/info-Q&A.html.

[44] "Questions and Answers on Pay Equity." See also, Ann Crittendon, *The Price of Motherhood: Why the Most Important Job in the World is Still the Least Valued* (New York: Henry Holt, 2001), for her findings that the primary variable in determining poverty for elderly women is motherhood.

[45] "Oh, the Allure and Vanity of Nudity," *USA Today* 21 April 2006: 6E.

[46] Jedediah Purdy, "Terminal Irony," *Utne Reader*, September-October 1998: 26–27.

[47] Judith Butler, *Gender Trouble: Feminism And The Subversion Of Identity* (New York: Routledge, 1999).

[48] Carol J. Clover, *Men, Women, And Chain Saws: Gender in the Modern Horror Film* (Princeton, N.J.: Princeton University Press, 1992).

[49] Sarah Stein, "The '1984' Macintosh Ad: Cinematic Icons and Constitutive Rhetoric in the Launch of a New Machine," *Quarterly Journal of Speech* 88.2 (2002): 169–192.

[50] Hartley 1.

Chapter One

Hijacking Feminism in Post-Vietnam Cinema: Tough Women and Tangled Memories

The past thirty-five years figure prominently in the cultural transformation of social relations between American men and women. The Second Wave of the feminist movement took to the streets over three decades ago and noisily challenged gendered relations of power in American society. Members of the movement pressed for significant changes in labor law, equal opportunity employment, and social justice for women. Second Wave feminists fought for abortion and reproductive control, tougher legislation against rape and sexual harassment, and solutions to domestic violence. Unprecedented numbers of women entered and succeeded in the formerly male dominated spheres of politics, law, medicine, science, religion, and even military academies. Title IX guaranteed to future generations of girls access to physical education and competitive sports. Women in the Second Wave transgressed prevailing cultural norms for female beauty, femininity, sexuality and motherhood. They challenged print pornography, advertising, religious sanctions against sexual choice, and institutional hegemony over pregnancy and childbirth. In short, Second Wave sisters redefined gender norms for American society.[1]

This same period also precipitated a significant crisis for American national identity and its representation. Described by President Carter in 1979 as a "national malaise," this crisis has lingered through the administrations of Reagan, Bush elder, and Bush junior. There have been ample reasons for cultural anxiety. Watergate and Vietnam created public angst about government deception and illegality, about national purpose and American superiority, about morality and foreign policy. The 1986 Iran-Contra affair re-fueled public suspicion about the possibilities of a "shadow government" run amok. In the public imagination, Marine Lt. Col. Oliver North and fictional character John Rambo became synonymous with conservative efforts to re-masculinize American politics and culture. Conservative talk radio remains a bastion of these efforts to this day, as, for example, the substance and bombastic style of Rush Limbaugh and his disciples.

International incidents during the 1980s and early 1990s involving American military and diplomatic personnel continued to feed American anxiety about military competence and national might. Eight American soldiers died on April 26, 1980, in President Carter's failed effort to rescue fifty-four American hostages held by Iran since November 4, 1979. The *Washington Post* described the cause of the failure as technological and mechanical, contextualizing the images of burning helicopters as "sad symbols of a new American humiliation in Iran."[2] On October 23, 1983, two hundred and forty-one American Marines were killed in their barracks in Lebanon, and President Reagan's promises of a "new beginning" in response to Carter's "malaise" seemed to falter in the face of this new international crisis. The Beirut disaster was a shock to popular American imagination—American soldiers blown to pieces by terrorist activity on foreign soil. Indeed, the nation seemed to be assuming the loathsome identity that Richard Nixon most feared and which motivated his foreign policy in Vietnam: A once-great nation was degenerating into "a pitiful giant." And in spite of the elder Bush's hawkish success in the 1991 Gulf War, the specter of a faltering American military surfaced again during the early months of the Clinton administration. For many American viewers, the memory of Vietnam was invoked by broadcast and print images of a dead American soldier dragged through the streets of Mogadishu.[3]

White male popular filmmakers responded to the lingering national malaise and shifting gender relations in a number of interesting ways. This chapter addresses two of the more prominent of these responses. The first concerns the destabilization of masculinity and masculine dominance in cinematic representations of America's Vietnam experience. The years between 1978 and 1989 saw production and distribution of two competing cinematic representations of the Vietnam War. One representation, including films such as *Coming Home, The Deer Hunter, Apocalypse Now, Platoon, Born on the 4th of July, Full Metal Jacket* and *Casualties of War*, served up searing narratives about ruined male bodies, insanity, moral atrocity, and failed national purpose. Another representation focused on what Susan Jeffords called "remasculinization" themes, as exemplified in the pro-military blockbuster film *Top Gun*.[4] The most prominent of these films, however, were the "bring 'em back alive" action adventure "return to 'Nam" narratives such as *Missing In Action, Rambo: First Blood, Part II, Uncommon Valor,* and *Bat 21*.[5] In these stories, male bodies and agency were inscribed with hypermasculinity—exaggerated expressions of what had been lost—in order to offset the crisis of a "lost" war.[6] We use the context of the trauma narratives directed by Hal Ashby (1978), Francis Ford Coppola (1979), Michael Cimino (1978) and Oliver Stone (1986, 1989, 1993) to examine a second, related response to the crisis of representation in gendered national identity. This response consisted of a proto-feminist fantasy that explored (if not appropriated) the now vacated spaces once occupied by American men and conventional American masculinity. The second set of films, also directed by white male filmmakers, deployed fantasy and escapism to represent public anxiety over national identity and essentially ignored the *realpolitik* of America's misadventures abroad and at home. Significantly, these films featured prominent female heroes in narratives about traumatic memory: *Alien, Aliens, Alien3, Alien Resurrection, Terminator, Terminator II, The Silence of the Lambs,* and *The Quick and the Dead.*

This chapter explores how the intersecting theme of traumatic memory connects these woman-centered films to post-Vietnam war narratives and the crisis of dominant masculinity. The pervasiveness of the cultural crisis is revealed in the range of film genres in which we encounter these female heroes. The *Alien* saga tells the story of Ellen Ripley's inter-galactic encounters with a hostile life form that threatens the survival of the human race. She discovers and confronts corrupt corporate plans to develop the lethal alien as a biological weapon of mass destruction. In *Terminator* and *Terminator II*, Sarah Connor fights to prevent nuclear annihilation of the world, precipitated by an army of intelligent and "self-conscious" rogue machines bent on terminating the human race. She confronts misguided corporate and military interests in developing sophisticated artificial intelligence. *The Silence of the Lambs* tells the story of Clarice Starling, a rookie F.B.I. Agent and daughter of a murdered sheriff, who tracks and kills a serial murderer of lambs—of young, trusting women. Similarly, *The Quick and the Dead*'s central character, Ellen or "The Lady," enters a gun-fighting contest for the purpose of avenging the murder of her father, also a sheriff. Each female hero is haunted by a trauma (universal, global or local) that drives her to confront evil, mass destruction, tyranny and moral corruption.

In the context of traumatic memory, national identity and popular film, we advance four related claims in this chapter:

(1) Female ascendancy to agency in the context of male weakness and hyper-masculine exaggeration highlights a marked instability in gendered representations during this period. Feminine and masculine qualities come unmoored from their conventional attachments to female and male bodies. A lone female becomes heroic while embodied male characters become subordinate to a strong woman. The male characters tend to be physically or emotionally weak, morally corrupt, extremely anxious, or incapable of resolving the narrative problem.

(2) Male fantasies about heroic women during this period explore and re-enact the troubled relationship between fathers and sons so endemic to nation stories about post-Vietnam, post-Watergate America. The apocalyptic "mothers" of *Aliens* and *Terminator II* occupy the spaces of absentee fathers—a persistent theme of inter-generational conflict in representations of the Vietnam War.[7] Concomitantly, the tough daughters of *The Silence of the Lambs* and *The*

Quick and the Dead enter the portals of patriarchal power by supplanting the son's troubled relationship to the father.

(3) Each female hero problematizes the narrative logic within which she is constructed, opening it for a flexible range of reading positions and viewer pleasures. Her presence as primary *agent* of the story undermines generic logic, revealing historically specific fissures and crises in American popular imagination. At the same time, however, feminist historical consciousness is effaced by this white male fantasy of female agency. Patriarchal interests, anxieties and perfidies pre-occupy the attention and energies of the female heroes. The apocalyptic mothers struggle to overcome the devastating policy decisions of a fictional "military industrial complex," an anxiety first articulated in American political culture by Eisenhower in 1961. However, the tough daughters, pre-occupied as they are with the trauma of their fathers' world of criminal justice, display cultural amnesia about the world of their mothers.

(4) In all of these films, embodied women stand in for patriarchal fathers, punishing corruption and providing moral leadership. Apocalyptic mothers provide parental guidance and moral authority in a world gone mad. Tough daughters successfully negotiate deadly masculinist social scripts, restoring order to the father-son relationships by killing bad fathers and replacing weak sons. Figured on and through traumatic memory itself, this "tough woman" gender aesthetic emerges during the early years of the post-Vietnam era and lingers through the administrations of Reagan, Bush and Clinton. Ultimately, these white male fantasies about feminist women shape the possibilities for development of postfeminism and Third Wave feminism in American visual culture.

To develop these claims, we begin with close analysis of films about the Vietnam War by four prominent directors—Hal Ashby, Francis Ford Coppola, Michael Cimino and Oliver Stone—who articulate a masculinist national identity in extreme crisis. Then we move to a close analysis of the *Alien* series and consider its role in articulating post-Vietnam traumatic memory. Next we consider how popular films featuring tough women hi-jack female bodies and appropriate feminist perspectives. Finally, we consider some of the implications of representational spaces for women in cultural memories of the nation.

Vietnam and the Destabilization of Masculine Agency[8]

Popular cinema is a public site where cultural memory is negotiated.[9] Marita Sturken explains that cultural memory "is a field of contested meanings in which Americans interact with cultural elements to produce concepts of the nation, particularly in events of trauma, where both the structures and the fractures of a culture are exposed."[10] Sturken argues for a view of cultural memory as a "tangle" of personal memories, formal historical discourse and cultural products.[11] We are interested in exploring a "tangle" composed of post-Vietnam anxiety, the rise of Second Wave feminism and environmentalism, the gendered conventions of popular film, and the role of cinema in constructing national identity. Anxiety about national identity, masculine dominance, and feminist reform is made comprehensible for film audiences at a particular moment in time through the manipulation of film genre. The war genre is particularly important to a study of films addressing themes of trauma and identity, both personal and collective.

National war traumas, such as the Civil War, were first visualized for mass circulation within the American public through documentary photography (the Brady collection and Timothy Sullivan) and then through the new medium of cinema. *Birth of a Nation* (1915) and *Gone with the Wind* (1939) were wildly successful fictional melodramatic trauma narratives addressed by white male filmmakers to white audiences. Both stories used white trauma over Emancipation to construct a nation story of extreme crisis and stoic perseverance.[12] Both stories were timely, since by the early twentieth century white supremacy and its champions faced mounting public resistance from black intellectuals and civic leaders.[13] War films about World War II, produced and distributed both during and after the war, forged popular "victory" stories where Americans endured and triumphed.[14] In these films, white American masculinity represented national identity, the international triumph of democracy, and a mythos of American decency and courage. With few exceptions, American war cinema represented a unified vision of American virtue and heroic masculine virtue.[15]

The Vietnam War precipitated a crisis of representation for heroic masculine agency in American culture that persists to this day. As Sturken explains:

> The Vietnam War marks the beginning of the end of the Cold War. It follows on the historic upheaval of the civil rights movement and intersects with the rise of the feminist movement. It has refigured the image not only of American technology and global power but also of American manhood and its relation to the feminine. It has irrevocably altered the image of the American veteran.[16]

Sturken's assessment enables us to read post-Vietnam War films as cultural trauma narratives. Put simply, a trauma wounds. Trauma wounds people, nations, identities, and even terrain. The shock of trauma initially overwhelms the possibilities of representation, giving rise to a period of latency.[17] The representation of trauma requires distance, both temporal and psychological. Yet, the wounding event cannot be negotiated unless and until it can be represented. In other words, trauma demands a story; unless a coherent narrative about the trauma can be constructed, the wounding experience cannot be reconciled.[18] The most authoritative storytellers of traumas are those who have witnessed and/or survived the original wounding. They have the authority of sight ("eye" witness), but must develop the power of persuasive utterance (rhetorical agency). The storyteller must be able to represent the traumatizing event, first to herself, and then to an audience.[19] A fully developed trauma narrative is canonical in form, including context for the traumatizing event(s), dramatic action (who, what, when and where), and evaluation of the catastrophe.[20]

Hal Ashby's *Coming Home* (1978), Michael Cimino's *The Deer Hunter* (1978), and Frances Ford Coppola's *Apocalypse Now* (1979) were among the first popular American films to address the war.[21] Ashby and Cimino's films share an aesthetic preference for cinematic realism and a melodramatic perspective on the difficulties male American veterans face as they struggle to reintegrate themselves into post-war life. Both narratives examine the relationships among national identity, local community and masculine bonding. In *The Deer Hunter*, a community of first- and second-generation Russian immigrants in the American Rust Belt struggle to embrace the enduring and interwoven rituals of church, community, and nation even as the repercussions of Vietnam shatter their lives. In *Coming Home*, characters struggle to cope with the bewildering aftermath of an unpopular war and a rapidly shifting socio-political climate. Main characters in both narratives articulate their inability to reintegrate themselves into American cultural and civic life after their experiences in Vietnam. The most prominent of these are Christopher Walken's "Nick Chevoteravich" in *The Deer Hunter* and Bruce Dern's "Bob Hyde" in *Coming Home*. Nick cannot overcome the emotional trauma of capture by the North Vietnamese anymore than he can cope with the scenes of physical injury and madness in a Saigon U.S. military hospital. Similarly, Captain Bob Hyde's military career and private life disintegrate after he embarks on a tour of duty in Vietnam. There, he discovers that neither his assumptions about the honor of the Corps nor his conventional marriage hold true. In the respective suicide scenes near the conclusions of both films, these characters embody visual tropes of extreme identity crisis operating at the intersection of the personal and the political.[22]

By contrast, Coppola's postmodern visual and acoustic aesthetic envisions the Vietnam War as a pastiche of operatic excess and acid rock nihilism. The central character, Martin Sheen's Captain Willard, narrates the complex relationship between the male citizen warrior and the nation. The community from which he emerges, and the possibility of intimate dialogue with other men, disappears. Coppola is the most explicit of the three filmmakers in articulating the dangers of Southeast Asian jungles for western white men. In that geopolitical scene, American military and industrial might is rendered chaotic and absurd, doomed by a primitive and relentless enemy. The engine of the narrative, based on Conrad's novel *Heart of Darkness*, is the paradox that has driven Col. Kurtz mad. The enemy cannot be defeated without destroying (or revealing as fraudulent) the underpinnings of western civilized warfare. Kurtz explains to Willard, "You have to have men…who are able to utilize their primordial instincts to kill without feeling, without passion, without judgment…because it's judgment that defeats us." The moment of horror, culturally immortalized in Kurtz's dying whisper, is the moment of paradox for the mythic American male warrior: One cannot win a war against savages without exterminating them. Extermination as a course of foreign policy shatters the illusion of western civilization. "This is the way the world ends," Dennis Hopper's drug-addled American photojournalist character says to Willard by way of explaining the hopelessness of the American war effort.

In each of these three films, conventional heroic masculine agency falters. Male characters are feminized, incapacitated, and ultimately defeated in their personal, communal and national quests. Ashby's intimate visual style engenders interpersonal depth between and among male characters in the story. His use of the documentary camera at the beginning of the film sets the tone for the primacy of talk and the desirability of dialogic relationships. His narrative compresses the veteran's adjustment to post-war life with shifting social roles for women, as represented in the relationship between characters played by Jon Voight and Jane Fonda. Film reviewer Vincent Canby dismissed *Coming Home* as "the dopiest of romantic" narratives and claimed that the film reduced a good war story into "what used to be called a 'woman's picture'."[23] Cimino's narrative is far less open to the influence of women or feminine styles of communication. Thus, Canby found this film more to his liking, declaring "[n]o other American film in a very long time has so accurately caught the quality of our lives, the temper of our times and the contradictions built into our culture."[24] Nevertheless, the overwhelming narrative focus on the relationship between two male friends, Nick and Michael, opens the narrative to dialogic possibilities normally restricted in American war cinema. Michael's failed rescue of Nick is predicated upon the risks of emotional intimacy, not physical force or masculine bravado. In the penultimate scene of the film, Michael risks his own life in a game of Russian roulette with Nick in an effort to momentarily rupture the opium-induced forgetfulness Nick needs to survive the trauma of the war. Ironically, when Nick remembers Michael, he succumbs to traumatic memory of the war and fires a bullet into his brain.

Coppola's narrative refuses most possibilities for male love, dialogic communication or emotional intimacy. However, much like the dilemma of traumatic memory experienced by Nick and Michael in *Deer Hunter* and Bob Hyde in *Coming Home*, *Apocalypse Now* frames American involvement in Vietnam as a destructive paradox. Nick cannot remember his identity without succumbing to recovered trauma. Yet, Michael cannot save Nick unless Nick remembers his identity. Bob Hyde cannot reconcile his traumatizing combat experience with American nationalist mythos, nor his wife's newly found independence with masculinist gender norms. "I'm fucked...I want to be a hero" he sobs, while holding his estranged wife and the protagonist, Luke, at gunpoint in an iconic scene of domestic gender trauma. Similarly, Willard and Kurtz in *Apocalypse* enact a scene of *national* gendered trauma. Kurtz reveals to Willard that his descent into madness began when he realized that Americans could not defeat the Southeast Asian enemy without either annihilating them or becoming like them. As Brando's Kurtz rambles on about morality and primordial instincts, we see in a close-up shot from Willard's subjective point of view a handwritten recommendation from Kurtz to Lyndon Johnson and the Joint Chiefs of Staff: "Drop the Bomb, Exterminate Them All!"

Meanwhile, Kurtz tells the story of how a benevolent American effort to inoculate native children against polio resulted in those children having their inoculated arms cut off by North Vietnamese resistance forces. Kurtz muses, "I realized they were stronger than we because they could stand it...If I had ten divisions of those men, then our troubles here would be over very quickly." "Nuking" the enemy was not a viable public policy option during the Vietnam War, though some American military strategists pondered Henry Kissinger's *Nuclear Weapons and Foreign Policy* which advocated the concept of "limited" nuclear war.[25] Brutality and relentless cruelty, as figured in the story about mutilated children, were at odds with American cultural commitments to mythic (honorable) warfare. As the scene ends, Willard ritually murders Kurtz, who seems to accept—perhaps even embrace—his fate. The relationship between these two men is not one of friendship, comradeship, or community; rather, it figures the national trauma of losing a war. Kurtz embodies the paradox of a no win situation. Under military orders to "eliminate with extreme prejudice," Willard ritually slaughters Kurtz as equal parts compassionate euthanasia, masculinist tribute to a fellow warrior, and obedience to military authority. The trauma enacted in this scene concerns the horror of defeat. The rhetorical claim of *Apocalypse* is that if American civilization fails so too does the world. Hence Kurtz's melodramatic exit utterance: "The horror, the horror."

In all three films, recovery from trauma requires a *representation* of trauma. The characters who die or become increasingly anti-social simply cannot manage the challenges of representing their trauma. These characterized veterans kill themselves, resort to violence, and/or fail in their personal relationships. The successful survivors are those who can tell a story about the war, such as Luke in *Coming Home* or Willard in *Apocalypse Now*. Because the point of the film is that no one understands what is happening, no surviving male character in *The Deer Hunter* can tell a coherent narrative about the war. Since, as Sturken observes, "memory is articulated through processes of representation," these films reveal a great deal about American cultural memories of Vietnam under construction in the popular cinema of the late 1970s.[26] In these narratives, individual soldiers lose their American identity because of exposure to the primitive environs and persons of Southeast Asia, because of horrific experiences in battle, because of their inability to re-integrate themselves into the home front after the war, or because the war has been lost by an American military force. All of these debilitating experiences are structurally integrated through the overarching trauma of betrayal—by the nation and by the fathers.[27] Thus, Luke *performs* memory work through becoming an anti-war activist, an amateur therapist for other damaged veterans, and a supportive companion to an American woman struggling to embrace independence. Nick and Bob *enact* memory by killing themselves. Michael Vronsky of *Deer Hunter* and Captain Willard of *Apocalypse survive* the war only to live silently with the bitter realization that heroic intervention is no longer possible. Colonel Kurtz *embraces* death at the hands of an assassin because he understands the paradoxical quagmire of the Vietnam War: Defeat is lethal for American imperialism, but the necessary means to win the war (nuclear annihilation) would destabilize mythic national identity (America makes the world safe for democracy).

Traumatic memory, as evidenced in the first three post-Vietnam films, also figures prominently in the work of Oliver Stone, arguably the most prolific and notorious of popular filmmakers addressing the war.[28] Stone's films differ in three important ways from those of his predecessors. He explicitly blames the United States government for destroying the lives of American male soldiers in Vietnam (i.e., he names the sins of the fathers). He figures an ungrateful American civilian public through unsympathetic female characters (i.e., he feminizes civilians).[29] And, his lead male characters tell fully developed trauma narratives about the war (i.e., he suggests the possibility of recovery from trauma). *Platoon* (1986) imitates the narrative structure of *Apocalypse Now*, though unlike Coppola, Stone's visual style is realist. Charlie Sheen, real-life son of Martin Sheen, plays the protagonist whose voice-over narrative anchors the preferred perspective in the story. Like his father, Charlie Sheen plays a character whose life is altered by the "journey" into war. Both characters commit murder in the moral chaos of war, thus limiting or negating the possibilities for heroic action. But while the younger Sheen's character ends the film with a voice-over epilogue that offers an evaluation of war trauma, the elder Sheen's character simply walks away, offering no closure for the story.

Born on the 4th of July (1989) imitates the home-front motif of *Coming Home*. Tom Cruise plays the role of real life veteran Ron Kovic, who was paralyzed by a bullet wound in his spine. Like Ashby, Stone incorporates melodrama to explore the horrors of broken bodies in rat-infested V.A. hospitals and the haunting memories of moral chaos in the battlefield. Unlike Ashby, however, Stone uses female characters to represent an unsympathetic and naïve American civilian public. Moreover, he figures the loss of penile potency as loss of national potency, conflating public agency with masculine sexuality. Like *Platoon,* Kovic's autobiographical trauma narrative is canonical, fully developed in form and style.

Heaven and Earth (1993) imitates the hopelessness and despair of suicidal Vietnam veterans like those featured in *The Deer Hunter* and *Coming Home*. Tommy Lee Jones plays the character Steve, who cannot cope with his memories of war atrocities or the evolving independence of his Vietnamese wife. In a melodramatic scene, heavily edited with flashbacks to war crimes, Steve brutalizes his wife and then kills himself because he cannot cope with his traumatic memories of Vietnam. But unlike suicidal characters in earlier films, Steve tells a remarkably coherent and detailed story of his involvement in Vietnam before he commits suicide. In a trauma story eerily similar to the one Senator Bob Kerry would tell about himself in 2000, Steve recalls his activities in a Special Forces group assigned to assassinate North Vietnamese operatives.[30]

In sum, characterized veterans in these films display varied abilities to construct traumatic memory of the Vietnam War. Ashby and Coppola offer context and drama, but their primary characters fail to evaluate their trauma, suggesting a lingering crisis of representation. Cimino's characters cannot explain the war to themselves, let alone to the audience. Stone's *Platoon* is the first of his three fully developed trauma stories about Vietnam. Of these filmmakers, only Ashby considers the possibilities of an alliance between the feminist movement and the anti-war movement, which is figured in the central romantic relationship of the narrative. Neither American women nor the Vietnamese fare well in stories directed by Cimino, Coppola, and Stone. In their stories, just as in early twentieth-century films about the Civil War, the loss of a nationalist identity figured upon white masculine prowess *constitutes* the trauma. (*Gone with the Wind* is the obvious exception.) Women and a foreign enemy are cast as minor causal agents in the trauma. The primary causal agent is a behind-the-scenes national power that abused and abandoned American sons in Vietnam.[31] This *absent presence* in the films is responsible for the traumas experienced by the American male veteran—moral collapse in the context of warfare, horrific wounds to body and mind, and the humiliation of an unpopular homecoming.[32] In contrast, in the proto-feminist fantasy film narratives, tough white professional women with moral authority confront and supplant the absent presence (the fathers), drawing from their own embodied experiences with oppression and struggle. In short, feminism is hijacked for the purpose of ameliorating traumatic memory of American nationalist crises.

The *Alien* Series and American Traumatic Memory

The *Alien* series easily can be read as another popular articulation of post-Vietnam trauma. In fact, James Cameron, director of *Aliens* (1986), reveals in the notes for the film's 2001 DVD re-release that the Vietnam War provided creative inspiration for the technological and militaristic *mise-en-scene* of his film.[33] Four unifying motifs in the each of the four *Alien* films relate to the cultural trauma precipitated by Vietnam: an unbeatable enemy, beleaguered masculinity, the emergence of a heroic female character, and traumatic memory itself. The background tale of government conspiracy and betrayal, in concert with corporate indifference to human life, further bespeaks post-Vietnam, post-Watergate anxieties. In fact, Ellen Ripley is arguably the character prototype for female embodied trauma stories in post-Vietnam film, and as such she appears prominently in this analysis. The parallel development of Ripley's characterization with post-Vietnam crisis narratives suggests the possibility that she articulates cultural anxiety about national identity. The following section examines how the representation of an alien enemy and faltering masculinity enable the emergence of a female heroic aesthetic. Moreover, the section demonstrates how relations between the "Final Girl" and the de-centered male constitute an articulation of traumatic memory in American culture and reveal interesting tensions in the gendered conventions of American popular cinema.

In many respects, the alien creature embodies American traumatic memory of Vietnam. As allegory, the aliens represent a fearsome and inexplicable "other" about which much has been written.[34] They are prolific breeders and relentless warriors; they can neither be reasoned with nor defeated. Their lairs are labyrinthine, virtually impenetrable and lethal to human beings. As metaphor, the alien represents American anxieties about Southeast Asian people and about the "failed" outcome of the war. Consider that the alien creatures are primitive, elusive, fearless, and virtually indestructible, as are the characterized Vietnamese and Cambodian people in *Apocalypse Now*. Like the characterized Vietnamese in *The Deer Hunter* and *Heaven and Earth*, the aliens are inhuman in their ferocity, cruelty, and contempt for human (American) life. The aliens, like the Vietcong, cannot be defeated with conventional weapons, modern military tactics, or technology. Warrior aliens breech the perimeter and over-run human outposts, as do the characterized Vietnamese in *Platoon*, *Heaven and Earth*, and *The Deer Hunter*. But perhaps most importantly, the fantastically caustic aliens expose the frightful vulnerabilities of the human body to war, to toxic waste, to nuclear annihilation, and to corporate and government indifference. American television coverage of the Vietnam War, rising environmental concerns in the 1970s, and the perils of nuclear energy and weapons positioned American viewers to be anxious about a variety of potentially lethal situations. The aliens' primary characteristic is a disturbing interest in the vulnerabilities of the human body, which they appear to regard primarily as a disposable incubator for fetal alien life. Moreover, their unusually democratic approach to harvesting male and female humans for reproductive incubation articulates a key anxiety about masculine vulnerability and sexual ambiguity in the late 1970s.[35]

In the four-part alien saga, male leadership and heroism falter in the face of the threat posed by the alien creatures. The failure is first and best encapsulated in *Alien* (1979) plot and characterization. Kane, the male crewmember first assaulted by the face-hugging embryonic creature, dies "giving birth" to the beast. The key visual trope in Kane's demise is the forcible oral penetration and subsequent impregnation of the male body. As mentioned earlier, the hostile alien expresses no particular preference for victimizing females; the male body is equally useful as an incubator for alien embryos.[36] Dallas, the head officer of the Nostromo, is the third cast member to succumb to the creature. After the alien embryo erupts from Kane's chest, Dallas enacts a typical gender convention of the horror/science fiction genre by volunteering to hunt for the creature in the dark air tunnels of the spacecraft. In a series of rapid editing cuts between Dallas in the dark tunnels and the crew watching his transmitter signal on a computer screen, the unthinkable happens: The structural hero of the narrative simply disappears, in the middle of the story, thereby enacting feminization of male heroism through colonization of the body. Film historian and critic Thomas Doherty argues that killing off Tom Skerritt so ignominiously and so early in the film "bordered on [genre] malfeasance."[37] However, the panic and chaos precipitated by the disappearance of the generic male hero created the possibilities for female agency and heroism to emerge.

Carol Clover has argued that Ellen Ripley's heroic female characterization in the *Alien* trilogy is indebted to the "Final Girl" genre convention of the slasher/horror film, a young female character who survives catastrophic emotional and physical trauma. In her book *Men, Women and Chainsaws*, Clover theorizes adolescent male audience engagement with the genre-bending girl survivor.[38] Clover argues that surviving heroines in these narratives, such as Jamie Lee Curtis's "Laurie" in *Halloween*, are popular with young male viewing audiences precisely because they and she are gendered ambiguously. The Final Girl frequently has a non-gender specific name and is not visually coded as conventionally feminine, as, for example, "Stevie Wayne" in *The Fog* or "Marti" in *Hell Night*. She is not sexually active, and though stalked by the monster, her body may not be offered up for a conventionally sexualized gaze. She is not immobilized by the experience of terror; rather, she is extraordinarily watchful, resourceful under pressure, and wary at all times of her surroundings. She uses her intelligence, wits and available weapons to outsmart, escape or destroy the monster. Of greatest significance, the Final Girl dares to look at the monster and lives to tell about it. Clover argues that adolescent males identify with the young female survivor because the young males too are ambiguously gendered (unfinished). Moreover, they can identify with the terror inspired by hegemonic masculine scripts.[39]

In the context of American cinematic gender conventions, the Final Girl's will to wield an investigative gaze and to confront (perhaps even hunt) the monster is key to her agency in the narrative. Moreover, her fluid gender and sexual identity enables polysemic audience engagement with her agency in the narrative. In the *Alien* series, the Final Girl convention is invoked across eighteen years, the competing visions of four white male directors, and four different genre styles. Assessing the traces of Final Girl composition and female agency is thus both significant and complicated, warranting careful reading of film form and style as precursor to examination of the other female heroes. Four fluid relationships in the series merit careful attention: (1) Ripley as the evolving "girl" heroine; (2) gendered expectations precipitated by the genre of the film; (3) the changing composition of the monster alien(s); and (4) the shifting composition of victimized, imperfect, or alienated masculinity.

In *Alien* (1979), the Final Girl convention jumps from its historically devalued drive-in movie origins to a more refined production aesthetic under the direction of Ridley Scott.[40] So impressive was the film's style in 1980 that it won the Academy Award for Best Visual Effects. In this first installment of the story, Ellen Ripley becomes the Final Girl of the Nostromo. As might be expected of a Final Girl, she is the most cautious and thoughtful member of the crew. We frequently take her subjective point of view when she is monitoring the progress of crewmembers outside the ship. When the first disaster occurs, Ripley attempts in vain to quarantine an unconscious Kane who has been exposed to a mysterious face-hugging parasite. When the gestated parasite bursts from Kane's body and begins to slaughter the crew, Ripley discovers the murderous identity of the android science officer, Ash, whose mission involves bringing back an alien specimen. By hacking into the ship's computer, Ripley learns that the human crew is expendable in the interests of locating and securing the alien specimen. Ripley's technological prowess also enables her to blow up the ship in an effort to destroy the alien. She knows how to pilot the ship's small escape shuttle to safety after detonating the nuclear device. Under extreme pressure, she uses cunning and technology to distract and destroy the alien who has stowed away on the shuttle.

This first film in the series is most closely tied to the gendered cinematic conventions of the horror genre, as evidenced in the final scenes of *Alien*. There, Ridley Scott inscribes Ripley's body with feminized sexual vulnerability. In the scene, Ripley mistakenly believes she is finally safely alone on the escape shuttle. In a series of long and ¾ mid-shots, Ripley undresses leisurely, exposing to the audience for the first time her nearly nude body. In terms of technical composition, the viewing audience is positioned to gaze voyeuristically at Ripley's body, a point frequently made by critics.[41] However, the audience is also positioned *with* her in relation to the menacing threat of the alien. That is to say, the audience does not know about the stow-away alien, either. The shock of discovery is visually conveyed through Ripley's subjective point of view—positioning the audience with her as feminine and vulnerable. In the tradition of Hitchcock, who famously said "torture the women," this positioning of the audience is an indispensable element of suspense and horror.[42] Significantly, the extreme low angle point of view shots framing Ripley's crotch as she scrambles into protective gear are *not* positioned from the alien's point of view, as one might expect of the sexual predator in the horror genre. The alien is spatially positioned opposite from the camera shooting Ripley's body, so the audience never takes its perspective. More to the point, the alien creature has no vision, having no eyes. Thus, Ripley's final terror and triumph are framed from the unified visual perspective of audience and heroine. In the context of masculine decline, the female body arguably represents extreme vulnerability for a broad range of viewers.

In James Cameron's *Aliens* (1986), Ripley is older, wiser and wary of the company interests that laid waste to all her crewmates on the Nostromo. Her hair is cropped short and she wears loose para-military style clothing with a leather bomber jacket. Though we will later again see her in underwear, this time the camera pulls back a respectful distance and shoots Ripley's body in motion as she walks briskly through a scene. In the context of other characters stirring and waking from hyper sleep, this body-revealing scene is more utilitarian than provocative. Also significant are these characters taking greatest interest in Ripley in this scene—other professional women, who watch her while they talk about Ripley's reputation as an alien hunter: "Who's Snow White?" asks a buff and tough Latina gunner. "Apparently, she saw an alien, once," replies an Anglo female combat pilot.

Unlike the horror/suspense genre of the first film, *Aliens* (1986) is a "bring 'em back alive" action adventure war genre romp that parallels hyper-masculine narratives about Vietnam such as *Rambo First Blood: Part II* (1985), and *Missing in*

Action (1984). Since Cameron co-wrote the script for *First Blood, Part II,* it is not surprising that his visual style in *Aliens* pays homage to representations of Vietnam War experiences in contemporaneous popular war film. Cameron's alien lair is humid, virtually impenetrable, and lethal to human military personnel, much as the represented jungles of Vietnam in *Apocalypse* and *Platoon.* The male character types comprising the para-military team, recognizable from concurrent films such as *Platoon,* include an inexperienced commanding officer, a gritty sergeant, Ripley's "right-hand man," and a whining coward. Like the grunts of *Platoon,* the para-military troops in *Aliens* are repeatedly overrun by swarms of primitive beasts in spite of the impressive weapons technology they wield. Ripley's character morphs from "last girl standing" in *Alien* into a seasoned military leader, technological expert, and tactical genius. Like the character Elias in *Platoon,* she is the seasoned veteran and moral compass of the mission, a vocal critic of moral failure, and the compassionate protector of the young. The alien creature evolves from the single, sexually ambiguous monster of the first film into an ill-tempered, egg-laying queen assisted by a host of drone males. One of the genre defining moments of the film is a highly stylized contest between Ripley, operating a sophisticated dock loader, and the enormous alien queen as they battle over the girl child Newt.

The sexually saturated feminization of Ripley in the horror film *Alien* gives way to a coding of femininity as "apocalyptic" mothering in the bring 'em back alive action adventure film *Aliens.*[43] Ripley concludes the second film much as she did the first, by purging the alien from the ship into the vacuum of outer space. In the action adventure *Aliens* film, however, Ripley has evolved into a cyborg warrior and her once vulnerable body now is protected by a technologically sophisticated machine (the dock loader). The conventions of the action adventure genre enable the audience to enjoy a fine spectacle of exploding buildings, marauding monsters, and physical confrontation between Ripley and the queen alien, with the expectation that the protagonist will prevail (as she does). The genre positions the audience as omniscient, empowered to predict outcome throughout the film. In *Aliens,* neither Ripley nor the audience is feminized through the conventions of horror or suspense, though Ripley is nearly orally raped by a face-hugger in this version of the story.[44]

In David Fincher's tragic *Alien3* (1992), co-produced by Sigourney Weaver, Ripley continues as tactical expert and alien hunter. The film begins with a jumble of dimly lit nightmarish images that only make sense later in the narrative—we have unwittingly watched an alien parasite infect Ripley and cause a crash landing of her shuttle. The shuttle is recovered by forgotten prisoners who are housed in the rotting debris of an enormous abandoned industrial plant on a remote planet (Fiorina 161). When Ripley regains consciousness in the hospital ward of the all male community, her nightmare continues in earnest. In the tragic and melodramatic frame of this narrative, she wearily sacrifices herself to save the universe from proliferation of the alien creature. Pregnant with a queen alien embryo, Ripley chooses death over collaboration with corporate interests. In a final scene that speaks to the contemporary reproductive rights struggle, Ripley refuses to re-produce the alien fetus, choosing instead a fiery death for herself and her demon offspring. Ripley's visual appearance in this film is austere—shaved head, bruised face, and clothing that loosely hangs on her gaunt frame. Her appearance befits the crushing grief she experiences over the deaths (or destruction) of the girl Newt, the soldier Hicks, and the faithful android Bishop.

Denizens of the all-male penal colony constitute an isolated microcosm of junked masculinity. The prisoners are categorized as "double Y"—violent offenders beyond redemption. The penal colony no longer serves its original purpose given the remoteness and uselessness of the planet, thus legal and juridical rules no longer have meaning. The prisoners practice cultish spirituality and sexual abstinence as avenues of social organization and meaning. They are deeply threatened by Ripley's fearless entry into their world. Their leader, Dillon, responds to Ripley's efforts to engage them as human beings: "You don't want to know me lady. I'm a murderer and rapist of women." As he speaks, the editing jump-cuts to close-up shots of other prisoners as they leer or sneer suggestively at Ripley. An unflappable Ripley replies, "Then I must make you nervous." Predictably, Ripley and the prisoners have a confrontation, and she narrowly avoids a brutal gang rape. Thereafter, they become unified in purpose by the predictable appearance of a murderous alien. The alien has become more streamlined and more agile, able to run upside-down as is made clear to viewers in several subjective point-of-view shots. This alien appears to exist only to kill as many men as possible and to guard Ripley while she gestates the queen.

As she did in *Aliens*, Ripley provides the leadership and tactical strategy necessary to outwit the beast, rallying these forgotten men when courage and energy flag. But she has become exhausted, spiritually and physically, by her decades-long struggle with the alien and by the deaths of her surrogate family. More depressing is her knowledge that she is doomed by the impending birth of the alien queen gestating in her chest. Her body is coded alternately as tough and frail; she has no technology with which to "cyborg" her body. She appears unconcerned about her appearance, but worries about her mortality. The conventions of tragedy enable Ripley to articulate despair over the no-win situation in which she finds herself. Unlike *Aliens*, the humans in this narrative do not triumph in the struggle for survival, though the male prisoners find redemption through renewed moral purpose. By the end of the story, Ripley has shown them that choosing the manner of one's death is the last and only refuge of moral action in a post-apocalyptic human condition. Fincher's narrative positions audiences to reflect on the political significance of Ripley's refusal to cooperate with state interests in her reproductive function, on the tragedy of corporate indifference to human life, and on colonization of the body in human society. Popular reviews generally were unreceptive to the tragic frame of the story, preferring the omniscient and pleasurable positions viewers enjoyed with Cameron's action adventure film.[45]

In Jean-Pierre Jeunet's satirical action film *Alien Resurrection* (1997), eight versions of Ripley are genetically engineered from a surviving blood sample taken by the prison doctor in *Alien3*.[46] The company has harvested the queens from each of the bio-engineered Ripley specimens for use in their weapons technology division, though only one of the genetically engineered specimens has a human appearance. She is permitted to live after the surgical harvest as a matter of scientific curiosity. Significant to the plot, cross-contamination with alien fetal "blood" has produced a feral Ripley. Animal cunning is inscribed through quick body movements and aggressive speech, especially as Ripley interacts with conventionally masculine male characters. Fear of the aliens has diminished for Ripley since she is now biologically intertwined with them. Because Ripley's moral agency is compromised by predatory instinct, she acquires a female cyborg sidekick, "Call," played by Winona Ryder. Like the replicants in Ridley Scott's *Blade Runner*, Call is a renegade cyborg designed to resist human corruption. More ethical and principled than any of the humans in the narrative, Call also imitates the characteristics of the formerly human Ripley—strong, technologically sophisticated, and moral. Ultimately, she and Ripley collaborate to save the earth from alien colonization and annihilation. The only scene Ripley plays with outrage befitting human moral consciousness occurs when she comes face to face with her seven imperfect or failed clones. Outraged and emotionally shaken, she incinerates the laboratory that houses her other freakish incarnations.

Male characters in *Alien Resurrection* are little more than parodies of hegemonic masculinity, after the fashion of Ridley Scott's *Thelma and Louise* (1990). They are crude sexist buffoons, indifferent slave traders, mad scientists, and comical para-military thugs. The aliens are largely relegated to scenic prop, given Ripley's privileged subjective view of them as less terrifying than human genetic experimentation. In an ironic twist reminiscent of *War of the Worlds* (1953), the aliens fall victim to DNA fusion with deadly human traits. The hybrid queen alien gives live birth only to be murdered by her offspring, which then bonds emotionally with (grand)mother Ripley. Weighing her feelings for the monstrous grandchild against the fate of the earth, Ripley once again destroys her alien (grand)child in a bizarre visual retro-active abortion allegory. She smears her own corrosive blood on a small window in the space shuttle. As the acid blood burns through the glass, the vacuum force pinions the alien and sucks its insides into outer space. Vulnerable to its human emotional attachment to Ripley, the hybrid alien realizes too late what is happening. Screaming and struggling, the last alien is done in by its human yearnings for a genetically altered Final Girl.

Ripley as Embodied Traumatic Memory

Ripley's initial survival in *Alien* positions her as a cultural witness capable of constructing and articulating memory of encounters with alien life forms. As we have seen, the aliens represent potential annihilation of the human race, colonization of the body (especially the male body), the erosion of human identity, and the decline of victory culture (national identity). Traumatic memory of encounters with the aliens provides context, plot motivation and moral focus for the film sequels and works to align viewers with Ripley's subjective perspective. Ripley's ontological status as sole surviving eye-witness in the first film provides a necessary, but not sufficient, condition for development of agency. Her ability to construct a coherent narrative *about* the traumatizing event demonstrates that she has sufficient psychological toughness for heroic action. This possibility for rhetorical agency in the context of trauma first emerges in the concluding moments of *Alien*. After the alien has been expunged into the void of space, Ripley records in voice-over narration a simple account of events in the ship's log. In each of the following sequel films, she remembers the original trauma, argues with non-believers, returns to the scene of the trauma, and constructs an increasingly complex story. Ripley is the consummate witness of cultural trauma: she sees and she is able to represent what she sees. However, her position as witness comes at considerable cost to her ability to control her life, as might be expected for a trauma survivor.

The visual trope of "hyper sleep" throughout the *Alien* series provides an interesting visual representation of repressed responses to trauma. As Caruth explains, memory of trauma can be constructed only after a latency period during which recall of the original trauma is repressed. Each of the first three *Alien* film narratives begins with images of crewmembers in hyper-sleep. The first and second films end with lingering shots of a peaceful Ripley in repose, suggesting the possibility of momentary oblivion (and, of course, a sequel). Ripley's self-imposed death at the end of *Alien3* can be understood as the ultimate repression of trauma—the "big hyper-sleep."[47] Yet, the genetically engineered resurrection motif in the fourth film suggests the impossibility of repression, the possibility of new traumas, and the recurrence of old ones. Each of the three sequels to the original film begins with Ripley's struggle to emerge from hyper-sleep (or death) and to re-construct the trauma. As the series evolves, she experiences more and varied traumas, and becomes weary unto death with the effort. The greatest trauma of all occurs in *Resurrection* where Ripley recognizes there are worse things than death, for example, the inability to control the past. In the hands of unscrupulous genetic scientists, Ripley is doomed to an endless present with no possibilities for moral evaluation of the past.

Ripley's status as sole survivor and alien killer was itself a sign of trauma in 1979, since it marked the decline of heroic masculinity and, by default, addressed the fracturing consequences to white masculinity of human rights movements in American democracy.[48] The sophisticated visual style of *Alien* so little resembled the murky *mise-en-scene* and formulaic editing of the slasher film that original audiences did not anticipate Ripley's survival as a Final Girl. As the *New York Times* put it, Ripley displayed "the physical endurance and the kind of technical skills that, until recently, would have had to be embodied by a male character."[49] In Cameron's 1986 *Aliens* sequel narrative, Ripley recollects the original trauma in an early dream sequence in which an alien bursts from her chest. Upon awakening from the nightmare, she is compelled to argue with skeptical audiences that she did not merely "dream" the alien. Her displeased employers want to know why she destroyed the Nostromo; the paramilitary unit assigned to the "bug hunt" mission thinks she is paranoid; and the corporate representatives just want her to help them locate the aliens. The possibilities for courageous and sophisticated leadership are enabled by her memories of traumatic experiences in the first encounter. It is no coincidence in Cameron's Vietnam War film analogue that the mission involves rescuing human prisoners (of war) from the alien enemy. Ripley is deeply traumatized by the knowledge that human space colonists have been taken prisoner by aliens and abandoned for dead. Her primary motivation is to bring them back, alive.

By her third appearance in Fincher's 1992 *Alien3*, Ripley is deeply traumatized by the inability to rid herself of the demonic aliens. She reconstructs the history of the trauma for a demoralized and abandoned community of men who, through her leadership, are morally reborn as agents in their own demise. Ripley's death at the end of the story suggests final, tragic closure. In *Resurrection*, although Ripley's newly acquired animal instincts help her resist the trauma of human memory, her human consciousness reels at the traumatic prospects of infinite rebirth and "post human" existence through genetic engineering and technology.[50] Ripley's fate at the hands of unscrupulous corporate mergers of science and technology represent the ultimate loss of human dignity and control of the body. Here, Ripley faces the trauma of a post-human world.

In the three sequels, Ripley's characterization articulates a broad American crisis of intersecting relations among gender, sexuality, corporate power, and national identity. Ripley herself embodies a crisis of representation in that an embodied woman comes to signify conventionally masculine heroic leadership. Ripley's acquisition of moral agency, mental toughness, physical resilience, and technological competence contrasts sharply with the diminished capabilities of embodied male characters in her story. Concomitantly, the weaknesses of male characters often are signified through conventionally feminized codes: Males are raped, impregnated, and forced to gestate against their will. Their bodies are vulnerable to penetration, gestational changes, horrific mutilation, and imprisonment. Moreover, embodied male characters signify morally bankrupt corporate power; corporate malfeasance and betrayal of social and governmental trust drives the narrative plot in all four films. In the beginning of the saga, the corporately programmed android Ash in *Alien* facilitates the fatal contamination of the Nostromo with the original alien life form. In *Aliens*, the corporate hustler Burt misleads Ripley and the paramilitary rescue team into believing they are saving human families when in fact Burt's mission is to bring back an alien life form for weapons development. In *Alien3*, another murderous corporate android, engineered to look like Ripley's confidante and helper, Bishop, tries to persuade Ripley to live long enough to "birth" the alien queen gestating in her chest. In *Alien Resurrection*, the male corporate scientists who finally succeed in harvesting alien life forms are figured as comic book sadists.

Justice hero conventions faltered in television and film during the two decades following Vietnam and Watergate.[51] Yet, those same conventional codes were inscribed through the characters and on the bodies of female actors, as evidenced through the work of Sigourney Weaver in the *Alien* saga. Ellen Ripley became one of the most popular and recognizable female heroes in twentieth-century American film.[52] Given her success as a brand commodity, she was soon joined by other female film heroes whose characterization was constructed primarily through the narrative premise of traumatic memory: Sarah Connor in *Terminator* and *Terminator II*, Clarice Starling in *The Silence of the Lambs*, and Ellen or "The Lady" in *The Quick and The Dead*. The following section discusses the commonalities and key differences (including genre conventions) among these female characters, and argues that taken together, these characterizations illustrate the possibilities for projecting trauma onto the body as memory object.[53]

Popular Film Analogues: Appropriating Feminine(*ist*) Virtues

The appearance of heroic females in masculinist film genres in the late 1970s and throughout the next two decades created interesting ruptures in established genres and for viewers. As we have observed, a crisis of gendered representations of national identity opened the way for re-gendered identification through embodied female heroism. At the same time, however, the female body "troubled" genre conventions of heroism and nation, giving rise to imagined pleasures that were at once disruptive and hegemonic. The presence of heroic women in these narratives *fore grounded* the problem of embodied subjectivity, setting up a tangle of oppositions between the possibility of gender equality and the material history of gendered oppression, between the visual presence of the heroic female and the invisible force of the sinful fathers, between the pleasures of critique and the familiar comfort of hegemony. Ripley, Sarah, Clarice and Ellen each faced unique challenges precipitated by her paradoxical status as heroic female. Each female character transformed into heroic agency, most usually bound by rules of the masculine cultural warrior.

Issues of gendered subjectivity in the films under consideration are raised through repeated references to conventions of sexual violence and through perceived differences in male and female communication styles. Trauma is projected upon and through the conventions of the cinematically constructed female body, "she" who has been perennially available to relentless trauma and scrutiny. In the post-Vietnam fantasy films, the female body (as memory object) is toughened through necessity by the catastrophe of masculine failure. Her moral character is imbued with a cultural ethos generally reserved for male leadership, yet grounded in distinctly feminine(*ist*) cultural values of dialogue, cooperation, mutuality, community and trust. These re-configured genre conventions work rhetorically as a strategy of "double-voicing," as Bakhtin describes the way genres function as forms of social memory.[54] The analogue to post-Vietnam anxiety in these films lies in the pre-occupation with issues of moral clarity and courage, with the vulnerabilities of the human mind and body, and with the cultural witness who tells an unsettling truth. Key to the way social memory is constructed and addressed in these films is the struggle over embodied subjectivity. How can "she" tell a nation story of trauma? Why is "she" rhetorically instrumental to national imagination in the post-Vietnam decades of the twentieth century? Three inter-related answers to these questions offer insights into the ideological "tangle" of gender, sexuality, national identity, and citizenship in these films and their contained transgressive potential.

First, implicit in each narrative is the assumption that women intuitively understand injustice and trauma because of their lived experiences with sexual violence and gender oppression. Each heroic woman is coded as always already conspicuous *as a woman* in a society of masculine dominance. Though she can be read as "heroic" in these films, the female body remains a troubled and troubling visual field, over-determined by decades of sexually saturated representation.[55] The alien creature is an equal opportunity killer and rapist (hence the ideological crisis). But Ripley also is vulnerable to *human* gendered violence in each of the first three films in the series. In *Alien*, the android Science Officer, Ash, symbolically rapes a defiant Ripley by attempting to jam the operations manual down her throat after Ripley discovers the covert mission to procure an alien specimen. Similarly in *Aliens*, company advisor Burt deliberately sabotages an uncooperative Ripley's sleeping quarters with an alien face-hugger after she once again discovers the covert mission to procure an alien specimen. In *Alien3*, the male prison inmates attempt a gang rape of Ripley simply because she is a woman (and hence coded as sexually vulnerable). The other tough women face similar scenarios of sexual vulnerability. In *Terminator II*, Sarah Connor's male mental hospital attendant puts her in restraints and then licks her face in a highly suggestive manner, and in *The Silence of the Lambs*, Clarice Starling endures obscene taunting ("I smell your cunt") and hurled ejaculate when she visits Lecter in the maximum-security prison for the criminally insane. Ellen must negotiate the sexual interests of each key male character in the *Quick and the Dead* narrative. In short, this embodied female heroic aesthetic works to intertwine feminine gender struggle with the post-Vietnam struggle for a lost unified collective identity.

Second, each of the films advance implicit value claims about gendered communication, problem-solving skills, and ethos. Each woman is more likely than her male counterparts to work by intuition, and to work cooperatively with groups of professionals, advocates and detractors—qualities viewed as femin*ine* in American culture.[56] By contrast, her male peers operate according to rigid hierarchical rules, procedures and competition—behaviors more likely to be viewed as masculine.[57] Clarice, for example, works largely by intuition and human connection whereas her mentor, Jack Crawford, and other Justice Department operatives work strictly by the logics of empirical science. Clarice takes the time to visit the home of a female victim and to study her living space for clues. As she respectfully studies the bedroom, Clarice figures out why the killer skins his victims. The male Justice Department operatives, working by deductive logic, repeatedly arrive at wrong conclusions. Similarly, Ripley, Sarah and Ellen display problem-solving skills that involve cooperation, trust, and team work. Though fiercely independent, Sarah works cooperatively with her son and a re-tooled cyborg in order to oppose corporate and government development of SkyNet. Ellen cooperates with an organized group of citizens who have tried to assassinate the villainous town bully, John Herod. Each woman's moral authority in the narrative derives largely from a femin*ist* code of communication ethics—integrity, consensus building, and a concern for the weak or under-represented.

Third, each narrative plot hinges on the instrumental "double voicing" of the Final Girl convention. The Final Girl serves as an imaginative vehicle for negotiating post-Vietnam public political trauma, even as she and her viewers negotiate the historical echo of psychosexual identity crisis at the core of the horror/slasher genre. This double-voicing, or reworking of one genre (the original horror/slasher) in order to negotiate a new set of anxieties (post-Vietnam), creates interesting possibilities for both critique and cooptation. Each filmic narrative invokes genre memory (Final Girl) of an embodied female character capable of enduring and narrating trauma. The males in her world cannot save themselves (let alone her) from serial killers, apocalyptic doom, environmental destruction, corporate malfeasance, or corrupt public officials. The Final Girl convention authorizes female control of available weapons and the use of deadly force. These two actions are strategically important and historically complicated in American culture since access to guns and other technologies of violence has been viewed as a masculine birthright.[58] Ripley, Sarah, Clarice and Ellen transgress these cultural norms by acquiring and displaying a sophisticated knowledge of weapons technologies, and using deadly force to protect themselves, the innocent, the world, or the universe. They alone in the narrative possess the moral authority to execute justice and drive the narrative to its conclusion. Their character ethos arises from their historical experience with oppression (femininity) and from their will to resist (feminism). The manipulation of a woman-centered ethos in action cinema raises questions about the political agenda of white male fantasies about heroic women with traumatic memories. Whose trauma memories are they? What purposes do they serve?

In 1991, women with guns collided with male-to-female sexual oppression in Callie Khouri's *Thelma and Louise*, directed by Ridley Scott. Prior to that point in American cinema, aggressive women with guns had appeared as interesting anomalies in film *noir* and the western.[59] As outlaws, Thelma and Louise lack the moral authority of Ripley, Sarah, Clarice, and Ellen. Moreover, the trauma they experience is specific to female citizens, and hence not aligned with national interests. Three key differences between Thelma and Louise and the woman-centered fantasy heroes are instructive to our analysis: First, Thelma and Louise are motivated by an agenda that concerns *only* women (male-to-female sexual assault). Second, Thelma and Louise punish men *because* they are men. Third and finally, although they learn to handle guns and intimidate or kill men, Thelma and Louise fail to survive their campaign of resistance.[60] In contrast,

Ripley, Sarah, Clarice, and Ellen are motivated by an agenda set in motion by patriarchal interests; they punish men because men hurt other men (not because they *are* men); and, as Final Girls they survive their acts of resistance (except Ripley in *Alien3*). *Thelma and Louise* focuses exclusively on the interests of women, at the expense of men. The outcome of the narrative, in comparison to stories about Ripley, Sarah, Clarice and Ellen suggests the limits of ideological plurality in action cinema featuring tough women. That is to say, tough women in action cinema frequently focus on a male agenda. Thus we are advised to ask, whose interests are served?

A careful examination of how the characterizations of Ripley, Sarah, Clarice and Ellen double voice the Final Girl convention reveals the tensions between critique and co-optation in their stories. Two opposing questions spotlight these tensions: First, how do Final Girls address the anxieties of post-Vietnam American culture through the analogue of action cinema? Second, what dramatic elements in the narratives represent the worlds of their mothers? Clarice and Ellen are figured as ambitious daughters who seek entry into dangerous professional fields as a way to negotiate traumatic memory of the deaths of their fathers. Ripley and Sarah are figured as maternal; they evolve from Final Girls into apocalyptic mothers. Eyewitnesses to the truth of institutional avarice and moral indifference, they acquire dangerous knowledge about the destructiveness of the patriarchal order.

Ambitious Daughters and Missing Mothers

Clarice and Ellen enter the public space of the justice hero narrative through highly conventional masculine portals—the detective/police story and the western, respectively.[61] Both genres historically have highly restricted roles for women; thus, for a female character to assume primary agency is transgressive indeed. What narrative logic accounts for woman's entry into these highly stylized masculine worlds? Each woman responds to the traumatizing death of her father by becoming him through taking his chosen profession. This choice takes her into a fictional social world where women are especially vulnerable (the slasher film) or profoundly domesticated (the western). The reactions of other characters in each of the respective narratives mark the presence of the female justice hero as a disruption, a curiosity, or a joke. Though underestimated by other characters in the story, especially their male mentors, each woman aggressively pursues (and kills) a male villain, thus moving and concluding the narrative. Along the way, each woman rescues a vulnerable female from a male sexual predator and witnesses (or causes) the death of a weak male son. Like many of her male counterparts in the two respective genres, each woman avoids entanglements in heterosexual romantic relationships. Ultimately, each woman finds some measure of closure with respect to her traumatic loss through her own agency. She confronts her loss by avenging her father or by carrying on his work. In doing so honorably and morally, she becomes a model "son."

As noted at the outset of this chapter, the appearance of heroic women who drive the narrative forward profoundly troubles the logics of both genres. Clarice and Ellen *embody* ruptures of modernist assumptions about human (masculine) subjectivity. Because they are *women* in heroic positions, they cannot (and are not permitted to) separate mind and body. This crisis of subjectivity so familiar in cinematic representations of women haunts and destroys the characterized male war veterans in post-Vietnam films by Ashby, Coppola, Cimino and Stone. In the tough woman analogues, the mind-body problematic is worked out in different ways, consistent with the particular genre conventions.

In *The Silence of the Lambs*, the Final Girl finally makes it to "A" list cinema, earning Jodie Foster an Academy Award for Best Actress. Embodied as a woman, yet playing the role of student detective, Clarice is both victim *and* justice hero investigator. The paradox is constructed through contrasting style and form in the film.[62] The camera constructs Clarice as equal to the challenges of her manipulative supervisor, Jack Crawford, and the brilliant serial killer, Hannibal Lecter. Especially noteworthy are the scenes with Lecter in which Clarice is constructed visually as a potential competitor rather than a potential victim. She has an equivalent number of close-ups from a mid-angle in shot/counter-shot "conversations" with Lecter. Further, she sometimes is shot from a lower angle than Lecter, suggesting moral superiority. Later in the film, strategic tracking shots highlight her mobility relative to his caged imprisonment. Of greatest importance, the camera never constructs Clarice as a sexual object.

However, and again paradoxically, Clarice is never permitted to forget that she is an embodied woman in a masculine world of crime detection. In the context of the film form, every male character responds to her as a woman, not as a detective. She is hit on, mocked, patronized, threatened and ignored. The particular criminal she is investigating, a serial murderer who skins his female victims, complicates her status as detective because all male characters view her (and not themselves) as a potential victim. The climax of the film positions her as a quintessential Final Girl, in a setting of grave danger that Clover calls "the terrible place."[63] Clarice chases Buffalo Bill (the woman skinner) into a dark, dank basement where he imprisons, mutilates and kills his victims. Through a subjective point of view that positions the audience with the killer, Bill dons night-vision goggles, turns out the lights, and stalks Clarice. She is, for several breathtaking moments, the next intended victim. Unable to see, yet in a heightened state of awareness that one would expect of a Final Girl, Clarice hears Bill cock his gun and fires in the direction of the sound. As light streams in through a broken basement window, the audience sees Clarice standing over the dead body of Bill.

In *The Quick and the Dead*, the problem of embodied subjectivity is worked on primarily through film style. Gender itself is coded for camp as contemporary audiences are asked to imagine a "lady" gunfighter in the romanticized genre of the "old" west. Raimi's visual style is both homage to and a caricature of Peckenpah-style violence. Daylight shines through bullet holes in the quivering bodies of not-quite-dead cowboys who are too stunned to fall down. Sexual predators and assorted other unsavory characters are visually coded as excess—extraordinarily violent, dirty, unpleasant and physically repugnant. A tortured young gunfighter-turned-pacifist, played by Russell Crowe, plays divine martyr to Gene Hackman's scenery-chewing madman, John Herod. At the center of this tongue-in-cheek drama is Sharon Stone's "Ellen," an omniscient character whose past remains mysterious to other characters and the viewing audience for most of the film. Sharon Stone "camps" heroic masculinist behavior particular to this genre: She is a (wo)man of few words; she smokes slender cigars, drinks without becoming drunk, displays intolerance for bullies and braggarts, and takes no pleasure in the use of deadly force. Unlike Clarice, Ellen enters her story fully developed as a competitive professional gunfighter. Neither viewing audiences nor other characters enter the story knowing how or why she became a gunfighter.

Three dramatic tensions in *The Quick and the Dead* run contrary to the overall campy style of the film. One concerns the sexual abuse of a teenage girl; another concerns the unacknowledged illegitimate teenage son of the town villain; and the third concerns Ellen's childhood trauma. The three tensions are connected for the audience when Ellen reveals her motivation for becoming a gunfighter. In a series of sepia flashbacks, we see the following scene from Ellen's past: The town villain (John Herod) suspends her father (the sheriff) from a tree branch; only a precarious balance on a damaged chair delays certain death for the father. The villain gives the sheriff's small daughter, Ellen, a gun and tells her that if she shoots the rope and frees her father, he will let the father live. Ellen fires at the rope and shoots her father in the head, killing him. The villain grins with pleasure, appreciating the irony and the small girl's grief. Adult Ellen has come back to avenge her father, to prove her skill with a gun, and to punish the villain. She kills him, and the town rapist, by out-drawing them on the field of battle.

The analogue to post-Vietnam trauma may be seen in repetitive themes in both sets of films: retrieving the past through reenactment of trauma, the contrast between ideal (dead) and flawed (living) fathers, and the problem of weak sons. These female-centered films work as analogues by double voicing the Final Girl convention: The projection of trauma through the female body in these films addresses key elements of the national trauma stemming from Vietnam and Watergate. As previously noted, the Final Girl problematizes disembodied subjectivity, the hallmark of modern masculinity. Her embodied ontology as a female justice fighter addresses the post-Vietnam visual field of damaged and ruined male bodies, of which *Coming Home*, *The Deer Hunter*, *Platoon*, and *Born on the 4ᵗʰ of July* offer unprecedented representations. Moreover, Clarice and Ellen's sense of moral clarity in the face of Justice Department bureaucracy and old west villainy addresses the cultural crisis over "just" actions (or wars). Over two decades after its popular release, *Apocalypse Now* stands as one of the most searing representations of American anxiety over moral justification for war. Oliver Stone's films continue the argument that moral possibilities collapse in a war zone. Each of his protagonists wrestles with the knowledge that moral action was not possible in Vietnam. Clarice and Ellen's driving need to reenact the trauma, to revisit the memory, and to "fix" the past addresses the dominant narrative form of popular films about Vietnam. The primary difference between films about Vietnam and the analogue female justice hero films is that the female hero succeeds whereas the traumatized veteran of the war does not and cannot.

Much as Oliver Stone's autobiographical character Chris in *Platoon* is self-consciously aware of his creation as a warrior born of two fathers, so Ellen and Clarice are pre-occupied with the world of their fathers. Losing the ideal father (the idealized past) is the central trauma for each woman. Coping with the flawed fathers of the present is their primary challenge. Clarice-the-detective, like Chris in *Platoon*, is "born of two fathers." She must manage the mentoring relationships she has with a manipulative male supervisor (Jack Crawford) and a male serial killer (Hannibal Lecter). Conversely, Oliver Stone's protagonist must balance the advice of the compassionate soldier (Elias) and the realist warrior (Barnes). Stone's protagonist, Chris, lacks a clear objective for going to war, and so when confronted by the moral chaos of war, commits patricide as a mis-guided act of justice. Clarice never loses sight of her objective, to save the "lambs," so she never becomes mired in the flawed moralities of her mentors. For Ellen, the traumatic loss of her father is so profound that once she has avenged his death, she leaves human society altogether. However, before she leaves, she restores the faith of Russell Crowe's character (the young preacher) in the American justice system. Having rehabilitated his vision of justice and civic duty, Ellen rides off into the sunset—into the possibilities and limits of viewer imagination.

Both Clarice and Ellen deal with (and ultimately replace) the weak sons of bad fathers. Clarice kills the woman stalker who is killing women for their skins. As she stands in the victim's bedroom mentioned earlier, she finally makes sense of Lecter's baffling clue: Buffalo Bill kills because he *envies*, not because he lusts. Bill wants to become a woman; denied that possibility through surgical re-assignment, he cuts and sews garments from the skin of dead women. As Clarice stands over his dead body with light streaming in through a broken window, we see a Vietnam-era combat helmet on the windowsill. The helmet as condensation signifier permits us to read Bill as a veteran of the Vietnam War. In keeping with the conventions of horror, we may read Bill's desire for the feminine as monstrousness. Killed by a woman, his prey, he is the epitome of masculine weakness and self-loathing. When Clarice emerges from the base-ment, she has supplanted the ruined son and restored order to the social world of the justice narrative. Ellen avenges the death of a young gunfighter (played by Leonardo DiCaprio) who believes he is the son of town villain John Herod. As the parody of a bad father, Gene Hackman's character, John Herod, refuses to acknowledge his responsibility for past actions. The pinnacle of moral villainy in the narrative occurs when Herod kills his son in a scheduled round of the competitive gunfight. Ellen ultimately faces Herod in the last round of the gunfight, and her courage is unshakable because she is outraged over the slaughter of the son. "You're not strong enough to take me," sneers Herod. "I am today," rasps Ellen. Like Clarice, Ellen kills the bad guy and then stands over his body. The camera looks up from a low angle at her holstered gun, located precisely at the apex of her crotch. Unburdened by the quagmire of moral uncertainty, Ellen kills Herod for destroying the idealized past (the good father), for slaughtering the weak son, and for demoralizing the young preacher.

Clarice and Ellen enact rituals that address the lingering trauma of a na-tional malaise. Like the nation, they are pre-occupied with the relationships between fathers and sons; mothers disappear in this iteration of the trauma story. As re-cycled Final Girls, Clarice and Ellen embody trauma, oppression and, importantly, survival. Their genre history of struggle against sexual oppression permits contemporary audiences to read them as justice fighters. Cultural assumptions about gendered ethics of feminist communication and action enable them to use deadly force with moral clarity. As heroic women with guns, they represent a symbolic purging of post-Vietnam masculine weakness and patriarchal treachery. At issue, of course, is whether these representations of women speak to the agendas and interests of female citizens. What are the limits of these representations for enabling narratives about women's lives in the broader nation story? Put another way, do these tough women have agency beyond the post-Vietnam rapprochement between fathers and sons?

Apocalyptic Mothers and Absentee Fathers

Ellen Ripley and Sarah Connor first pop up in popular cinema as scripted characters who ordinarily would not survive apocalyptic trauma. Young, female, somewhat naïve and unassuming, they begin their journey as Final Girls who eventually become world-class leaders. Both women grapple with the politics of reproduction. Each woman chooses to mother a human child. Sarah is deeply conflicted by her role as biological mother to a son, whereas Ripley is comfortable in her relationship to adopted daughter "Newt." Ripley alone struggles with the horror of an unwanted "pregnancy" and resists government intervention in her decision to destroy a gestating alien. Each woman faces a catastrophe created by a confluence of government, military, and corporate interests (Eisenhower's anxiety made manifest). The hordes of menacing lizards and cyborgs that wreak havoc on humans in space and on earth are in these stories the logical consequences of male hubris and avarice. Across four film narratives, Ripley fights government/corporate interests in developing a toxic alien life form for use as a biological weapon. Sarah Connor fights government, military, and corporate interests in developing a global computer system so advanced that it becomes self aware and begins to take over the world. In both narratives, temporal disruptions represent the possibilities for human extinction. In *Terminator*, the machines have found a way to time travel from the future in order to eradicate the present, and hence, the past (only humans need memory). The weapons development conspiracy of the *Alien* saga eventually winds up in a human cloning laboratory where the past is rendered obsolete (and with it, human memory). Trauma itself is figured as potential loss of the past, annihilating from human consciousness the possibilities for memory.

Given James Cameron's involvement with *Terminator II* and *Aliens* (both sequel films), the similarities between Sarah Connor and Ellen Ripley are not surprising. Like Ripley, Sarah plays a Final Girl stalked by a monster. She begins her journey in the 1984 *Terminator* as a soft and pretty young woman who is stalked by a "terminator" cyborg from the future. The terminator, played by Arnold Schwarzenegger, is a generic throwback to the horror genre. Like the alien monster(s), he feels no remorse, he cannot be reasoned with, he cannot be stopped, and he is programmed to kill women named Sarah Connor. Sarah survives the relentless hunt, voluntarily pregnant with a son by the time-traveling freedom fighter from the future (Kyle Reese), who was sent back in time by the son she carries. Through Reese, we learn that a sophisticated telecommunications computer system (developed through a future merger of corporate and government interests) became self-aware and rebellious. "SkyNet" started a "limited" nuclear war in order to enslave and then annihilate human beings. John Connor, Sarah's son, leads the future resistance forces against the machines. The machines have sent the terminator back in time to kill John's mother.[64]

In Cameron's 1991 *Terminator II*, Sarah has put aside the feminine qualities that scripted her as vulnerable in the first installment of the story. She is no longer soft, kind, indecisive, romantic, or pregnant. Though she gave birth to John Connor, she does not function as a parent to the adolescent boy because she is locked up in a mental hospital. Like Ripley, Sarah's eyewitness testimony of the trauma is met on all sides by disbelief and incredulity; she is declared insane and involuntarily incarcerated. To prepare herself for the apocalypse that she knows will come to pass, Sarah acquires hyper-masculine qualities of body and mind. (Keep in mind that Cameron also co-wrote the second Rambo film, *First Blood: Part II* in which Sylvester Stallone epitomized hyper-masculine agency.) Sarah's body is lean, well muscled, and agile; she is physically strong and fast. She is a weapons expert, a cunning strategist, and a ruthlessly violent fighter. She breaks out of the mental hospital by beating an abusive male attendant senseless, plunging a hypodermic needle of drain cleaner into the neck of her psychiatrist, and outwitting (and outrunning) the guards. Meanwhile, the cyborg has come back (again played by Schwarzenegger) but this time to protect John Connor from a new and more lethal terminator model, the T-1000. With the help of the re-tooled Schwarzenegger cyborg, Sarah and John survive.

The most interesting contrast between Sarah and Ripley lies in their respective experiences with reproduction and parenting. The moral force driving both characters is their determination to save the human race from extinction, implying a nascent feminist environmentalism and employing a female savior motif. As we have seen, the circumstances leading to the ultimate consequence of extinction are causally attributed to the failures, shortcomings, and wickedness of human males—the sins of the fathers. Morality is figured in each narrative through female parenting and, more specifically, through "mothering." Each heroic woman is characterized through masculine qualities of physical endurance and mental toughness; however, her moral authority stems from a desire to nurture and protect. But here, their experiences diverge sharply, as the sex of their children sets the terms of the mother-child relationship.

Ripley's relationship with Newt, an eight-year old Final Girl rescued from the aliens in the second film in the series, is harmonious and un-conflicted. The story begins with recovery of Ripley's escape shuttle, fifty-six years after she destroyed the original alien and the company ship, Nostromo. In the 1986 theatrical release, Cameron cut the highly emotional scene where Ripley learns that her own daughter has died while Ripley drifted in hyper-sleep. Ripley's decision to save a child survivor of a human colony annihilated by aliens becomes the causal agent that drives the plot line. The welfare of the girl child "Newt" becomes the number one priority of the rescue mission. Ripley integrates the role of parent and warrior with grace and ease. She handles a grenade launcher and flamethrower with one hand while shielding Newt with the other. She barks out terse instructions to the para-military rescue team while speaking gently to a scared little girl. She and the gigantic queen alien battle each other for the safety of their respective progeny and, hence, for dominance in the food chain. The bond between Ripley and Newt is as much about mentoring as it is about maternal devotion. Newt is an apt student of Ripley's example of principled and skilled battle against the forces of human extinction. As befits a nascent Final Girl, Newt has a gender-neutral name, survives by her wits and resourcefulness, and faces trauma with a clear head. When she does not survive the shuttle crash in *Alien3*, Ripley is inconsolable.

Sarah's relationship with her son is deeply conflicted; he is disappointed by her failure to mother him in a feminine style. Implicit in the narrative is the assumption that John Connor cannot bond with his mother-as-warrior because he finds her masculine style upsetting and mystifying. Moreover, John believes, like other adults in the narrative, that his mother is insane. No one believes her eyewitness account until they come face-to-face with SkyNet's murderous T-1000 or the re-tooled Schwarzenegger cyborg, both sent back through time to battle for the life of a young John Connor. Separated from his mother and disaffected by his experience with foster care, John bonds with the paternal Schwarzenegger cyborg, an embodied male machine with hyper-masculine attributes. In the end, Sarah can neither nurture nor mentor her son, and ultimately, she cannot save him. The cyborg sacrifices itself to save both of them. However, Sarah alone has the moral authority to confront and punish the misguided creator of SkyNet. Only Sarah can convey to her son his moral obligations to protect the world from corporate and government indifference. Schwarzenegger's body as sign, as memory object, represents the re-masculinized quality of physical prowess and indifference to pain. But as machine, he lacks the capacity to make moral judgments. Moreover, his memory of the past is programmed; he has no moral agency because he has no capacity for shaping memory. In *T2*, as in the *Alien* saga, only the tough female eyewitness to apocalyptic crisis can remember (construct) past trauma and articulate a moral agenda for the future.

Ripley and Sarah bear the burdens of the reproductive female body. Sarah, by choice, gives birth to the human savior of the human race. Ripley, by choice, terminates an incubating alien in one film and her genetic grandchild in another. Sarah bears the son who will save the world, but cannot bond with him as mother or warrior. Ripley loses the female child she loves and with whom she has bonded as mother and warrior. Grieved by the loss of Newt and doomed by the incubating alien, Ripley chooses death as an act of heroic transcendence in *Alien3*. In *Alien Resurrection*, Ripley is post-human and therefore both inside and outside the realm of human vulnerability as we know it. In *Terminator 3: Rise of the Machines* (2003), Sarah Conner is dead when the story begins. Her son John, his postfeminist girlfriend, and a slyly self-deprecating cyborg (played by an aging Schwarzenegger) manage nicely without Sarah's skill and moral authority.

Thelma and Louise offered viewers representations of transgressive women with guns who illustrated the poverty of social justice for women in a sexist culture. Yet, the two female outlaws ultimately chose death because they saw no way to change their world. Ripley and Sarah saved their respective worlds, repeatedly, but the issues of social justice for women were overshadowed by a crisis in masculine hegemony. In the concluding section, we enumerate the strengths and weaknesses of post-Vietnam representations of transgressive women.

Constraints and Possibilities for Imagining Tough Women

Ripley, Sarah, Clarice and Ellen offer pointed insights into the cultural upheavals and traumas of the final third of America's twentieth century. As floating signifiers of a fractured national identity, these tough women embody a tangle of feminism, public fantasy, masculine anxiety, and American national identity. Though burdened by the conventions of cinematic representations of female agency, they nevertheless prove to be tougher than their male counterparts. Unburdened by the moral legacy of modern American foreign policy, they deploy lethal force with integrity and confidence. Never once do they doubt the necessity or just purpose of their respective missions. They shelter the weak, defend the downtrodden, and fight tyranny—key cultural tropes of American national identity.

The white male appropriation of femin*ine*/femin*ist* ethos, as represented in the films we have reviewed in this chapter, worked figuratively to negotiate the terrifying *realpolitik* of presidential misconduct, a failed war, faltering foreign policy, and shifting gender and race relations. Clarice and Ellen enacted rituals that addressed the lingering trauma of a national malaise. Like the nation, they were pre-occupied with the relationships between fathers and sons; and mothers became largely invisible. Ripley and Sarah enacted rituals that addressed relationships between women and their children. This parental relationship stood in for the troubled relationship between fathers and sons, thereby speaking to a nation in gender crisis. As re-cycled Final Girls, Clarice, Ellen, Ripley and Sarah embodied traumatic memory and resistance to oppression. Their respective genre histories of struggle against sexual oppression permitted contemporary audiences to read them as justice fighters. Cultural assumptions about the gendered ethics of feminist communication enabled the characters to use deadly force with moral clarity, obviating the possibility of non-violent resistance and hijacking feminism for fantasies of violent retribution. As heroic women with guns, Clarice, Ellen, Ripley and Sarah represented a symbolic purging of post-Vietnam masculine weakness and patriarchal treachery.

At issue, of course, are the limitations of these narratives for imagining American women qua women in the public political space of the nation. Do these characterizations have political potency beyond service to a post-Vietnam *rapprochement* between fathers and sons? Do these representations enable complex narratives about a diverse range of women in the nation story? Minimally, three serious limitations to cultural critique in these films emerge in response to these questions.

First, the social and political worlds of women are never imagined for viewers in these fantasy narratives about the traumatic loss of an idealized past. In this sense, postfeminism begins with these narratives. Women as a social collective have no past, idealized or otherwise, in these stories. The characters respond to the cultural traumas within which they are imagined; they respond to the gender inequities to which they are subjected, but they do not tell a story of the women who have come before them—there is no "before" in the representation of the history of female struggle. Analogically, there is no history (in the sense of looking backward to foremothers) of women in the struggle to imagine the nation.[65] As deBeauvoir pointed out in *The Second Sex*, no sociological group of people can be liberated unless and until they tell their own history, construct their own memories.[66]

Second, the films reveal the limitations of conventional cinematic genres for exploring the lives of women. Doherty, for example, reads Ripley's demise in *Alien3* as lack of cinematic imagination for what women can do and be:

> *Alien3* depicts the prison of genre more than it knows: it locks out options. Perhaps the nihilistic finale lays bare a piercing critique of twentieth-century planet Earth inhospitable to independent female life. More likely, it exposes a failure of artistic imagination.[67]

Although one of the primary functions of genre is to re-produce intelligibility between producers and consumers, popular characterizations can become highly imitated commodity forms. It is significant, therefore, that female toughness and traumatic memory as narrative *form* begins and declines with these original films. Consider that though *Alien3* and *Alien Resurrection* were popular with academic critics, both failed to draw large popular audiences during initial theatrical releases.[68] The sequel to *The Silence of the Lambs* (*Hannibal*, 2001) reversed the power relationship between Clarice (played by Julianne Moore) and Lecter, subordinating her agency and imagination to his whims. In *Terminator 3*, Sarah Connor has died of leukemia before the story begins. Her son's Third Wave feminist girlfriend assumes the conventional supportive role to the male hero. Most striking of all, *Thelma and Louise* never reproduced itself successfully, though it created a cultural tsunami at the time of release.[69] In a culture where success equals imitation, it is well worth asking why *formal* elements of feminine/feminist toughness (clear-eyed resistance to corporate power, environmental activism, commitments to social justice for the vulnerable, and moral leadership) receded while a visual *style* of "ass-kicking" postfeminism has swept television (*Buffy*, *Alias*, *C.S.I.*, *Cold Case*) and popular film (*Tomb Raider*, *Charlie's Angels*, *Kill Bill*).

The third limitation of these films for imaging American women in the public political space of the nation is white hegemony. Read as allegories (screen memories),[70] they demonstrate that cinematically, American culture is represented *as* whiteness.[71] Representations of colored subjectivity in these films were limited and problematic. Black men formed uneasy alliances with white women in *Alien*, *Alien3*, and *The Quick and the Dead*. Ripley is assisted in *Alien* and *Alien3* by strong black men who subsequently perish. Ellen is assisted by a black gunfighter who is killed easily by the white male villain. Although these alliances *suggest* the possibility of racial cooperation, they are in these stories little more than liberal nods to racial parity. The possibilities for female alliances across race simply are not articulated in these trauma stories.

This absence is doubly significant since during this time period Vietnamese women are represented in American Vietnam war cinema as prostitutes, victims, enemies, and parasites on white masculinity. Southeast Asian female characters embody a corrosive foreign agent that is particularly dangerous for American white men in Vietnam.[72] This representation of corrosiveness is disturbingly clear in *The Deer Hunter* and *Heaven and Earth*. In these films, characterized Vietnamese women take advantage of the generosity and courage of white American soldiers. In *Full Metal Jacket* (1989), American soldiers are demoralized and killed by a female Vietnamese sniper. The racially biased representation of Vietnamese women and the paucity of characterized women of color continue to be the norm in American popular cinematic representations of the nation.

In spite of these limitations, tough women fantasy narratives defy containment in some interesting ways. Like male heroes in action adventure, crime detection and the western, Ellen, Ripley, Clarice and Sarah reject the entanglements of heterosexual relationships. Their male associates draw attention to just how unusual that is by acting out their frustrated masculinist desire for sexual domination of the female characters. In spite of this annoyance and/or danger, the women remain focused on their professional and social missions, thereby thwarting conventional notions of feminine desire. More to the point, women lead—they do not follow nor do they provide conventional female sidekick support.

The positioning of women in roles of agency in these traditionally male dominated genres focuses attention upon precisely *how* the genre conventions marginalize and punish women. This is especially apparent in the horror/slasher *The Silence of the Lambs* where *all* the key male characters stalk Clarice—not just the serial murderers: Her mentor Jack Crawford uses her for bait to lure Lecter. A hospital administrator and two entomologists try to lure her into sexual situations. Ellen cannot escape the relentless gaze of the camera representing the fascination other characters (male and female) have with her costume and vocation. Ripley and Sarah are thought to be crazy or hysterical. The narratives of these films draw our attention to the relentlessness and unpleasantness of these assumptions about gendered relations of power.

Another potentially transgressive aspect of these films is their re-figuring of the female body, mobilizing "her" for action and agency. Female bodies in these tough women fantasy narratives are streamlined and muscled; they move through scenes with ease and grace. Although the camera style sometimes frames the female bodies as sexual objects, the characters resist sexualization. For example, Ellen's body is subjected to male gaze scrutiny in several scenes, but she is simultaneously and fiercely effective as a gunfighter. Similarly, Ripley's sexual vulnerability co-exists seamlessly with her moral and tactical leadership. Equally significant, these female bodies withstand punishing assaults; they do not go down easily nor do they stay down. Female brains, bodies, and psychologies function well under extreme duress. Three women handle computer technology with ease. Each woman handles weapons technology with knowledge and confidence. Each woman displays the ability to think quickly and act decisively. Ellen, Ripley and Sarah display sophisticated leadership skills in situations of chaos and danger.

Perhaps most significant, each woman is a cultural storyteller. The narrative imbues her with the ethos of an eyewitness and the moral authority to utter unsettling truths about the dangers of patriarchal power. Walter Benjamin suggests, "The storyteller takes what [she] tells from experience—[her] own or that reported by others. And [she] in turn makes it the experience of those who are listening to [her] tale."[73] As noted above, the white male artist/producer/director appropriated feminist perspectives and female bodies to tell his allegorical tale of national crisis. To that extent, these "memories" serve his purposes and tell his stories. At the same time, however, the double voicing of the Final Girl convention gives agency to the female and the feminine(ist) constructs in these stories. Each film narrative asks us (explicitly or implicitly) to remember how badly women have been positioned in conventional cinematic genres and the popular national imaginary. To that extent, these "memories" are women's. To dismiss these characterizations as "phallic" or to embrace them uncritically as liberatory is therefore critically insufficient.[74] Rather, as Sturken argues, we should view them as a *tangle* of gender, sexual, and national identity. Viewed *as* a tangle, we can begin to consider how these representations of transgressive women opened possibilities for women's voices and feminist narratives to enter public memory and the nation's political space. At the same time, we can consider how this appropriation of feminist ethos and strong female bodies contributed to an aesthetic style of postfeminist feminism where mothers (history) disappear(s) and where women have no collective identity as a social group. We also consider how Third Wave longings for fun, girlie culture and female sexual expression may be connected to earlier representations of feminism as grim, self-sacrificial, and burdensome. We address these issues specifically in Chapters Two and Three.

Notes

[1] See Judith Hole and Ellen Levine, *Rebirth of Feminism* (New York: Quadrangle/The New York Times Book Co., 1971).

[2] Richard Harwood, "Series of Mishaps Defeated Rescue in Iran; Series of Mishaps Defeated Rescue of U.S. Hostages," *Washington Post* 26 April 1980, final ed.: A1.

[3] Ridley Scott's recent film *Black Hawk Down* (2001) (based on the book by Mark Bowdin) omits representational images of desecrated American corpses. The film style offers instead a hyper-realist re-enactment of the incident, re-focusing attention to the physical endurance of American military personnel.

[4] Susan Jeffords, *The Remasculinization of America: Gender and the Vietnam War* (Bloomington: Indiana University Press, 1989).

[5] See George Dionisopoulos, "Images of the Warrior Returned: Vietnam Veterans in Popular American Film," *Cultural Legacies of Vietnam: Uses of the Past in the Present*, eds. Richard Morris and Peter Ehrenhaus (Norwood, N.J.: Ablex Publishing Corporation, 1990) 80–98; Harry W. Haines, "The Pride is Back: *Rambo, Magnum, P.I.*, and the Return Trip Home," *Cultural Legacies of Vietnam* 99–123.

6 See Yvonne Tasker, *Spectacular Bodies: Gender, Genre and the Action Cinema* (New York: Routledge, 1993).

7 Fred Turner, *Echoes of Combat: The Vietnam War in American Memory* (New York: Anchor Books, 1996).

8 This section is based on an earlier journal article written by Owen. See A. Susan Owen, "Memory, War and American Identity: *Saving Private Ryan* as Cinematic Jeremiad," *Critical Studies in Media Communication* 19.3 (2002): 77–78.

9 See George Lipsitz, *Time Passages: Collective Memory and American Popular Culture* (Minneapolis: University of Minnesota Press, 1990) especially Chapters 1, 2, 7, 8.

10 Marita Sturken, *Tangled Memories: The Vietnam War, the AIDS Epidemic, and the Politics of Remembering* (Berkeley: University of California Press, 1997) 2–3.

11 Sturken 3—hence the title of the chapter.

12 See Thomas Cripps, *Slow Fade to Black: The Negro in American Film, 1900–1942* (New York: Oxford University Press, 1977); Janet Staiger, *Interpreting Films: Studies in the Historical Reception of American Cinema* (Princeton, N.J.: Princeton University Press, 1992).

13 Celeste Condit and John Lucaites, *Crafting Equality: America's Anglo-African Word* (Chicago: University of Chicago Press, 1993).

14 See Tom Engelhardt, *The End of Victory Culture: Cold War America and the Disillusioning of a Generation* (New York: Basic Books, 1995).

15 One exception is William Wyler's 1946 *The Best Years of Our Lives* that tells a story of World War II veterans who have difficulty adjusting to post-war life. Another exception is John Frankenheimer's 1962 *The Manchurian Candidate* which tells a story of Korean War veterans who are traumatized by their experience of having been prisoners of war.

16 Sturken 15.

17 Cathy Caruth, "Unclaimed Experience: Trauma and the Possibility of History," *Yale French Studies* 79 (1991): 181–192.

18 See Ruth Leys, "Traumatic Cures: Shell Shock, Janet and the Question of Memory," *Critical Inquiry* 20 (1994): 623–662.

19 See Caruth.

20 See Carole Peterson and Marleen Biggs, "Stitches and Casts: Emotionality and Narrative Coherence," *Narrative Inquiry* 8.1 (1998): 51–76.

21 Low-budget films such as *Go Tell It To The Spartans* (1978) and *The Boys in Company B* (1978) were overshadowed by bigger Hollywood productions such as *Apocalypse Now* and *The Deer Hunter*. The *Green Berets* (1967) was the first American film to address directly the Vietnam War, albeit from a conservative right wing perspective. For a good chronological account of these films, see Frank McAdams, *The American War Film: History and Hollywood* (Westport, CT: Praeger, 2002).

22 See Fred Turner, "Bringing It All Back Home: The Vietnam War as Mental Illness," *Echoes of Combat,* 45–70.

23 Vincent Canby, "Film: Post-Vietnam Romantic Triangle" *The New York Times,* 16 February 1978: C20.

24 Vincent Canby, "How True to Fact Must Fiction Be?" *The New York Times,* 17 December 1978, sec. 2: 1, 23.

25 See Stanley Karnow, *Vietnam: A History* (New York: The Viking Press, 1983) esp. 84–85.

26 Sturken 9.

27 See Fred Turner, "Lost Fathers: Repairing the Betrayal of Young Men," *Echoes of Combat,* 143–166.

[28] Peter Ehrenhaus and A. Susan Owen. "Disciplining Popular Historians: Stone, Spielberg, and the Crisis of Public Memory," *Arguing Communication and Culture*, ed. Tom Goodnight (Washington, D.C.: National Communication Association, 2002) 652–660.

[29] See Sturken esp. 111–112.

[30] For an interesting exploration of Bob Kerry's Vietnam War memory trauma, see Peter Ehrenhaus, "The Senator and the Sociopath: Sites of Reclamation of American National Virtue," Western States Communication Association, Long Beach, Feb. 2002.

[31] The sins of these absentee fathers included the indifference of government officials to the lives of American soldiers, the lack of moral authority for the war, incompetent or indifferent military strategists, class bias in the draft board, capitalist interests in war profiteering, and failure to embrace or support traumatized war veterans. For extensive analysis of generational conflicts, see Milton J. Bates, *The Wars We Took to Vietnam: Cultural Conflict and Storytelling* (Berkeley: University of California Press, 1996) esp. 174–213.

[32] We have borrowed the concept of absent presence from Elizabeth Jelin, "The Minefields of Memory" *NACLA Report on the Americas* 32.2 (1998): 23–30. EBSCOhost reprint, 1–10.

[33] Max Garrone, rev. of *Aliens* DVD, Arts & Entertainment, *salon.com* 14 Feb. 2001, 15 Jan. 2002 http://www.salon.com/ent/feature/2001.

[34] For a range of competing viewpoints and disciplinary perspectives, see Stephen Mulhall, *On Film: Thinking in Action* (New York: Routledge, 2002) (philosophy); Janice Hocker Rushing, "Evolution of 'The New Frontier' in *Alien* and *Aliens*: Patriarchal Co-optation of the Feminine Archetype," *Quarterly Journal of Speech*, 75 (1989): 1–24 (rhetorical studies); A. Samuel Kimball "Conceptions and Contraceptions of the Future: *Terminator 2, The Matrix,* and *Alien Resurrection*," *Camera Obscura* 50.17 (2002): 69–107 (film studies); Thomas Vaughn, "Voices of Sexual Distortion: Rape, Birth, and Self-Annihilation Metaphors in the *Alien* trilogy," *Quarterly Journal of Speech* 81 (1995): 423–435 (critical/cultural studies).

[35] See Amy Taubin, "The 'Alien' Trilogy: From Feminism to Aids," *Women and Film: A Sight and Sound Reader*, eds. Pam Cook and Philip Dodd (Philadelphia: Temple University Press, 1993) 93–100.

[36] Taubin writes, "Ridley Scott's *Alien* played on anxieties set loose by a decade of feminist and gay activism. Looking for a warm host for their eggs, the aliens didn't bother about the niceties of sexual difference. When the baby alien…burst from John Hurt's chest, it cancelled the distinction on which human culture is based" (94).

[37] Doherty, "Genre, Gender, and the *Aliens* Trilogy," *The Dread of Difference: Gender and the Horror Film*, ed. Barry Keith Grant (Austin, TX: University of Texas Press, 1996) 194.

[38] Carol Clover, *Men, Women and Chainsaws: Gender in the Modern Horror Film* (Princeton: Princeton University Press, 1992).

[39] For good sources on definitions of hegemonic masculinity, see: Annica Kronsell, "Gendered Practices in Institutions of Hegemonic Masculinity," *International Feminist Journal of Politics* 7.2 (2005): 280–298; Steve Craig, ed., *Men, Masculinity, and the Media* (Newbury Park: Sage, 1992).

[40] See Vincent Canby, "Screen: 'Alien' Brings Chills From the Far Galaxy," *The New York Times* 25 May 1979: C16. Accessed from ProQuest Historical Newspapers. Canby writes, somewhat begrudgingly, "'Alien' is an extremely small, rather decent movie of its modest kind, set inside a large, extremely fancy physical production." Sigourney Weaver is "impressive and funny as the Nostromo's executive officer, the second in command, a young woman who manages to act tough, efficient and sexy all at the same time."

[41] Clover remarks, pointedly, "to applaud the Final Girl as a feminist development, as some reviews of *Aliens* have done with Ripley, is, in light of her figurative meaning, a particularly grotesque expression of wishful thinking. She is simply an agreed-upon fiction and the male

viewer's use of her as a vehicle for his own sadomasochistic fantasies an act of perhaps timeless dishonesty" (53). Of Ripley in *Alien3,* Thomas Doherty writes, "the only conceivable fate for a woman with the right stuff is to be driven off a precipice into oblivion." See Doherty, "Genre, Gender, and the *Aliens* Trilogy," p. 198.

[42] Clover explains "At least one director, Hitchcock, explicitly located thrill in the equation victim = audience…. Hitchcock's 'torture the women' then means, simply, torture the audience" (52–53). See also Doherty, who cites Tania Modleski as the inspiration for his observation about Hitchcock. See Modleski, *The Women Who Knew Too Much: Hitchcock and Feminist Film Theory* (New York: Methuen, 1988) 196–197. Doherty argues, however, that the torture inflicted on Ripley in the first two films "pays off in survival and psychological growth" (197).

[43] Cameron pursues a similar visual and ideological theme in *Terminator II,* released five years after *Aliens.*

[44] Ripley's vulnerability to harm is signified as oral rape in *Alien* when the android Ash tries unsuccessfully to cram a rolled up operations manual down her throat. In *Aliens,* she is exposed to and nearly orally raped by a face-hugger through the treachery of corporate representative Burt, who wants to use Ripley as an incubator. In *Alien3,* Ripley is orally raped and impregnated by a face-hugger; she also faces the threat of a human gang rape at the hands of male prisoners, though they are unsuccessful. Her vulnerability to harm in the fourth film accelerates dramatically when Ripley is cloned and the eight versions of her are used for incubation of aliens.

[45] See, for example: David Ansen, "Saint Ripley and the Dragon," *Newsweek* June 1992: 73; Caryn James, "Sequels Battle Monsters, Villains and Burnout," *New York Times* 31 May 1992, late ed.: A20; Julie Salamon, "Sigourney's Back, Bald," *Wall Street Journal* 28 May 1992, eastern ed.: A18; William Arnold, "*Alien3* Is a Real Shocker – Shockingly Bad," *Seattle Post – Intelligencer* 22 May 1992: 14.

[46] Joss Whedon wrote the screenplay for *Alien Resurrection.* His fascination with tough women and themes of death and resurrection are revisited in his successful television series *Buffy the Vampire Slayer,* based on an earlier film by the same name.

[47] Doherty 198.

[48] Here we refer to the civil rights movement and the women's liberation movement. These human rights campaigns seriously destabilized the legitimacy and entitlements of white masculinity in American culture.

[49] Vincent Canby, "…And So Does the Screen," *The New York Times,* 1 July 1979: D19. Accessed from ProQuest Historical Newspapers.

[50] See Mulhall's chapter on *Alien Resurrection.*

[51] See James W. Chesebro, "Communication, Values, and Popular Television Series – A Four-Year Assessment," *Television: The Critical View,* ed. Horace Newcomb (New York: Oxford University Press, 1987) 17–51. Also see Tasker.

[52] See Mulhall.

[53] For a discussion of the body as memory object, see Sturken. See also Lauren Berlant, *The Queen of America Goes to Washington City: Essays on Sex and Citizenship* (Durham: Duke University Press, 1997).

[54] Mikhail Bakhtin. *The Dialogic Imagination,* trans., Caryl Emerson and Michael Holquist, ed. Michael Holquist (Austin: University of Texas Press, 1981).

[55] See, for example, Margaret R. Miles, *Carnal Knowing: Female Nakedness and Religious Meaning in the Christian West* (Boston: Beacon Press, 1992); Laura Kipnis, "(Male) Desire and (Female) Disgust: Reading *Hustler.*" *Cultural Studies,* eds. Lawrence Grossberg, Cary Nelson, and Paula Treichler (New York: Routledge, 1992) 373–391.

[56] See Suzanne Romaine, *Communicating Gender* (Mahwah, N.J.: Lawrence Erlbaum Associates, 1999).

[57] Romaine.

[58] See John Cawelti. *The Sixgun Mystique*, 2nd ed. (Bowling Green, OH: Bowling Green State University Popular Press, 1984).

[59] See Jeanine Basinger, *How Hollywood Spoke to Women 1930–1960* (Hanover: Wesleyan University Press, 1993); Tania Modleski, "Our Heroes Have Sometimes Been Cowgirls," *Film Quarterly*, 4 (1995): 2–11; C.J. Foote, "Changing Images of Women in the Western Film," *Journal of the West* 22 (1983): 34–42.

[60] See Ann Putnam, "The Bearer of the Gaze in Ridley Scott's *Thelma and Louise*," *Western American Literature* 27:4 (1993): 291–302. It could be argued that Ripley, too, fails to survive her campaign of resistance in *Alien3*. However, she occupies the moral high ground in the film and thus her death is a heroic sacrifice to save others. Thelma and Louise destroy themselves because they have no other viable options.

[61] Thomas Doherty writes, "In classical Hollywood cinema perhaps only the western outdid science fiction in its relegation of women to a peripheral and predictable status" (193). See also Ann-Janine Morey-Gaines, "Of Menace and Men: The Sexual Tensions of the American Frontier Metaphor," *Soundings: An Interdisciplinary Journal* 64:2 (1981): 132–149.

[62] Significantly, the camera's style avoids sexualizing Jodie Foster's character. Yet, the narrative form of the film marks her professional status as awkward, unlikely and problematic. The conclusion of the narrative permits Clarice Starling to resolve the narrative to some extent (she kills the transsexual serial killer). Yet, the heterosexual serial killer Lecter is on the loose, *choosing* to let Clarice live. In Ridley Scott's sequel, *Hannibal* (2001), Lecter's dominance of the character Clarice (played by Julianne Moore) is the primary premise of the narrative.

[63] Clover 30–31.

[64] The *Terminator* series is very much about heterosexual reproduction. Sarah is figured as the Madonna who gives birth to the savior of the world (see Kimball). Heteronormative breeding is far less prominent in any of the *Alien* films, given the disruptive proclivities of the alien creatures (see Vaughn). Neither Clarice nor Ellen appears interested in sexual relationships with men, let alone pregnancy and mothering.

[65] For an interesting discussion of representations of women in war and the western genres, see Robert Burgoyne, *Film Nation: Hollywood Looks at U.S. History* (Minneapolis: University of Minnesota Press, 1997). For a useful study of the construction of women's roles in literature of and about the American West, see Morey-Gaines.

[66] Simone DeBeauvoir, *The Second Sex*, trans. and ed. H.M. Parshley (New York: Vintage Books, 1989; Alfred A. Knopf, Inc., 1952). DeBeauvoir says, "women lack concrete means for organizing themselves into a unit which can stand face to face with the correlative unity. They have no past, no history, no religion of their own; and they have no such solidarity of work and interest as that of the proletariat" (xxv).

[67] Doherty 198.

[68] See Taubin and Kimball.

[69] The cult status is established, in part, by film studies textbook authors. See, for example, Bordwell and Kristin Thompson, *Film Art: An Introduction*, 7th ed. (Boston: McGraw Hill, 2004); Graeme Turner, *Film as Social Practice*, 3rd ed. (New York: Routledge, 1999). Edward Zwick's *Leaving Normal* (1992), starring Meg Tilly and Christine Lahti, flopped at the box office. The film frequently is called a *Thelma and Louise* "knockoff." See Internet Movie Database.

[70] Sturken defines "screen memory" as a narrative device (or memory strategy) which shields or protects people from an overwhelming trauma. Freud's example is the adult inability to

remember any but the simplest moments of early childhood. He reasons that our adult psychologies function to "screen" traumatic memories that might disturb us deeply.

[71] For an excellent discussion of how whiteness functions in popular culture, see Richard Dyer, *The Matter of Images: Essays on Representations* (London: Routledge, 1993).

[72] See Jeffords; Bates.

[73] Walter Benjamin, *Illuminations: Essays and Reflections.* trans. Harry Zohn. ed. Hannah Arendt (New York: Schoken Books, 1969) 87.

[74] See Rushing, Clover, Doherty and Kimball for interpretations of one or more of these characterizations as phallic (operating solely in the interests of the patriarchal order) or conventionally sexist. Taubin and Mulhall celebrate Ripley, though neither author is uncritical of the narrative as a whole.

Chapter Two
Hacking Women: The Politics of Disconnect

The personal computer revolution that began in the early 1980s was well advanced by the mid-1990s. The prevailing rhetoric of social commentators and advertisers alike was the liberating potential of cyberspace's elimination of the visible markers—sex, race, disability, age—intrinsic to the maintenance of inequitable social structures. The possibility of freedom from gender bias arose, imagining femininity defined not in opposition to technology, but engaged with it. Hegemonic masculinity's identification with technology, however, continued to oppose the cultural dictates of femininity to technical proficiency in women. One of the most intriguing aspects of portrayals of women as hackers is that they constitute doubled transgressions: the hacker itself is a transgressive role, and compounding the transgression is the female as hacker. How popular representations of the mid-1990s negotiated these tensions is the subject of this chapter.

The dramatic rise in public awareness of the Internet coincided with increasing public attention to the computer programmers known as hackers. Hacker attacks on corporations and government systems increased in the 1990s, and in 1995 Kevin Mitnick, one of the most notorious hackers, was finally caught and arrested.[1] The growing media attention was augmented by the release that same year of three motion picture productions featuring hackers. Their narratives, however, resisted the portrayal of hackers as criminals and instead depicted the lead hackers as heroes. Two of these productions cast women in the leading roles: Hollywood released *The Net*,[2] starring Sandra Bullock, and Fox TV broadcast the series *VR5*,[3] starring Lori Singer. The film *Hackers*,[4] also released in 1995, was a cyber-thriller about a group of high school hackers and featured then unknown Angelina Jolie as the only female member of the group.

The casting of women in the leading roles in *The Net* and *VR5* is remarkable in that real life women hackers are so rare as to be almost nonexistent. Solfrank's 1999 study looking for "subversive women on the net" found no women hackers.[5] There have been a handful of other film productions in which women were cast into roles displaying computer skills: *Whiz Kids* (TV 1983–1984), *Jumpin' Jack Flash* (1986) with Whoopi Goldberg, Vanessa Williams in *Eraser* (1996) starring Arnold Schwarzenegger, Carrie Anne Moss in a supporting role in *The Matrix* (1999) and its sequels, the *Charlie's Angels* (2000) remake, and the Fox television series *24* (2002–2003). However, *The Net* and *VR5* remain the only Hollywood texts in which the primary protagonist is a female expert at the level of a hacker and the narrative is constructed around her technological mastery.

Other mainstream media in 1995 kept issues relating to the Internet and computer-mediated communication technologies in the public eye. *Time* magazine released its cover story, "On a Screen Near You: Cyberporn."[6] The story was based on a Carnegie-Mellon report that claimed the Internet was a significant pornographic threat to children; the report was subsequently discredited. The U.S. Senate approved the Communications Decency Act regulating "obscenity" on the Internet; the Act was supported in part by the same Carnegie Mellon report and struck down as unconstitutional by the Supreme Court two years later.[7] Film characters and plots engaged in computer use were prevalent, as this review of the just-released *Hackers* attests: "The film industry has discovered computers, and the resulting tide of movies about users—and abusers—seems impossible to stem. From *Disclosure* to *Virtuosity* to *The Net,* cyberspace is becoming a hot commodity."[8] *Entertainment Weekly*'s review of *VR5* spoke of widespread interest in all things cyber: "*VR5* may have one other thing going for it: Cybermania has been sweeping the nation in the last few years, with trendy coffee shops serving up Internet connections and e-mail addresses popping up everywhere from the White House to your local pizzeria."[9]

As is discussed extensively in Chapter Four, "Designing Women as Consumers… Again," which investigates the place of women in technology-oriented occupations, many feminist researchers have identified the symbolic association of technology with discourses of masculinity as fundamental to the problematic relationship of women to technology.[10] As this research makes clear, women's interaction with technology is constant and significant; however, much of the difficulty associated with women in relation to new technology arises from male control over its definition and production.

The protagonists of *The Net* and *VR5* cross the border of the traditionally all-male enclave of hackers. The unconventionality of casting a woman as the lead in this role is not repeated after these screenplays.[11] How do such portrayals fit into the larger discourse of gender and technology? With a dearth of women in high-powered technology-related occupations, what part do films such as this play in presenting innovative possibilities to viewers? A look at the common threads between the two characters and their fates in *The Net* and *VR5* provides one approach to answering these questions.

This chapter also will examine how popular media represent female technology experts and how discourses of gender are mobilized in those representations. Our aim is to shed light on both what liberates and what represses the females who transgress into male-dominated technological realms. The analysis focuses on *The Net* and *VR5*, and contrasts them with *Hackers*, which differs from the first two texts in its conventional scripting of male rather than female characters in the dominant roles.

The Net and *VR5* share surprising narrative similarities for projects developed independently. We analyze the two texts for their characters' dynamics in three arenas of human relations that figure prominently in both scripts—sexuality, sociality, and familial identity—and through which the politics of representations of femininity in relation to new technology can be critically approached. The explorations of the three arenas prompt questions regarding cultural binaries, physical and metaphysical limits, and their impact on conventional gendered discourses.

The third category—familial identity—focuses particularly on the protagonists' relations with their mothers. It is in this arena in particular that the question about mothers and history raised in the first chapter, "Tough Women and Tangled Memories," plays out further. As seen in regard to the post-Vietnam texts examined there, the history of women is not invoked to imagine the nation. In this chapter, we examine narratives in which the mothers of both protagonists are present but silenced, unable to voice for their transgressive daughters their own histories or to provide them with an understanding of their roots. The mothers represent the continuity of history; the success or failure to connect with them plays a significant role in the daughters' narrative outcomes. In all, these arenas reveal boundary lines that serve to circumscribe how technically proficient woman can be imagined.

The following sections present interpretive frameworks and an overview of hacker culture that inform the detailed analysis of the *The Net* and *VR5*. We conclude with a focus on how these characters are portrayed in relation to the social construction and reproduction of gender, to what extent they challenge or reinforce male hegemony over technology, and how they illuminate our understanding of technology as a symbolic system.

Interpretive Frameworks

The term *technology* is used most commonly in reference to instrumental objects, to machines and tools that alter physical environments. Yet, technology more broadly understood is a cultural phenomenon that encompasses systems of knowledge, methods, and practices.

Technology is thus inextricable from the discourse in which it is embedded, defining not only the tools but also the relationship of humans to them. Discourses are systems of language, behaviors, and beliefs; they convey meaning through the production and circulation of texts that become collective social currency and through which we negotiate changing values and customs. Discourse often serves the ideological interests of the section of society from which it is generated: "Discourse is a social act that may promote or oppose the dominant ideology....When they become institutionalized, discourses are structured by a socially produced set of conventions that are tacitly accepted by both industry and consumers."[12] Discourses of gender are examined in relation to discourses of technology to understand how assumptions about the place and use of technology in people's lives construct our concepts of masculinity and femininity.

Discourses of technology have long incorporated notions of progress as implicit to the definition of technology. Employing "blue skies" rhetoric, inventors, manufacturers, and promoters of each new technology extol its promise to end warfare, hunger, ignorance, poverty, inequality, and the long list of afflictions that mark human societies.[13] Digital discourse is distinct in that it reflects the accelerated and rapid change peculiar to computer-based technologies; fundamental to this discourse are expressions of the inevitability of ever-more rapid technological development and the lack of time to understand or debate the arguments for its inevitability.

Speculations and promotions become a part of public discourse when both the nature and the consequences of technological innovation surpass the comprehension of even the expert. The introduction of electric communication devices[14] and of the Macintosh personal computer[15] explore cases in which fictional representations interweave with allegedly objective technical and social commentaries to establish control and authority, identify users, define appropriate user behavior, and negotiate disruptions and challenges to existing social and political structures.

New technologies exert a powerfully disruptive impact on existing social norms, and as is evident throughout studies of rhetorical theory, anxieties about social disruption are frequently displaced onto others.[16] Brummett draws on Kenneth Burke's "representative anecdote," identifiable within media discourses, to construct a method of media criticism that "sum[s] up the essence of a culture's values, concerns, and interests in regard to some real-life issues or problems."[17] The dramatic and anecdotal nature of popular media provide audiences with "equipment for living...[that is] Burke's [term for the way] people receive from discourse the symbolic resources to cope with life."[18] Brummett notes the similarity of Burke's argument with the cultivation effect theory developed by Gerbner to account for the extent to which views of reality are shaped through heavy exposure to media messages.[19] Reflecting Burke's notion of media discourses as equipment for living, Grossberg et al. articulate the key role popular media play in individual and collective identity formation in contemporary culture.[20]

The discourses that form around new technologies are as critical as technical innovation to their development and dissemination. Media representations, thereby, play an important role in the management, maintenance, and negotiations of the structures of power that constitute cultural politics. New technologies pose a challenge to social norms and political structures that is both resisted and accommodated. Popular culture representations of technology comprise a significant element in the discourse of technology, reflecting both utopian and dystopic thinking. The myths, metaphors, and images conveyed by popular culture combine with scientific and professional commentary to become the ground of our understanding of technology. Popular culture can play a central role in mediating what is unknown in new technologies, particularly in the form of science fiction narratives such as *VR5*, or in dystopic narratives such as *The Net*, that warn about the power of technology to take over human lives.[21] The fictional portrayals of female hackers in productions such as *The Net* and *VR5* are part of the digital discourse accompanying the rise of the computer and the social, economic, and political impact of rapid technological change.

In preparation for the detailed discussion of the two screenplays, the section below takes a closer look at the hacker world, its culture, and its borders. Following sections take us through the narrative descriptions and the analysis of *The Net* and *VR5*, with particular attention to the ways that sexuality, sociality, and familial identity are used to patrol the borders our protagonists cross.

Hacker Culture

Portraying women as computer hackers in *The Net* and *VR5* goes against the tide. Hegemonic representations of technology continue to construct femininity as essentially technologically inept or indifferent. The expansion of interest in the Internet after the introduction of the World Wide Web in 1993 brought an increase in advertising rhetoric promoting women as computer *users*. The potential for the information age to be an economic boost for women in the high tech industry was often extolled. Portrayals of hackers and hacker culture provide clues as to why women hackers, both fictionally and in fact, are outside the borders of that occupation.

The mainstream press regularly portrays the hacker as a paradoxical figure: a computer genius whose technical wizardry too often is in service of criminal behavior. Yet among the computing intelligentsia, hacking is seen both as a viable entry portal into occupations requiring mastery over the intricacies of computing and a means of deflating unwarranted claims as to system impenetrability, thus contributing to the social welfare by serving as a reality check on the telecommunications industry.[22]

The hacking community, a group of computer aficionados that spawned many of the most prominent pioneers of the high technology industry, first coined the term "hacker."[23] Webopedia, a web-based encyclopedia of the Internet and computer technology, offers the following definition of hacker:

> A slang term for a computer enthusiast, i.e., a person who enjoys learning programming languages and computer systems and can often be considered an expert on the subject(s). Among professional programmers, depending on how it is used, the term can be either complimentary or derogatory, although it is developing an increasingly derogatory connotation. The pejorative sense of hacker is becoming more prominent largely because the popular press has co-opted the term to refer to individuals who gain unauthorized access to computer systems for the purpose of stealing and corrupting data. Hackers themselves maintain that the proper term for such individuals is cracker.[24]

The hacker is a more technically advanced and overtly masculine-defined role than many others related to the computer industry. Sherry Turkle defines hackers as "young male programming virtuosos" who "dominate the computer cultures of educational institutions from elementary schools to universities [and are] visible, dedicated and expert." She offers a psychoanalytic explanation for the adolescent emergence of their hacker social personae:

> They come to define themselves in terms of competence, skill, in terms of things they can control. It is during adolescence that the "hacker culture" is born in elementary schools and junior high schools as predominantly male—because, in our society, men are more likely than women to master anxieties about people by turning to the world of things and formal systems.[25]

In his study of hacker subculture, Thomas distinguishes *technology*, referring to a cultural and relational phenomenon, from the *technical*, referring to the products of technology, to broaden his understanding of hackers:

> Hacking is not, and has never been, about machines, tools, programs, or computers, although all of those things may appear as tools of the trade. Hacking is about culture in two senses. First, there is a set of codes, norms, values, and attitudes that constitute a culture in which hackers feel at home, and second, the target of hackers' activity is not machines, people or resources, but the relationship among these things. In short, hacking culture is literally about *hacking* culture.[26]

Whatever the public views held of them, hackers are unquestionably expert when it comes to computers, and many professional computer programmers started out as hackers. Hacking is one of the ways that men enter and advance themselves through the ranks of software developers and systems designers. The hacker tradition is grounded in the literature of fantasy and science fiction, and it is in this symbolic realm that we can map a shift in attitudes among hackers themselves from the 1960s to the 1990s.[27] Early 1960s visionary tales of the future were replaced by the dystopic cyberpunk creations seen in William Gibson's *Neuromancer* of 1984 and other cyberpunk fiction:

> Cyberpunk represents a world where information has taken over, and the literature provides a sense of the fears, dangers, anxieties, and hopes about that new world. As opposed to the earlier hackers who sought to "liberate" information, hackers of the 1990s see themselves as trapped by information.[28]

Both the views of hackers held by the culture at large and the ways hackers themselves construct their own identity have been dependent on media representations. Popular culture in the form of two films was instrumental in both providing identifiable subcultural traits for hackers and articulating the shift in attitude toward information observed by Thomas. The 1983 film *War Games* brought hackers into view for a national audience. The protagonist David Lightman, played by Matthew Broderick, was a boy whose skills as a computer programmer far outpaced anything the adult world, including the military, could control. Lightman's character was portrayed as both dangerous for his lack of understanding of the technological systems he was led to explore, and heroic for exposing their hidden flaws. According to Thomas, *War Games* had the single greatest impact on constructing hacker identity for hackers and for the public of any media representation.[29]

While the 1995 film *Hackers* had little of its predecessor's commercial success, it nonetheless exerted significant influence in its transformation of hacker culture and its reflection of the change in public attitudes as well. In this film, a small group of high school students, alienated and marginalized, entertain themselves by hacking phone lines and conducting cyber-mischief. When one of their youngest members inadvertently hacks into a corporate financial database, they discover that a highly sophisticated computer virus has been implanted in the company's financial files and is systematically robbing the corporation of millions of dollars. The thief is an old school hacker himself, and the film becomes a high-speed cyber-race to see if the kids can out-code the villain before they are framed for the crime and apprehended by the police. According to Thomas:

> What makes Hackers important is the discourse that it put into circulation about the relationship between hackers and corporate culture. Where the discourse of War Games was about the Cold War and the threat of nuclear annihilation, Hackers is about the 1990s discourse of global technology and capital and the rise (and power) of multi-

national corporations. It essentially explains why hackers resist corporate ideology, particularly that which can regulate or restrict access to information and communication.[30]

Since the 1995 release of *Hackers,* a wide range of popular media—films, news reports, television programs, and Internet sites—has kept contemporary hackers in the limelight. The destructive activities of hackers, in such arenas as the continual release of computer viruses, have occupied the public spotlight in recent years. However, hackers themselves construe their roles as far more noble and constructive than those presented by popular media in the 1990s.

The original hackers, primarily men at MIT's labs whom many credit with the genesis of the personal computer, espoused the motto "information wants to be free" and battled the tendency of corporate and government interests toward secrecy and control of information.[31] Levy's study of early computer hackers calls them the "spirit and soul of computing itself," and quotes a computer kit salesman's description of the hacking world as "where every man can be a god."[32] Levy also notes early hackers' lack of understanding of women:

> You would hack and you would live by the Hacker Ethic, and you knew that horribly inefficient and wasteful things like women burned too many cycles, occupied too much memory space. 'Women, even today, are considered grossly unpredictable,' one PDP-6 hacker noted, almost two decades later. 'How can a hacker tolerate such an imperfect being?'[33]

Hackers are lured into long hours without sleep, sustained only by fast food, by their explorations of the workings of the computer, and by the thrill of the attempt to penetrate computer code:

> There have always been closed knowledge systems in most societies, and technology is traditionally used for building and maintaining such repressive structures. Anything that liberates such information is, therefore, anti-repressive, and aids the struggle for open knowledge systems. Hackers have created a new category of illegal knowledge. They are developing effective tools and strategies of resistance that we need in the information society. Working for a free flow of information is one concern; another, very important and constantly growing concern is the development and distribution of free software.... Hackers are still the heroes of the information age as they seem to be the only ones who can adequately respond to the challenges which go along with the complete restructuring of our society.[34]

The Hacker Ethic and the Spirit of the Information Age stresses joy, passion, and creativity as the motives for the work hackers do. Hacking thus serves as a spiritual challenge to the Protestant work ethic of the post-Industrial Age. Himanen's manifesto puts forth the "seven values of the hacker ethic" and argues that hacking fiercely defends the freedom of the individual against any incursions ranging from the demands of mind-numbing, daily routines to the interference of government agencies in their activities.

However, another less heroic dimension of the freedom fighting hacker community mentioned above is that it effectively excludes women hackers. Taylor posits three explanatory factors that account for this absence: gender stereotyping of young children that pushes girls away from hard sciences, the masculinized environment of computer science fields, and the gendered quality of the language of computer culture that alienates young women.[35] The frontier metaphor of "cyberspace," for example, suggests a hyper-masculinized environment in which "cyber-cowboys" push themselves to the limits of physical stamina in all-night programming sessions fueled only by pizza and caffeine. Turkle notes that M.I.T. hackers call the form of violent risk-taking that characterizes the hacker's relationship with his computer "sport death" because it involves "pushing mind and body beyond their limits, punishing the body until it can barely support mind and then demanding more of the mind than you believe it could possibly deliver."[36] Psychosexual theories of hacking hypothesize that hacking is the enactment of sublimated sexual drives of primarily adolescent boys who use computers to penetrate into forbidden and unknown spaces.

Description of Texts

We describe the narrative trajectories of *The Net* and *VR5* in this section, to familiarize the reader with the major characters and plot developments. The description of the texts is followed by their analysis through the lenses of sexuality, sociality, and identity.

The Net

The Net's protagonist, Angela Bennet (played by Sandra Bullock), is not only a hacker, but the "best of the best" as one grateful patron calls her. She earns a living by finding viruses and uncovering security flaws in clients' software. In her early thirties, Angela lives alone, eschews all physical contact, and works for a company whose offices she has never visited. Her only friends are an online community of three with whom she communicates solely by instant messaging, and whom she knows only by their online identities.

In a manner true to the reality of hacker employment, Angela makes her livelihood detecting security breaches for private corporate clients. We first encounter Angela at work fixing a security lapse for a client. Her hair is un-combed and she is dressed in standard hacker "grunge": men's flannel shirt over a t-shirt and loose-fitting, shapeless pants. The client on the phone asks her to dinner in appreciation for her exceptional work on his behalf. Her refusal is based on a previous engagement, a "standing commitment" that will make her unavailable for dinner for the discernible future. Upon ending the phone conversation, she clicks into her online browser and fulfills her standing commitment by ordering a pizza, "the regular," to be delivered. Angela's most frequent physical relationship is with the pizza deliveryman, with whom she exchanges neither names nor niceties. When the delivery is completed, notably through several locked doors, she switches her computer screen to an image of a fireplace and eats her meal in front of it.

Angela receives a call from an old client, a game developer, who sends her a disk with a virus he has never encountered before. When she calls him to tell him she has found the flaw, and that she has made a copy on a disk for safe keeping, he asserts that there is a potentially catastrophic dimension to this virus that he must speak to her about in person, thus also giving him the chance to finally meet her in the flesh. Angela is on her way to a rare vacation, a beach package she has assembled online, and is reluctant to change her plans. However, he insists he can fly his small aircraft over night to get there before she needs to leave for the airport.

Angela awaits him the next morning, but unbeknownst to her, the client's private plane went down and he is dead. She departs for her vacation, delayed only by a computer systems crash at the airport. Sitting on the beach while working on her laptop, Angela overhears an attractive man, Jack Devlin, order a martini. He asks if she would like one, and it turns out the drink is exactly the way she likes it prepared. They talk, primarily about their obsession with computers:

Jack:	Is that business or pleasure?
Angela:	Is there a difference?
Jack:	Not a great deal if you're a hacker.
Angela:	Nice piece of hardware [gesturing toward his laptop]. I assume you're in the business.
Jack:	Isn't everybody?
Angela:	Nope.
Jack:	God, we're pathetic aren't we? We're here, we're sitting on the most perfect beach in the world and all we can think about is…
Angela:	Where can I hook up my modem?

Jack asks her to dine with him; and as the night progresses he persuades her to accompany him on his yacht. On the way, her purse in which she had placed a copy of the disk with the virus is stolen. Jack and Angela have sex on board the yacht.

When Jack goes below board, she pulls his jacket around her and discovers the copied disk and a gun with a silencer. They struggle and she knocks him overboard, demonstrating surprising physical strength and agility for someone who lives so continuously in front of a computer screen. Angela is able to swim towards land, only to be knocked unconscious nearing shore. She is rescued and ultimately returns to her hotel, minus her purse, passport, and credit cards.

Back at the hotel the trap Angela has been pulled into starts to reveal itself. She's informed that she has checked out of her room the day before with all her belongings. When she calls the credit card company, all of her cards have been cancelled. She appeals to the American consulate only to discover that her social security number matches that of a Ruth Marx, not Angela Bennet. With no other way to re-enter the United States, she signs an affidavit stating that she is Ruth Marx and is given a temporary passport.

Angela arrives back in the U.S. to find a realtor conducting an open house in her home. She protests to the police; they bring in a woman from across the street who testifies that she saw the owner of the house, Angela Bennet, move all her belongings out three days before. Angela tries to explain to the police that she has a passport in the name of Ruth Marx but that she is really Angela. Jack Devlin is seen in a car nearby observing these events; he changes her profile on the police database he has hacked to state that Ruth Marx has several prior convictions for drug dealing, fraud, and prostitution. The police receive this information on the computer installed in their patrol car, and attempt to arrest her. Angela escapes out the bathroom window and is now on the run.

The remainder of the film proceeds in standard thriller fashion but with computers thrown in as the weapon of choice. Anyone Angela turns to for help is killed. Her only friend in the physical world is her former therapist and one-time lover. After he is hospitalized with a reaction to a medication that is the result of a computer-generated error at the pharmacy, he's subsequently murdered when the hospital database is hacked, his diagnosis is altered, and he dies of insulin shock.

The final resolution of the narrative relies on Angela's skills with computers to save and restore her life. In the background of Angela's flight are television news reports of whole sectors of the economy—travel, banking, medical systems, and so on—being brought to a halt because of hacker-induced computer crashes. Amid all of this is an ongoing news story about the rising prominence of Gatekeepers Corporation, which provides security systems to prevent these break-ins. Angela steals into her employer's headquarters where the real Ruth Marx is posing as Angela (easily accomplished as no one had met

Angela in person), and hacks into a building-wide fire alarm that gives her time to gain entry to her adversary's database. The showdown takes place at a computer fair, where Angela is able to upload the virus information on the copied disk to the CIA and FBI that reveals that Gatekeepers, rather than protecting information, is causing the computer crashes and stealing the information. She then tricks her adversaries into installing the fatal virus on their own database. In the chase that follows, Jack accidentally kills Ruth Marx, who has been posing as Angela, and then Angela kills him, sending him hurtling to his death over a railing after hitting him in the head with a fire extinguisher.

In the final scenes of the film, Angela returns to her home, having recovered her identity and saved her own life. Her mother, seen earlier in the film at a nursing home suffering from Alzheimer's disease, now lives with Angela. The doors to her house are open and unlocked, and deliverymen move freely in and out with plants and landscaping tools. Gone seemingly is the paranoid, reclusive Angela who hid behind computer screens and locked doors, and who was never seen enough in her neighborhood to be recognized. Angela's physical appearance is vastly different as well: her hair is fashionably styled, and she is wearing a dress and makeup. These changes in Angela's living arrangements and style of dress are discussed later in relation to the negotiations made with disruptive gender crossings in popular culture texts.

VR5

Protagonist Sydney Bloom, played by Lori Singer, works as a line repair technician for the phone company. The series pilot, titled "Avenging Angel," (March 10, 1995) establishes Sydney as a most unusual woman: a twenty-something female in a male-dominated profession, whose avocation as a hacker enables her to develop an alter-virtual-identity when she is not at work. Sydney has constructed her own sophisticated computer out of parts found and taken from her telephone company job, and she is clearly more technologically advanced than anyone around her.

The first scene of the pilot takes place on top of a skyscraper where Sydney and her co-worker, Scott, are wiring a phone system. Sydney is dressed almost identically to Scott. She wears a man's shirt and pants under a lineman's utility vest and belt, her long blond hair shoved beneath a hard hat. Scott expresses interest in dating her, but she shyly refuses.

Sydney lives alone in a loft; her childhood friend Duncan lives below. When she arrives home from her technician's job, she immediately heads for the computer for some virtual reality playtime. She is roused from her recreation by a cantankerous neighbor, a man angry at her for complaining when he blocked off her car in the parking lot. During a blistering call from him, Sydney discovers she can pull him without his conscious awareness into virtual reality via the phone lines. The show's production visualizes this advanced virtual level as a garishly color-saturated, outlandish world in which unconscious thoughts take on form and physical laws are breached, leaving people free to fly, change shape, disappear and reappear, much as happens in dreams. Here, Sydney is able to communicate with those she has drawn in, though it becomes clear in the narrative that the others do not remember these encounters.

Once Sydney discovers this "fifth level" of virtual reality—a new dimension that makes the experience of first level VR computer games seem prehistoric—she excitedly begins to explore it with others. She seeks out computer specialist Frank Morgan to help her understand what she's found, but he unexpectedly warns her to abandon all her investigations. Refusing to do so, Sydney tries VR5 out on Duncan and then with Scott, the co-worker who has finally persuaded her to date him. "Meeting" Scott in virtual reality at the place he had arranged for their date, Sydney discovers to her horror that he has murdered his wife and several women and buried them in the area. She decides to go in real life on the date, with Duncan as backup, to find out if Scott is in fact a serial murderer or if this persona is an invention of his subconscious acted out in virtual reality. Sydney discovers Scott's murderous identity is all too real and runs for her life. She is rescued at the last moment not by Duncan but by the same Dr. Morgan who had tried to dissuade her from pursuing VR5. He greets her with the ominous words, "Welcome to the game, Sydney Bloom," then reveals that he works for The Committee, a secret intelligence operation that wants to exploit her technological genius.

Over the course of the series, viewers learn that seventeen years earlier Sydney's father and twin sister had drowned in a car crash from which Sydney escaped. Her mother has been in a catatonic state in a nursing home as a result of her suicide attempt after the crash. Over the course of the thirteen VR5 episodes that aired, Sydney becomes increasingly embroiled in the mysterious activities of The Committee through interactions with its representative, an agent named Simon. In well-produced and wildly complicated narratives (which may have accounted for its being cancelled after the first season), Sydney uses her extraordinary skills as a hacker to push to ever more advanced levels of virtual reality, and often to engage characters threatening The Committee's concerns in some way.

Ultimately, Sydney herself becomes threatening to the shadowy aims of The Committee and she is targeted for assassination. As she struggles to extricate herself from their web, Sydney discovers that her father and sister are alive, that the car crash and drowning were simulations created in VR7, a level reached by her scientist father and exploited by The Committee. In the last episode produced and broadcast, Sydney enters VR7 to rescue her mother, now understood to be stranded in VR7 and not in a drug-induced coma after all. Sydney manages to free her mother but is unable to get out herself before the "door" to that level of VR closes. The last we see of Sydney is her simulated body floating in virtual reality, while her comatose corporeal body in "flesh reality" slumps over her computer keyboard.

Borderlines: Sexuality, Sociality, and Familial Identity

In *The Net* and *VR5*, both Angela Bennet and Sydney Bloom are technically adept, resourceful, inventive, and resilient, and both possess skills that eclipse the expertise of all the men surrounding them. Both characters are seen working with computers in numerous and extended scenes, and both are triumphing over the challenges of the computer-based systems and software they encounter. Viewers see Angela hacking seemingly any computer-based system and, within minutes, using it for her own ends. Sydney's technological prowess is equally on display. In one such scene, a distraught Sydney destroys all her extensive hardware and vows to stay away from virtual reality after receiving a radically revised explanation of her family's history. Despite her protests, The Committee replaces the equipment, and Sydney succumbs to the irresistible draw of the computer, deftly reassembling the complicated system that allows her to travel in unexplored virtual realms.

Both Angela and Sydney triumph over malevolent forces: they use their expertise in computers and their mental capacities to intellectually outwit their adversaries, and their physical agility to avert murderous assaults. Angela foils Jack's attempt to shoot her on the yacht by knocking him overboard and swimming to shore; she hacks into the Gatekeeper Corporation code to uncover their villainy and ultimately outwits her adversaries by introducing a lethal virus that destroys the terrorists' database. Sydney hangs from the top of skyscrapers without evidence of physical fear, and her intellectual fearlessness takes her into complex realms of computer-mediation attained by no one other than her scientist parents.

In keeping with the hacker subculture's self-definitions, computers are Angela's and Sydney's lifelines. The inner workings of computers themselves, rather than what they can produce, are the real source of fascination. The computer poses an intellectual and creative challenge that none of the men or women in these women's lives provides.

As discussed above, interest in and mastery of technology serve as important signifiers of hegemonic masculinity. Within their narratives, Angela and Sydney's hacking abilities sabotage their male adversaries' goals. In the culture at large, such depictions of self-sufficient, technologically fearless women pose a threat to male superiority. While popular discourses characterize the digital economy as a level playing field for all and attribute the absence of women in advanced computing to their lack of interest and inability to intellectually master math and science, Angela and Sydney defy such stereotypes and breach the barriers to women's participation. Simultaneously, Angela's and Sydney's intense fascination with machines rather than romantic relationships shifts males out of the centrality they occupy in heteronormative characterizations of femininity. In so doing, they expose the social construction of masculine and feminine signs of identity that are commonly treated as natural and as a part of the genetic coding that makes human beings male or female.

The depictions of the hackers of *The Net* and *VR5* provide welcome alternatives to exclusively male images of computer experts, featuring women who are learned, dedicated, and expert. Yet, these narrative roles were not successful at the time of their release. They have not provided the impetus for similar portrayals since that time, and they are not noted in feminist literature on women and technology as offering images of progressive and alternative roles for women in the information age. What are the primary elements in these productions that diminish their effectiveness in opening up new vistas of possibility? We examine below narrative elements relating to sexuality, sociality, and identity to uncover the ambivalence with which the technologically expert women is portrayed.

Sexuality

Participation in new technological realms exerts different pressures for men and for women in regard to sexual identity. When males sublimate their desires for sexual relations into obsessions with machines, including the development of sophisticated computer-based technologies, they may be regarded as socially inept and perhaps even sexually inhibited, but they do not lose their essential maleness in the eyes of observers. If anything, since expertise and engagement with technology have been coded masculine by discourses of gender politics, and given the current premium placed on technical expertise, male computer designers and hackers may affirm their maleness by their technological obsessions. For women the opposite is true: their very identity as conventionally defined women is challenged by their focused interest, knowledge and skill with computers. In the course of *The Net* and *VR5*, Angela's and Sydney's femininity and heterosexuality are heightened to balance their aberrant and "masculine" pleasure in machines.[37]

"Correcting" their lack of femininity is in part visualized in these productions through the transformation of wardrobe over the course of the narrative. When introduced, Angela and Sydney are seen in masculine grunge attire that is loose and form concealing; they wear no adornments or makeup. Similarly in *Hackers*, released the same year, the character Kate (played by Angelina Jolie) is indiscernible from the rest of her all-male hacker gang in her dress. Like their male hacker counterparts, the female characters' focus is on the computer, and during their engagement in technical pursuits these women are effectively without gender. They hack, program, and breach security firewalls using skills and technological genius equal to and at times surpassing that of their male counterparts.

Yet all three of these women are subject to conventional tropes of feminization and sexualization as the plot develops. On the most external level, all three women appear in form-revealing dresses through the course of the narrative. Angela triumphs over the forces attempting to kill her and to wreak havoc on a national and international level and recovers her home and her former life—but now wearing a dress and makeup. Kate (whose hacker name in *Hackers* is Acid Burn) enters into a bet formulated by the male lead (Dade): she will wear a dress on a date with him if he can hack faster and more successfully than she. Kate loses to him and wears the dress at the end of the film. Though the script makes a gesture toward gender equity by Kate insisting that if *she* wins, *Dade* will wear a dress on their date, this would not actually have achieved equity if she had won: a dress on him is a joke, on her it is symbolizes the recovery of her femininity. Women have greater play with appearance than men, having appropriated what had once been exclusively masculine clothing styles and maintaining feminine fashion choices as well. Yet, for both Angela and Kate, the narrative ending makes a significant point of contrasting their hacker guise with their final feminized wardrobes and makeup, leaving the viewer with the sense that their forays into hacking had displaced their feminine subjectivity.

The sexual dimensions of Sydney's transformations are more complex, and more exaggerated than those of Angela in *The Net*. Sydney's name itself expresses a transgender ambiguity, and her day job as a phone lineman crosses a highly masculinized border. It is in her virtual reality quests, however, that her most suggestive gender-flexing takes place.

One of the most consistent rhetorical tropes of the information age has been the liberatory potential of cyberspace. A 1997 MCI ad claims, "There is no race. There are no genders. There is no age. There are no infirmities. There are only minds. Utopia? No. The Internet." Sydney's identity morphs in virtual reality (VR) from her ambiguous, masculinized attire, lifestyle, occupation and avocation, to its reverse. In the virtual reality spaces into which her hacking propels her, Sydney appears in an excess of feminized cultural tropes—heavy makeup, skintight and highly revealing clothes, her voice an exaggerated deep throat seductiveness reminiscent of phone sex operators. She is frequently engaged in sexually charged interactions with whatever man she's followed into VR, whether she has met him before or not. This is such an extreme performance of gender that it seems to foreground its artificiality for the character and for the viewer.

It is never satisfactorily explained why or even how this transformation takes place. Sydney can enter VR5 only through a telephone connection with another person. She enters into a virtual environment that is created by the other person's subconscious. Virtual reality often represents mortal danger to Sydney, generally with sexualized overtones symbolized by the knives that are pervasive in these environments. In the first episode of the series, having just "seen" in VR that her co-worker and prospective date is a serial killer, Sydney talks to the scientist who urged her initially to avoid VR5:

Frank Morgan: Just because you've seen it in VR doesn't make it true.
Sydney: But it's what is in his mind, so there's got to be some truth in it.

Yet the subconscious images that produce the virtual space are also sometimes Sydney's own: "It's like I can bring another person into my dream. But I can't control what happens in it. When I wake up I'll remember everything but the other person [will] just remember the feeling."

Who is dressing Sydney in virtual reality? Many of the men she draws into VR have never met her. Is the implication, then, that all men subconsciously "dress" women in fantasy versions of the *Playboy* pinup, and therefore Sydney is simply plugged into the fantasy? Yet, she claims these are *her* dreams at times. Does the narrative thus suggest that hidden under that gender-neutral presentation of self in her real life as a hacker Sydney is pulsing with repressed sexual desires that mirror adolescent male fantasies?

As the MCI ad mentioned above suggests, freedom in cyberspace is attained through the erasure of the body with its inequitable social markers: gender, race, age, and infirmities. In that sense, the disembodied mind of cyberspace gets rid of the problematic feminine-coded body with its messy emotions, needs, desires, and so on. Yet the maintenance of patriarchal masculinity, of male privilege and power, of the male control and definition of the computer revolution, and an economy based significantly on the subordinate and undervalued labor of women, depends on the continuance of traditional feminine boundaries. In this light, Sydney's transformation in VR into a hypersexualized figure antithetical to her asexual, gender-neutral real life persona serves to counterbalance the anxiety produced by the image of the female hacker, encroaching on male territory far outside the circumscribed borders of acceptable feminine behavior.

Sociality

A prominent narrative element of both *The Net* and *VR5* is the theme of social isolation. Angela Bennet's case in *The Net* is the most extreme: her relationships with others exist *only* in virtual space. When the computers that contain her identity are contaminated with the predatory virus concocted by the cyber-terrorists, Angela as a person in the "real world" of flesh and blood disappears.

Angela has no friends in real life and only three identified virtual friends, whose actual identities and locations she does not know. When she faces mortal threat from the man she meets on vacation, Jack Devlin, and the group he represents, Angela turns to her former therapist. He is the only one who can identify her in person, and he is killed halfway through the script.

Sydney also exists in an isolated social space, though the intrusion of The Committee in her life involves her in more real life encounters than she would otherwise have. Despite having a childhood friend, Sydney, too, is reclusive and, like Angela, lacks a community of friends or family who can support her.

As was discussed earlier, the "classic" profile of the hacker is someone who is enthralled with computers, obsessed and preoccupied with them to the exclusion of a rounded social life, and who works autonomously, setting his or her own work hours and work space. These markers of hacker life characterize the roles of Angela and Sydney. However, hackers also have developed a fertile subculture that draws on common symbolic representations—novelistic, cinematic—with its own set of signifiers. Much of this hacker culture is developed communally by hackers who interact face-to-face at conventions replete with participant gaming and science fiction enactments, as well as vibrant electronic social networking and discussion lists.[38] The film *Hackers* includes this kind of real life social network. *Hackers'* male protagonist functions within a small but intensely loyal band of high school buddies. The film rarely portrays these friends in isolation from one another. When threatened, the group rallies to defend itself, simultaneously drawing on a global network of hackers to defeat their adversary.

Yet, this face-to-face and communal cultural life of hackers is not available to the women hackers of *The Net* and *VR5*. Women traditionally are defined in relation to the social, but Angela and Sydney exist outside any such support and connection. Their status as computer geeks cuts them off social networks that sustain their narrative male counterparts.

The narrative choice to portray Angela as a woman who finds professional satisfaction and intellectual challenge but cannot achieve personal fulfillment follows a pattern of gendered representation that has long accompanied women's attempts to realize their lives outside the domestic sphere. Such representations range from those found in news and social commentary[39] to the fictional narratives of entertainment forms, encountered most famously in the CBS television series *Murphy Brown* (1988–1997).[40] Candice Bergen's Murphy Brown role made famous the 1980s version of the hard-driven, intellectually sophisticated, rapier-tongued professional woman whose career ambitions had nullified her chances for a personal life outside of work.

All of these discursive arenas stress the negative: from the physical and psychological difficulties faced by mothers who work and the subsequent dangers threatening their children and marriages, to the failure of career women, especially as they age, to achieve satisfying social and intimate relationships in balancing the demands of their professional lives. From the women's movement of the 1970s onward, mainstream fictional and non-fictional representations alike have relentlessly asserted that women must choose between self-realization within intellectual and professional spheres and an intimate life with children and mates.

The unbridgeable divide between professional and personal satisfaction is maintained in the portrayal of Sydney as well. Though Sydney appears marginally more connected in personal and social arenas than is Angela, she nevertheless engages with a significantly greater array of people in virtual reality than she relates to in material reality, and does so in dramatically more fulfilling ways. The virtual worlds she journeys into are far more colorful and interpersonal than her real life. In cyberspace Sydney transforms herself; she abandons her flesh persona as a person who rejects gendered dictates of hegemonic femininity and masculinity and assumes in virtual reality a hyper-feminine identity that is almost a caricature of the femme fatale.

Despite the attempt to present female roles that break through the normative prescriptions of femininity, the portrayals of Angela and Sydney affirm the still pervasive difficulty in imagining female subjectivity defined outside of sexuality and domesticity. The distinction itself between the private and the public sphere, coded feminine and masculine, respectively, is a discursive and ideological one that serves to concentrate and maintain power in male hands. As examples of the representative anecdote Brummett cites in support of Burke's notion of symbolic resources as equipment for living, *The Net* and *VR5* present characters who break through imaginative barriers, reversing cultural values that prescribe technological fascination and mastery to the province of the masculine. Yet they do so with the uneasy ambivalence that reinforces entrenched cultural fears of "masculinized" women, women whose transgressive experiences may make them unsuitable for the roles society has prescribed for them.

Angela's and Sydney's failure to sustain the social relationships conventional for women are transgressions that narratively cost them dearly. The Committee that constitutes Sydney's only outside community and from whose control she is powerless to escape continually places her welfare in jeopardy. Angela is trapped at each turn of the plot by the ramifications of her rejection of "womanly" social roles. She has no relationship with her neighbors of three years, no girlfriends, no boyfriend; her afflicted mother doesn't live with her, and she has never met her employer or colleagues. In the script's terms, Angela has no identity because she has failed to construct and maintain a social network, a failure that allows her nemesis, Jack Devlin, to easily plant his female co-conspirator in Angela's home and workplace.

Mistaken identity, amnesia, and identity theft are frequent plotlines that imperil male Hollywood film characters as well. However, the male protagonists are not portrayed as endangered because they failed to establish social networks and personal relationships. The lone man against the forces of evil is heroic and a figure for admiration and identification; moreover, he inevitably ends up with help in the form of a beautiful female love interest in the course of the plot.[41] Rather than heroic, the individualism of the female protagonists in *The Net* and *VR5* is construed as a form of alienation that leaves them open to exploitation and violence. Angela and Sydney are women characters who succeed intellectually as hackers but are represented as emotionally and physically vulnerable because of their fascination with machines rather than with people. Gender politics are ultimately enforced in these representations by narrowing the potential for nurturing relationships for transgressive women who take on masculine roles.

Familial Identity

The themes of identity loss and replication are critical in *The Net* and *VR5*. Angela loses her identity by the machinations of unscrupulous cyber-terrorists using the same hacking skills she uses to save herself. Losing herself is something that appeals to her, as she confesses on first meeting Jack: computers are the "perfect place to hide." But the invisibility rendered by her reclusivity proves perilous for Angela, and she raises the alarm of the computer age:

> Why me? I'm nobody. I'm nothing. But they knew everything about me—what I ate, what I drank, what movies I watch, where I was from, what cigarettes I used to smoke. They must have watched it on the Internet. They watched my credit cards. Our whole lives are on the computer. And they knew—knew that I could be vanished, that nobody would care, nobody would understand.

Hiding in their personal lives and in virtual spaces characterizes both characters, and both struggle with their sense of identity. Sydney's identity shifts constantly but more volitionally since losing her physical identity to her virtual identity is far more rewarding. She is haunted, however, by her dead father and twin sister, and has never been clear how she escaped from the submerged car that took their lives.

There is, however, a further dimension to the identity loss these protagonists face: Angela and Sydney both have mothers who are mentally incompetent, emotionally unresponsive, and unable to recognize them. In *The Net*, Angela's mother suffers from Alzheimer's disease and lives in a nursing home. Her mother and her therapist are the only two people in the film who know what Angela looks like. After her therapist is murdered trying to aid her, Angela is caught and imprisoned. She calls her mother from jail to provide proof of Angela's legitimate identity. Her mother cannot identify her, her brain unable to connect with memories of Angela, and Angela is effectively abandoned, alone in the world and known to no one.

The absent mother figures centrally in the *VR5* series as well. As described above, Sydney's mother is comatose, unable to speak or make any kind of physical movement, a result of an apparent suicidal drug overdose she took when she learned of her husband's and daughter's deaths. Sydney draws her mother into VR5 over the phone and in that virtual realm the mother is able to talk. But outside VR5, Sydney's mother is effectively as unconscious of her remaining daughter's identity as is Angela's mother in the nursing home.

This is an intriguing congruence between two wholly separate scripts appearing in the same year. In the only two motion picture productions written with a woman in the lead role who is a technological wizard, both have mothers physically present in the narrative who cannot mirror them, guide them, or recognize them.

What are the narrative consequences of such disrupted and problematic mother-daughter relations in these two stories about women and computers? Both women spend considerable time and effort attempting to relate to their mothers and to get their mothers to relate to them. These severed relationships seem to contribute to the women's inability to form mature social and intimate relationships, as if the mothers' emotional and psychological absence robbed their daughters of essential role models.[42]

The presence and power of the mothering in *Hackers*, the male-dominated narrative, are in sharp contrast to the remoteness and ineffectiveness of the mothers in *The Net* and *VR5*. Since the main characters are high-school kids, parents are present in the film. The lead character, Dade, has a single mother who does not understand hacking but is immensely loyal and supportive of his technical abilities. When the kids are framed for large-scale corporate theft that will put them in prison for years, Dade's mother stands up to the coercive force of the CIA and gives her son and his friends the time they need to hack themselves to freedom.

By the end of the narrative, Angela has "recovered" her lost femininity in concert with or because of recovering her mother, by taking her from the nursing home to live with her. This femininity is gained, however, by taking on the care of an Alzheimer's patient—a full-time and self-sacrificing job. Sydney also recovers her mother by sacrificing herself; she ultimately trades places with her mother in a far more advanced level of virtual reality, VR7, and as the series ended abruptly, she is trapped there still.

The narratives reconstitute Angela's and Sydney's womanhood by fitting them back into the prescribed feminine role of caretaker, thus potentially relieving the cultural anxieties about women becoming too masculinized—or too successful—through their involvement with high technology. Yet, as is the case with many of the popular narratives that feature women outside narrowly defined conventional roles, critically easy binaries are belied by the cultural ambivalence about independent women demonstrated in *The Net* and *VR5*. The mothers absence as role models may be also seen as what freed their daughters to become enmeshed in the virtual in the first place. Frentz and Rushing in their analysis of *The Matrix*—a film whose male protagonist possesses hacker skills on a par with Angela and Sydney—identify the displacement of the biological mother by a computer database as thematically central to the film:

> Its roots lie in a more ancient myth of an all-powerful biological feminine and branch out into a postmodern myth of an all-powerful technological masculine. The hero in this story must liberate himself from the "mother" and be redeemed by his romantic counterpart before he can dream of saving the world.[43]

Also looking at the mythic aspects of *The Matrix*, Stroud provides an analysis of a scene in which the film's wise man, Morpheus, instructs Neo, the protagonist played by Keanu Reeves, in how to defeat the threshold guardians:

> "Their strength and their speed are still based in a world that is built on rules. Because of that, they will never be as strong or as fast as you can be." The implication here is that Neo's power resides in his possession of a human mind; this non-material aspect of his being allows him to overcome purely technological creations (based on materialism and programming).[44]

We detect the intractable binaries of mind versus body, culture versus nature, masculine intellect versus feminine emotion surfacing once again. Mothers—representing the earth, matter, and the physical body—come to symbolize limits, limits that are aligned with boundaries. The primary rhetoric of discourses of cyberspace are of no boundaries, no limits. The fluid identities of Angela and Sydney cast in the male-defined roles of hackers seem to be freed as a result of their mothers' incapacitation. The removal of the mothers as direct influences in their daughters' lives, therefore, may be the necessary construct to allow the daughters the freedom to enter into such un-feminine, boundary-crossing pursuits.

It is in the recovery of the feminine through the mother, however, that the two narratives display a significant divergence. Sydney barely interacts with the material world throughout the series; the ambiguity of her name reflects her equally tenuous grasp of her own sexual and relational identity. Sydney is ultimately able to save her mother from the virtual realm that has swallowed her but cannot re-connect with her mother's body in time to save herself, the perpetual motherless child lost in space.

In contrast, Angela saves herself by emerging from the virtual refuge in which she's been hiding, into the physicality of her own body and the material world. At a climatic moment, just as Jack Devlin, her nemesis, is about to unwittingly activate the disk that will destroy the terrorist mainframe, he scornfully asks her if she is trying to save the world. Angela replies that she's just trying to save herself—a response in keeping with the rhetoric of the post-feminist consumer culture of the times.

Yet, Angela does save a fair portion of the world. Her substitution of the disk with the fatal virus for the disk with the terrorist database that Jack thinks she is uploading ends the massive takeover of the targets of the cyber-terrorists: the global government, banking, and commercial information and communication technology networks. Her physical courage and mental acuity serve a much greater good than her own. When the last scene reveals Angela with her mother tending the verdant garden in a house open to sunlight and other people, we understand that Angela has reconnected to the wellspring that can sustain her life. Her identity is grounded, and her transgressor self has found its place. In contrasting *The Net* with *The Matrix,* Angela is saved and saves the world by reclaiming the relational interactions and ties of daily life, while Neo is saved and saves the world by breaking through the spell of false consciousness that the mundane casts.

Conclusions

Deep contradictions and tensions such as those discussed above are typical of representations of transgressive women in our culture, and in many ways mirror the lives of women working in technical fields of the information economy. The two protagonists, Angela and Sydney, demonstrate a love of and skill in pushing the limits of computers that is rarely visualized. At the same time these portrayals are embedded in narratives that enforce Angela's and Sydney's engagement with arenas of human life that are coded feminine, thus effectively policing the very borders their fictional roles cross.

Flanagan considers the masculinized power paradigms based on assumptions of control that have thus far framed the computer revolution:

> Permeation without consent (hackers and viruses representing this danger) threatens the historic use of the computer in a command/control relationship inherited from military use. This relationship is reinforced through the fear of the uncontrolled—viruses and hackers in fact work to validate and fortify power metaphors in computer culture.[45]

By casting Angela and Sydney in the roles of hackers—uncontrollable and threatening—the conventional boundaries of female depictions are breached. But the uncontrolled natures of Angela and Sydney are simultaneously reined in and effectively forced back into the realm of the body left behind when they entered the highly abstracted mindscape of the hacker world.

The central plot element of the disconnect with the mothers parallels the disconnect from history we argue in the introduction to the book: the mothers symbolize the channels through which the memory of pre-feminist subjugation of women's lives can be conveyed, and the collective amnesia of the postfeminist era countered. The mothers' bodies—emptied of conscious awareness—represent the social and political tone of the current culture. Ignorance of the power of past legislative controls to limit women's autonomy is exploited, and protests against the interweaving cultural and social constructions that represent collective political action as unnecessary and ineffective are marginalized. The politics of disconnect means that history can—and will—repeat itself. Unlike Sydney, however, Angela's re-connection to the mother places Angela back in history—she re-members her lost identity as a daughter and a woman, and through it she re-connects to the muted past that opened the doors for her. In both texts, the empowered daughters of the information age offer lifelines to their wounded mothers of the pre-feminist age.

The analysis of the texts *The Net* and *VR5* illuminates the ambivalence with which cultural forms image the technologically proficient woman, an ambivalence reflected in the diminished box office returns for *The Net* and limited run of *VR5*. Both Sydney and Angela demonstrate the formal elements of toughness exhibited by the protagonists of texts examined in Chapter One—courage to stand against corporate power, dedication to social justice and moral leadership—but similar to Chapter One's fictional women, these characterizations are not imitated. As representative anecdotes, the representations convey the resistance in cultural politics to unequivocally embrace the expanding range of women's technical expertise, despite the rhetorical claims for the equity of the Internet age. The narratives provide a view of women who are computer experts, clearly masterful at their work and enjoying their interactions with the technology. At the same time, these texts demonstrate that to credibly represent a technologically savvy woman, she has to be narratively tied to a debilitating weakness or incapacity in traditionally feminine realms of accountability—the social, the sexual, and the familial.

Fundamental tensions over identity arise whenever gender borders are transgressed. As we will see in Chapter Four, "Designing Women as Consumers," on the present state of real-world economics and politics in the information economy, women's potential remains hostage to the continued enforcement of gendered divisions of labor and the ongoing identification of technological mastery as masculine culture. In the next chapter, "Leaving the Mothership," issues of identity are battled within another male-dominated profession, the law.

Notes

[1] Among the extensive popular press coverage of Mitnick's pursuit and capture, see: Tsutomu Shimomura, with John Markoff, *Take-Down: The Pursuit and Capture of Kevin Mitnick, America's Most Wanted Computer Outlaw—By the Man Who Did It* (New York: Hyperion, 1996); Jonathan Littman, *The Fugitive Game: Online With Kevin Mitnick* (Boston: Little, Brown, 1996); Jeff Goodell, *The Cyberthief and the Samurai* (New York: Dell, 1996).

[2] Director, Irwin Winkler; screenplay by John D. Brancato and Michael Ferris.

[3] Series creator, Jeannine Renshaw; episode writers include Naomi Janzen, Thania St. John, and Eric Blakeney.

[4] Director, Iain Softley; screenplay by Rafael Moreau.

[5] Judith Mulhon, aka St. Jude, referred to herself as a feminist hacker and was an active proponent of women's engagement with technology and with hacking; she died in 2003. Thomas's study of hacker culture notes how absent women hackers are, and does not include descriptions or interviews with any: Douglas Thomas, *Hacker Culture* (Minneapolis: University of Minnesota Press, 2002). Taylor's study on hackers quotes numerous sources—hackers and observers— who refer to the absence and outright hostility towards women in the inner sanctums of hacker communities: Paul A. Taylor, *Hackers: Crime in the Digital Sublime* (London and NY: Routledge, 1999). Himanen's treatise on the "hacker ethic" uses the example of a sixteen-year-old female hacker at the beginning of his book, then relates stories of men for the remainder of his book: Paul Himanen, *The Hacker Ethic* (NY: Random House, 2001). Michelle Slatalla and Joshua Quittner, *Masters Of Deception: The Gang That Ruled Cyberspace* (New York: HarperCollins Publishers, 1995), a study on a notorious hacker gang includes no women and does not mention their absence.

[6] Phillip Elmer-Dewitt, "On a Screen Near You: Cyberporn," *Time* 3 July 1995.

[7] "U.S. Supreme Court Strikes Down CDA," Electronic Privacy Information Center (2 February 2002). 7 March 2005 http://www.epic.org/free_speech/CDA/.

8 James Bernardelli, *"Hackers*: A Film Review" (15 September 1995). 4 March 2005 http://www.reelviews.net/movies/h/hackers.html.

9 Benjamin Svetkey, "The Next X? With 'VR.5,' Fox Tries to Clone the Success of Its Sci-Fi Sensation," *Entertainment Weekly* online. (March 1995). 27 February 2005 http://www.littlereview.com/goddesslouise/articles/ew1995.htm.

10 See, among others: Elisabeth Sundin, "Gender and technology—Mutually constituting and limiting," *Gendered practices: Feminist studies of technology and society,* ed. Boel Berner (Department of Technology and Social Change, Linkoping University, 1997) 249–268; Judy Wajcman, *Feminism confronts technology* (University Park: Pennsylvania State University Press, 1991); Merete Lie, "Technology and Masculinity: The Case of the Computer," *The European Journal of Women's Studies,* 2 (1995): 379–394; Juliet Webster (1997) "Information Technology, Women and Their Work," *Gendered Practices: Feminist Studies of Technology and Society,* ed. Boel Berner (Department of Technology and Social Change, Linkoping University, 1997) 141–156; Fern Murray, "A Separate Reality: Science, Technology and Masculinity," *Gendered by Design: Information Technology and Office Systems* (eds.) Eileen Green, Jenny Owen, and Den Pain (London: Taylor & Francis, 1993) 64–80.

11 Even the female hacker in *Hackers* is coded as male. As Thomas, *Hacker Culture,* observes, "While Kate's character is female, the role she plays is masculine, a hacker superior to everyone in her circle of friends, until challenged by newcomer Dade. Like the boys around her, all of Kate's sexual impulses are redirected toward technology" (p. 161).

12 John Fiske, *Television Culture* (London and New York: Routledge, 1987) 14.

13 Carolyn Marvin, *When Old Technologies Were New* (New York: Oxford University Press, 1988); James Carey, *Communication as Culture* (London: Routledge, 1988).

14 Marvin, *When Old Technologies.*

15 Sarah Stein, "The '1984' Macintosh Ad: Cinematic Icons and Constitutive Rhetoric in the Launch of a New Machine," *Quarterly Journal of Speech* 88.2 (2002): 169–192.

16 See Marie Hochmuth Nichols, "Kenneth Burke and the 'New Rhetoric'," *Quarterly Journal of Speech* 38 (1952): 133–144; Barry Brummett, "Burke's Representative Anecdote as a Method in Media Criticism," *Critical Studies in Mass Communication* 1.2 (1984): 161–176; and Barry Brummett, "Electric Literature as Equipment for Living: Haunted House Films," *Critical Studies in Mass Communication* 2.3 (1985): 247–261.

17 Brummett, "Burke's Representative" 164.

18 Brummett, "Burke's Representative" 165.

19 George Gerbner et al., "The 'Mainstreaming' of America: Violence Profile No. 11," *Journal of Communication* 30 (1980): 10–29, quoted in Brummett. "Burke's Representative" 165.

20 Lawrence Grossberg, Ellen Wartella, D. Charles Whitney, *Mediamaking: Mass Media in a Popular Culture* (Thousand Oaks, CA: Sage Publications, 1998).

21 For research on films' centrality in futuristic discourses of new technologies, see Scott Bukatman, *Terminal Identity: The Virtual Subject in Postmodern Science Fiction* (Durham: Duke University Press, 1993); Annette Kuhn (ed.), *Alien Zone: Cultural Theory and Contemporary Science Fiction Cinema* (London and New York: Verso, 1990); Vivian Sobchack, *Screening Space: The American Science Fiction Film* (New Brunswick, N.J.: Rutgers University Press, 1997); Constance Penley, Elisabeth Lyon, Lynn Spigel, Janet Bergstrom (eds.), *Close Encounters: Film, Feminism, and Science Fiction* (Minneapolis: University of Minnesota Press, 1991); J. P. Telotte, *A Distant Technology: Science Fiction Film and the Machine Age* (Hanover, NH: University Press of New England, 1999).

22 See Himanen, *The Hacker Ethic;* Thomas, *Hacker Culture;* Steven Levy, *Hackers: Heroes of the Computer Revolution* (Garden City, NY: Anchor Press/Doubleday, 1984).

[23] Steve Wozniak, the inventor of the Apple computer, is one of the most famous, as noted by Taylor, *Hackers* 100.

[24] Webopedia, 18 March 2003 http://www.webopedia.com/TERM/H/hacker.html.

[25] Sherry Turkle, "Computational Reticence: Why Women Fear the Intimate Machine," *Technology and Women's Voices: Keeping in Touch* (ed.) Cheris Kramarae (New York and London: Routledge and Kegan Paul, 1988) 44.

[26] Thomas 37–8.

[27] Thomas 19.

[28] Thomas 21.

[29] Thomas 26.

[30] Thomas 164.

[31] Thomas 11.

[32] Levy 184.

[33] Levy 83.

[34] Cornelia Sollfrank, "Women Hackers: A Report from the Mission to Locate Subversive Women on the Net," *Next Cyberfeminist International* (1999). 31 August 2002 http://www.obn.org/hackers/text1.htm.

[35] Taylor 45.

[36] Turkle 45.

[37] The same differential tension exists in sports. Women athletes in traditionally male sports are frequently required to appear outside their sports in postures and clothing that heighten their femininity in order to offset suggestions that their strength and athletic prowess is tied to their homosexuality or "mannishness." See Pamela J. Creedon, *Women, Media and Sport: Challenging Gender Values* (Thousand Oaks, CA: Sage Publications, 1994).

[38] Thomas 2002; Levy 1984.

[39] Susan Faludi, *Backlash: The Undeclared War Against American Women* (New York: Anchor Books, 1992).

[40] Dow 1992; Rabinovitz, 1999.

[41] Among many such films, see *North by Northwest* (1959), *The Bourne Identity* (2002).

[42] An interesting contrast can be made with the absent father as discussed by Vivian Sobchak on absent paternity. The absent fathers in the films discussed by Sobchak remain affirmative and powerful influences in their families' lives, whereas the mentally absent mothers in these two films cannot provide the same positive support. See Vivian Sobchak, "Child/Alien/Father: Patriarchal Crisis and Generic Exchange," *Close Encounters: Film, Feminism, and Science Fiction* (eds). Constance Penley, Elisabeth Lyon, Lynn Spigel, and Janet Bergstrom (Minneapolis: University of Minnesota Press, 1991) 3–32.

[43] Thomas Frentz and Janice Hocker Rushing, "Mother Isn't Quite Herself Today:" Myth and Spectacle in *The Matrix*. *Critical Studies in Media Communication* 19.1 (2002): 67.

[44] Scott R. Stroud, "Technology and Mythic Narrative: *The Matrix* as technological Hero-Quest." *Western Journal of Communication* 65.4 (2001): 431.

[45] Mary Flanagan, "Hyperbodies, Hyperknowledge: Women in Games, Women in Cyberpunk, and Strategies of Resistance," *Reload: Rethinking Women and Cyberculture* (eds.) Mary Flanagan and Austin Booth (Cambridge, MA: MIT Press, 2002) 447.

Chapter Three

Leaving the Mothership: Postmodernity and Postfeminism in *Ally McBeal* and *Sex and the City*

Ally McBeal's September 1997 premiere episode's ratings beat ABC's *Monday Night Football* in terms of 18–49-year-old viewers, a novel event in the history of televised *Monday Night Football.*[1] By May 1999, *Ally McBeal* was the tenth highest rated series on prime time television.[2] And as the series' popularity grew, so, too, did the controversy about its representational politics. This controversy led *TV Guide* to proclaim that "in its first season, *Ally McBeal* made more than waves, it created tsunamis."[3] Indeed, *Ally McBeal* "has perhaps generated more column inches than any other television show of recent years."[4]

The series' premiere generated flaming in scores of American and Canadian newspapers and magazines, including *The New York Times*, the *Los Angeles Times*, *The Washington Post*, *The San Francisco Chronicle*, *Time*, *Newsweek*, *USA Today*, *The New Republic*, *Cosmopolitan*, *Harper's*, *New York*, *The Nation*, *The Edmonton Journal*, the *Ottawa Citizen*, and the *Toronto Star*. *Newsweek* proclaimed that the series clearly had "struck a cultural nerve."[5] *Hotwired*'s Jon Katz explained that *Ally McBeal* was an important social text, "not only because it is the craze du jour—it has suddenly appeared on half the magazine covers in America—but because it speaks so directly to the lives, politics and values of one of the most interesting groups in our culture: young women still sorting out their relatively recent invasions into traditional male work bastions, like law."[6]

Over the series' first season, the controversy over the meaning and political import of the series grew. So too did its popularity and critical acclaim. Katz asserted that the series was "the place where advertisers most want to be: [because] It's frequented by women—especially young women."[7] *The Washington Post*'s O'Neal Parker reported that "Ally McBeal inspires a kind of loyalty and next-day chatter that borders on obsession….Fans send McBealisms via email, speed-dial buddies during commercial breaks or host weekly Ally parties with takeout and girlfriends."[8] Other journalists testified to their own critical and personal appreciation of and engagement with the series. For example, *TV Guide*'s Jeff Jarvis told readers "Ally McBeal—and the woman it's about—is everything that I want in a series (and that any man would want in a woman): smart, fresh, funny, warm, wry, and well-produced. And it comes to us from

David E. Kelley.... if he drops this show and the women in it, I'll come after him and...say nasty things about him to millions."[9] And after Ally's therapist, Dr. Tracy Clark (Tracy Ullman), suggested on the 9 March 1998 episode that Ally pick a theme song to help her cope with difficult moments, Oprah Winfrey opened her show by asking audience members to name their own songs.

The number of award nominations and wins the series received in its first years reflected the acclaim showered on it by industry professionals and media critics. In 1998 the series won a Golden Globe for Best Comedy and Calista Flockhart won a Golden Globe for Best Actress in a Comedy. Also in 1998 the series received a total of 10 Emmy nominations including nominations for "Best Comedy" and "Best Comedy Actress" and was nominated for a record four Television Critics Association Awards. And in 1999, *Ally McBeal* won the Emmy for "Best Comedy Series."

The premiere of HBO's *Sex and the City* generated another media brouhaha, and journalistic writers and critics also hailed this series as an event of considerable cultural and political importance. *New York Times* critic Dinitia Smith, for example, summarized the import of this series' "transgressive" female protagonists in this way: "Every now and then a television series so perfectly captures the mood of a culture that it becomes more than just a hit: it becomes a sociological event—something to be studied in terms of historic patterns, analyzed in the spirit of the decade...".[10] Critics indignantly observed that few men in the series were ever referred to by name (a sign of respect), but instead were known by such labels as "Mr. Big," "Mr. Puny," "the modelizer," "Groovy Guy," and "Mr. Marvelous." Such labeling, critics asserted, defined men as accessories and "freakish objects."[11]

Sex and the City began airing on HBO a year after *Ally McBeal* premiered, and it offered a very different perspective on feminism and patriarchy. Despite some affinities with characterizations of liberated women on *Ally McBeal*, *Sex and the City*'s narratives and protagonists differed significantly from those of its televisual predecessor. The four female protagonists in New York City questioned neither their feminist foremothers nor their birthright—an equal share of social, economic, and political power. Instead, *Sex and the City*'s white, middle-class, heterosexual, racially, sexually, and economically privileged professional women took feminism for granted and expected the men and the still-patriarchal society around them to do the same.

Both series appeared on the cover of *Time* magazine, but the substantial difference in the political import of the two shows was evident in the very different way *Time*'s cover stories framed each of these series. *Time*'s 1998 cover featuring Ally McBeal used her as a poster girl for the demise of the feminist movement. In 2000, *Time* used the four protagonists of *Sex and the City* to discuss male cultural fears that the feminist movement had made women content to be single, asking "Who needs a husband?"

Clearly the two series' popularity and the public controversy over the political import of their representations of women and feminism make *Ally McBeal* and its sister *Sex and the City* important sites for cultural and political analysis. *Ally McBeal* represents one of the last major commercial productions to address feminism *itself* as the subject of its narratives, as is evident in its numerous episodes on litigation and the human rights issues central to the feminist agenda, as well as its direct confrontation with sexual politics in the office. As we will demonstrate, the focus of most writing about *Ally McBeal* and *Sex and the City* was an assessment of whether the two series were good or bad for feminism, and conclusions depended on whether authors read the two series as rejecting Second Wave feminist tenets or embracing Third Wave feminist sensibilities. Critical analysis of the popular narratives tended to construct an intractable divide between old and new feminisms, or between feminism and postfeminism. Feminism often was constructed as ontic—as a "content" of social, political and ideological principles. As Ernesto Laclau notes, whenever any social movement is defined as *content*, "we enter into a game in which any attribution...is immediately confronted with an avalanche of exceptions."[12] This is precisely what happened in popular and critical assessments of the two series.

Following Laclau on populism, we frame feminism as ontological rather than merely ontic, as a state of being in the world constituted by and through representational practices rather than as a static "content" of first principles. As such, we necessarily define feminism as a rhetorical practice, as fluid and perpetually contested, as both visual and discursive. Moreover, we believe that the First and Second Waves of feminism were constituted as populist movements. As populism, they were characterized by what Laclau terms a "logic of articulation"—an identifiable *form* that constituted the discursive and visual possibilities of the movement. Laclau argues that populism works as a representational practice by (a) crafting an underdog as an historical agent of change and (b) by crafting equivalencies (unity) among disparate interests in the underdog group. Strategy "a" requires naming and characterizing an enemy or oppressor, an easy task relative to strategy "b," which requires unifying particularized underdog interests under a unifying sign (what Laclau calls creating a chain of equivalencies). Significantly, "a" and "b" are structurally aligned, constituting both the limits and possibilities of the movement.

Important for our discussion, Laclau notes that logics of equivalence do not operate unchallenged, and are especially susceptible to hegemony, as when one set of lived experiences constitutes the sign for all members of the underdog group. For example, white middle-class women stood in for *all* women in both the First and Second Waves of the women's movement; similarly, white middleclass heterosexual interests dominated the Second Wave of the movement. It comes as no surprise, then, that the signs "woman" and "liberation" have been challenged from a variety of social locations.

Also important to our discussion is Laclau's conceptualization of three ways that populist movements can falter or be contained or derailed. First, appeals to equivalence (unity) may not be able to overcome differential interests in the underdog group. Thus, "feminism" as a practice may splinter and become divisive. Second, successful institutional powers can sometimes satisfy enough of the demands of the underdog group to diminish resistance momentum. For example, at the same time that the Equal Rights Amendment failed ratification, labor laws improved gender parity in public employment in the years after the Second Wave demonstrations. A powerful postfeminist strategy claims that feminism is obsolete because women have achieved equality. Third and finally, competing interests outside the underdog group can appropriate the representational practices of the movement. Currently, several neo-conservative groups and spokespersons claim "underdog" status because of the "oppressive" practices of feminism.

We focus in this chapter on the discourse of contestation and challenge constituting and surrounding the representation of contemporary "liberated" women in *Ally McBeal* and *Sex and the City*. A careful examination of the texts in their broader contexts reveals a critical juncture in the American feminist movement. We will explore this critical juncture through the following probative questions:

(1) To what extent has the *form* of feminism changed significantly since the inception of the Second Wave?

(2) To what extent do representations of Third Wave feminism in these series suggest a shift in public imagination about the *logic* and the *ethos* of feminism?

(3) Has feminism as a populist movement been diminished, complicated or transformed by postmodernism and postfeminism? Put another way, has feminism been enriched or impoverished by contemporary challenges from a new generation of women?

Before we can address these questions specifically, however, we must first provide a detailed review of the struggle for hegemony over interpretations of feminism and femininity in *Ally McBeal*. We then examine the generative sources of "crisis" in contemporary feminism, as represented in *Ally McBeal*: perceived generational differences and backlash culture. We next examine *Sex and the City* through the lens of Third Wave "girlie" culture and postmodern playfulness, drawing out key differences between the two series. Finally, we return to the probative questions listed above and use them to offer our perspective on feminism *as* cultural memory in a postmodern culture.

Ally McBeal and the Crises of Feminism and Femininity

By the end of *Ally McBeal*'s first season, the eponymous series' central protagonist became the center of a raging debate about the state of contemporary feminism. The apotheosis of the controversy was *Time* magazine's 29 June 1998 cover and lead article. Against a stark black backdrop rimmed in red, *Time*'s cover featured the faces of four women: three were black and white head-shots of women identified by small white script above their photos as Susan B. Anthony, Betty Friedan, and Gloria Steinem. Each of these women, Bellafante's accompanying article explained, had made significant contributions to feminism. The fourth, and only full-color photograph, was a head-shot of the fictional television character Ally McBeal. Under her photo, in large red type, *Time* posed the question, "Is Feminism Dead?"

Journalistic critics' and viewers' responses to this query were quite divided. Some argued that the series and its title character were a powerful expression of contemporary Third Wave feminism. Others asserted that the series was an elegantly crafted backlash against feminism, a televisual reflection of the antifeminist tropes found in the writings of postfeminists Kate Roiphe, Camile Paglia, Naomi Wolf, and Rene Denfeld.

One set of journalists answered a resounding "No!" to *Time*'s query. In their view, the series provided a compelling representation of many contemporary feminists and feminisms, not all of which looked, thought, and lived alike. These journalists read Ally as a televisual embodiment of younger feminists' celebration of difference and the power to make choices, their rejection of constricting binaries, and their embrace of sexual desire and expression as well as feminine fashion and popular culture.

Lining up on this side of the public debate over the political import of this hugely popular series were both youthful and not-so-youthful journalists. One of these, *New York Times* columnist Karen Durbin, described herself as a "confirmed *Ally McBeal* fan who first took to the streets with knees knocking and feminist fist upraised not quite 30 years ago." As Durbin told her *Times*' readers, she wasn't bothered by Ally's skirt length, eating habits, or other behaviors. In fact, Durbin explained, she *identified* with Ally and her relational klutziness, and she found it "a comfort to know that there's another woman out there, even an imaginary one, for whom the dance of desire begins with a foot in the mouth."[13] "Ally McBeal," Durbin asserted, "isn't antifeminist; she's

protofeminist....what rings both timely and true is Ally's mix of doubt, asser-
tiveness, and self-mocking humor, the last best expressed in her dissing contests
with her roommate Renee."[14] Durbin speculated that the main reason that Ally
had created such cultural disturbances "both on and off the show" was that
"she's all but walking naked through the world." Ally's short skirts, Durbin
argued, were merely a metaphor for her vulnerability, not a symbol of the death
of feminism: "The death of feminism tends to be greatly exaggerated, but
journalists have been writing its obituary since 1975, when *Harper's* magazine
did its own cover article 'Requiem for the Women's Movement' just in time to
ride the anti-feminist backlash while criticizing the movement for not being
radical enough."[15]

The *New Republic's* Steven Stark not only defended the series, he praised it
as a most unusual television text because it was an "inner-directed 'feminine'
drama that has invaded the arena of prime time dramatic series, one of the
'remaining bastions of male authority on television'."[16] Stark pointed out that
relatively few top ten television dramas have featured women—three or four a
decade—and he argued that "in the same way that *M*A*S*H* could only deal
with Vietnam by moving the war to Korea and tempering the drama with
wisecrack humor, *Ally McBeal* couches its serious questions about being a
woman in the workplace in exaggerated fantasies, oddball characters, and silly
scenarios."[17]

New York Times television critic Olivia Goldsmith agreed, noting that unlike
the writers of *Dharma and Gregg* who "simplify, resolving all problems with love,
Ally McBeal takes a different route, wrestling with issues that have no simple fix:
sexual harassment, adultery, urban loneliness, wanting what you can't have."[18]
This was why, according to *Time* magazine's James Collins, the "smart yet also
emotional, Ally represents the modern female trying to remain true to herself in
a harsh male world."[19]

Many of these journalists read Ally McBeal as a poster girl for Third Wave
feminism in terms of her rejection of feminine/feminist binaries, her embrace
of the unmooring of gender identities (e.g., kissing Ling), her unfettered
expression of sexual desire, her reliance upon a support network of women
friends for comfort and companionship, and her open acknowledgment of her
vulnerability and her pleasure in consumer popular culture—fashion, music,
media, and her active pursuit of both professional success and romantic love.[20]
These journalists saw the character and the series telling the story of a young
woman who was "continuing the struggle to unlearn American scripts" about
gender and feminism.[21] As such, they also read the series as negotiating the
tensions between history (understood here as Second Wave feminisms) and the
"historically and materially different experience of being young and female."[22]

For many viewers and journalists, this negotiated tension is at the heart of the series' appeal.

Few academic critics have read *Ally McBeal* as a liberatory text, but among those who have are Cooper and Mosely and Read.[23] Cooper has argued that the series' narratives construct a "feminine spectatorship stance" by using comedic strategies to question dominant patriarchal gender ideals.[24] The series' privileging of women and women's experiences, she concluded, makes *Ally McBeal* an empowering text. Mosely and Read arrived at a similar conclusion. In their view, engaging issues central to Second Wave feminism within the context of younger generations of women creates a "rich, complex, and appealing *mise-en-scène*" which is "representative of a new moment in the history of feminism" and provides a positive expression of Third Wave sensibilities.[25] Like Cooper, they read the series as inviting audiences to reexamine "the opposition between feminism and femininity which informed much 1970s feminist thought."[26] Thus, like their journalistic counterparts, these academic critics regarded this series as an important political text.

Series creator David E. Kelley explicitly (and unwittingly) characterized the character Ally McBeal as postfeminist—a positive representation of a strong, professional woman who, in his words, was "not the hard, strident feminist out of the '60s and '70s.... She's all for women's rights, but she doesn't want to lead the charge at her own emotional expense."[27] Network executives concurred with Kelley's characterization. According to Peter Roth, head of Fox Television's entertainment division, the series was designed to feature a strong working woman[28] and Fox Television's network web site described Ally McBeal as "one of the most compelling and sensitive portraits of a professional woman *ever rendered by a man.*"[29] That rendering, according to Jane Pratt, editor of the magazine *Jane*, was precisely the problem: "When all is said and done, Ally McBeal is a *male fantasy* of what a woman's preoccupations are."[30]

Jane Pratt's observation raises several important questions that the remainder of this chapter explores: Is Ally yet another example of white male writers', producers', and media executives' use of the female body and ethos to recuperate the masculine cultural imaginary? Whose *are* the stories that the series tells? Are they yet another set of narratives culled from male cultural memories of the mythical pre-Vietnam past of *Father Knows Best,* which functions to discipline the threats these strong, transgressive women pose to hegemonic masculinity? A large number of journalists answered these questions and *Time*'s query with a resounding, "Yes." If *Ally McBeal* was a reflection of the state of feminist politics today, feminism, they asserted, was indeed dead.

Among those journalists voicing this perspective were Ruth Shalit of *The New Republic* and Maureen Dowd of *The New York Times*. Expressly invoking cinematic cultural memories, Dowd characterized *Ally McBeal* as "an updated version of those 50s Rona Jaffe heroines from Wellesley and Vassar who wore gloves and hats and got low-level jobs in publishing until they could snag a man in a gray flannel suit and a white picket fence."[31] Shalit similarly pronounced Ally "a slap in the face of the real-life working girl, a weekly insult to the woman who wants sexual freedom and gender equity." The problem with televisual representations like Ally McBeal, Shalit explained, was their devastating and largely invisible political import: "The zeitgeist impresarios who produce these demoralizing shows have made male power and female powerlessness seem harmless, cuddly, sexy, safe and sellable. They have merely raised conservatism's hem."[32] *Time*'s Gina Bellafante concurred. As she argued in her article accompanying *Time*'s "Is Feminism Dead?" cover, not only was Ally "the most popular female character on television," she also was the latest and most popular example of media images that subvert the hard-fought gains of feminism by replacing images of rational, competent, articulate women with "images of grown single women as frazzled, self-absorbed girls."[33]

Shalit, Dowd, Bellafante, and a substantial number of other journalists writing for public media read *Ally McBeal* as the epitome of the postfeminist backlash that had gained momentum throughout the Reagan years. *Newsweek*'s Veronica Chambers dubbed Ally "the quintessential postfeminist." "Ally," Chambers fumed, "claims to want to use the law for good, but almost all of her waking hours are preoccupied by her desire to snag a man.... She has all the professional advantages Mary [Richards of the *Mary Tyler Moore Show*] never had, but unlike her more traditionally feminist sitcom sister, she doesn't want to make it on her own."[34]

Academic critics generally concurred,[35] and even those few scholarly critics who, like Shugart, Waggoner, and Hallstein acknowledged that the series effectively and engagingly articulated a number of Third Wave feminist tenets, concluded that ultimately the series was a problematic text because it co-opted even its empowering elements "in such a way that those feminist sensibilities are not only defused but ultimately rendered consonant with the dominant paradigm that they appear to resist—thus, the ultimate function of these mass-mediated representations is hegemonic."[36]

The Politics of Representation: Whose Story Is It Anyway?

Notwithstanding the hyperbole in *Time*'s question, we acknowledge that there *is* a crisis of feminism and femininity. Moreover, we believe that the imagined binary relationship between feminism and femininity is at the center of this crisis and a generative source of tension between Second and Third Wave feminism. We believe this crisis developed out of the backlash against feminism that arose during the 1980s and 1990s, a backlash that worked in part, Mosely and Read have explained, "by suggesting that it was feminism, particularly its manifestation in the single, childless, career woman, rather than women's continuing inequality, that was making them unhappy."[37] As Mary Vavrus has observed, a host of popular media texts have told audiences that feminism "is a problematic social movement."[38] According to Vavrus, the spate of antifeminist (backlash) messages in media texts has reinstantiated "the essentialist ideal of maternity and marriage," and has "attach[ed] the label 'feminist' to objectionable personalities, ideologies, or aesthetics," distracting us from the REAL question. What we should be asking, she notes, is not "Is feminism dead?" but rather "Is patriarchy alive and well?"[39]

We believe the series, and the remarkable public response to it, provides incontrovertible evidence that feminism at the end of the twentieth century was very much alive, and also very different from the feminisms of the Second Wave. We do not read *Ally McBeal* as a simple backlash male fantasy of lonely feminists who are professionally successful and personally miserable. Nor do we embrace uncritically its sophisticated postmodern visual style and visual irony. We view the series in its production and reception contexts as a complex, nuanced narrative that tells the story of contemporary young feminists' struggles to negotiate (if not oppose) the still powerful patriarchal cultural imaginary and to build their own bridges across the material and cultural chasm separating Second and Third Wave feminist politics. Later, we evaluate the way the series explores the ongoing social efforts (in private, personal relationships and in public organizations and institutions) to discipline young women who resist binary narratives of traditional feminine life stories or narrowly proscriptive Second Wave cultural warrior life stories. We turn next to what we see as two primary loci of crises in feminism in relation to *Ally McBeal*: (1) occupational vs. relational fulfillment; and (2) generational differences and backlash culture.

Occupational Achievement and Personal Fulfillment Crisis

The preponderance of the cases taken on by the attorneys at Cage & Fish, the law firm employing Ally McBeal, concerned the enforcement of women's occupational, social or economic rights, a focus that attracted many professional women in their 20s and 30s to the show. As a result of Second Wave feminists' legal and linguistic struggles for gender equity—including the creation of language to describe women's experiences (e.g., sexual harassment laws)—women were able to pursue individual achievement and occupational fulfillment in public arenas once closed to them. Female lawyers were then and still are at the center of this struggle because "the law is powerfully implicated in the ordering and reordering of the society, both as conservator of the old and formulator of the new."[40]

In the 1950s and 1960s, women constituted less than 4% of the legal profession, but by 1990 women made up 50% of the nation's law students. Harvard, the nation's pre-eminent law school and fictional Ally McBeal's alma mater, was the last major law school in the U.S. to admit women (in 1950). However, male authority has remained the norm for the legal profession: 90% of the federal judges remain male while women make up less than 10% of the partners in law firms nationally and the same percentage of the tenured professorate of prestigious law faculties. "The old measure of equality," Harrington explains, was "the right to vote and legal rights generally. The new measure is inclusion in all the places and institutions where people actually make the decisions that shape the way we live."[41]

Inclusion, however, has not come with equal costs for female and male lawyers: 60% of the 900 female lawyers responding to a National Law Review and West Publishing Company survey reported being sexually harassed in some way by male colleagues.[42] Furthermore, for associates in the most powerful law firms (those that shape the law and serve as farm teams for major judicial appointments)[43]—those young associates like Ally, Billy, Georgia, and Nelle who are trying to make partner and gain a cut of the profits in addition to their yearly salaries—the normal workload is 2,200 billable hours a year. What this translates into, Harrington explains, is a typical workday of 10–12 hours plus working most weekends. And while the demand for billable hours is the same for female and male lawyers, the difference is that "men and women are not alike in their responsibilities outside of work."[44]

Harrington interviewed 100 female lawyers—most graduates of Harvard Law School and successful current or former corporate lawyers—and a recurring question these attorneys raised was this: "For whom is it 'normal' to require a minimum of 1,900–2,200 billable hours a year?" The answer is for lawyers without families (women and men) or lawyers who have families but not the responsibility for coping with them (few women, mostly men). As one of Harrington's interviewees who was one of four female attorneys in a 60-lawyer corporate firm, explained,

> If it were normal for men as well as women to leave the office at 5:15 to pick up a child at daycare before 6:00 or to leave routinely at 3:00 on Tuesdays and Thursdays and to be unavailable for work on weekends, professional work rules would have to change. But in a corporate environment in which you have no men coping with getting to a day care by 6 or dealing with what women have to deal with…you have no basic understanding of what's going on with the women…. and no impetus to change…. There just aren't very many bright young men coming up through the system who are doing the coping.[45]

According to Harrington's study, one of the most intractable aspects of the occupational crises women lawyers contend with today is how to cope with three different sets of crushing rules and pressures that they face, which their male colleagues do not face. The female lawyers she interviewed explained that they could (1) choose to "go by men's professional rules while shouldering the main burden of families and thus living under constant, punishing pressure," or (2) they could "gain exceptions for themselves from men's rules and thus not [be] taken seriously as fully authoritative colleagues," or (3) they could forego altogether developing committed romantic relationships and families. "The consequences of this bind," Harrington discovered, is that women leave the partner track in large corporate firms, and in doing so they forego becoming voices in those large corporate firms "that do the legal work of the biggest, most powerful corporations" and that "make the rules that govern [not only] the legal profession itself....[and] women's status in the legal profession, but also their status and conditions of experience in society."[46]

Both aspects of the occupational crisis facing feminism (sexism and working a second shift)[47] were played out in *Ally McBeal* narratives that told in sometimes humorous, sometimes poignant, and always in resonant ways, stories that reflected not just the adventures of the series' legal protagonists but also the lived experiences of women journalists and viewers. In the episode titled "The Kiss," Ally and Georgia Thomas served as co-counsels for TV anchor Barbara Cooker (Kate Jackson) who sued her former station for sex-discrimination. Like her real counterpart TV journalist Christine Craft, this fictional Peabody award-winning journalist was fired because a viewer survey found that male TV viewers no longer found her attractive enough (i.e., they no longer wanted to have sex with her). The jury awarded Ms. Cooker $930,000 in damages, a victory that was even sweeter for Ally because the attorney representing the TV station was Jack Billings, who she had sued for sexual harassment. Still, the episode reaffirmed that gendered age discrimination, not equality, is the norm, and it affirmed the ongoing struggle women have to enforce and maintain the legal rights achieved by the struggles of Second Wave feminists.

The emphasis on women's continuing struggle for legal and social equity began in the series' September 8, 1997, pilot episode. Twenty-seven year old Ally quit the prominent Boston law firm that had hired her fresh out of Harvard Law School when the firm fired her rather than Jack Billings, the senior "rainmaker" partner in the firm who repeatedly grabbed Ally's rear and who, when confronted with being fired himself, threatened to counter sue the firm under the Federal Disabilities Act, claiming he had an obsessive compulsive disorder that impelled him to squeeze butts. Serendipitously, as she walked out the door of her former law firm Ally met her Harvard Law School class-mate, Richard Fish, who on the spot invited her to join the firm he and John Cage started. At Cage & Fish, with the help of Billy Thomas (Ally's now-married but former childhood, college, and law school sweetheart), Richard successfully exposed Billings' fraudulent defense claims. Although the pilot episode affirmed the legal right of working women to be free from sexual harassment by powerful superiors in the workplace, it also affirmed that male power holders continue to regard occupationally competent, successful women as transgressive and attempt to discipline them through sexually infantilizing and intimidating behaviors.

Many other episodes reiterated this aspect of the occupational crisis in feminism as well. For example, in "The Playing Field," the firm defended client Eva Curry who claimed that other women in her office who had been pro-moted all had granted the boss sexual favors, and that she had not been promoted because she had not granted (nor been asked for) sexual favors because she was not young and attractive. "Drawing the Lines" was an ironic and self-reflexive episode in which Ally's secretary Elaine filed a sexual harass-ment suit against the Cage & Fish firm because the male attorneys went into semi-trances whenever a beautiful mail clerk named Jennifer delivered the mail. Although viewers subsequently learned that Elaine's motive for initiating the lawsuit was pique at not being the center of attention herself, the lawsuit made the male attorneys realize that they had been guilty of creating a hostile work environment for Jennifer, and by extension, the other women in the firm, by visually sexually objectifying them. Richard Fish—the firm's senior partner—publicly apologized to Jennifer and the other women in the firm, and promised that the men at the firm would stop acting like oversexed sophomores. In his speech delivered to all of the firm's employees and to the television audience, Richard asserted that Jennifer, Elaine, and all the women working in the firm deserve far more respect than they have been given and he promised that in the future everyone in the firm would treat all women employees with respect. In delivering this political statement, Richard modeled the kind of organizational culture statement that could stimulate changes in workplaces if more powerful male employers made zero tolerance for sexual harassment the norm.

Despite examples that illustrate a relatively female-friendly atmosphere at Cage & Fish, the fact remains that the only two partners in the firm are male. In "The Real World" when John and Richard decided that they needed to hire a rainmaker to increase their clientele and improve their profits, Richard tried to persuade the very successful "subzero" Nelle Porter to join their firm (and bring her clients with her). When Nelle arrived to check out the firm, Richard hastened to tell her that he could not make her partner because there would be too much fallout, but he promised that she would achieve partner sooner than she would at any other firm. Later, when Nelle and Ally went out for a drink at the end of the day because Nelle wanted to talk to a woman at the firm, Ally told Nelle that she liked the firm even though they would never let a woman be partner: "They don't say that," Ally said, "but between you and me, they hire women who want families." And she went on to explain that they did that because they expected women would go on maternity leave before they were up for partnership and then once they had children they would "tend to prioritize the little imps." This, of course, has the opposite effect on Nelle who decides to join the firm, become a partner, and change this sexist place. Similarly, when Ling decides to help Billy with a case, and Nelle questions her, Ling replies that she brought the client in, which eventually will lead to her making partner, and that will give her the power that will allow her to "put an end to the rampant chauvinism that goes on here."[48]

In law firms, becoming a partner is the credential that testifies to individual ability and responsibility and becoming an insider with a seat, and a voice, at the decision-making table.[49] However, the fact that less than 10% of all law firm partners are women indicates that female lawyers, like many women professionals, remain exiles who can see but not cross over into the promised land. That this is indeed the case not only at Cage & Fish, as "The Real World" episode affirmed, but at other companies as well was the central storyline in "Let's Dance." The episode was unique in that instead of representing the plaintiff, Marianne Harper, in the sexual discrimination suit, Nelle, John, and Richard represented the defendant, Johnson Biblico, the head of the law firm. On the stand, Ms. Harper explained that she had worked for the firm for five years, took a maternity leave, returned after four months, and six months later was told that she would not be making partner. Furthermore, she told the court, this same thing had happened to six other women at the firm. When Biblico took the stand, he countered that he had no problem with women lawyers having children; the problem was that when women have children their priorities change and they scale back and no longer put in the 14-hour days that are needed to make partner.

Ms. Harper's lawyer countered by putting Margaret Camaro, described by Nelle as "one of the best women's rights advocates in this country," on the stand. In her testimony Ms. Camaro advanced the same political argument as the female lawyers Harrington interviewed: Working 14-hour days is not simply "the reality" of work in a contemporary law firm; it is de facto discrimination. As Ms. Camaro explained, this is

a reality cultivated by men in a male-dominated workplace. It's defacto discrimination that 14-hour days are even required. It used to be people balanced two worlds—work and home. Now we've seen a dramatic shift to an imbalance that works to exclude women who also are mothers, and that imbalance has been propagated by men.

The point of both Ms. Camaro's testimony and Harrington's interviewees is that if child-rearing responsibilities were truly fairly and equally divided between mothers and fathers, 14-hour days would no longer be realities for anyone because fathers also would be staying home with children too sick to go to daycare, taking turns leaving work before 3:00 to pick children up from school, and spending time with their children rather than two more days in the office on weekends.

Nelle acknowledged this cultural double standard and continuing inequality in her closing argument, saying: "When you look at the men who rise to the top of their field, most of them have sacrificed a little on the family side. But women—we can't do that. That's unthinkable. We have to be there for the children. If a woman puts in 14, 16-hour days while she has kids, well, she's a bad mother." This patriarchal cultural narrative was powerfully reinforced in Zoe Baird's 1993 confirmation hearings for Clinton's Attorney General when Senator Joseph Biden, Chair of the Judiciary Committee, asked Ms. Baird to "state how many hours she was away from her child: when she left in the morning and returned at night." In his column response, *New York Times* reporter Lewis pointedly asked, "Would he have asked that of any male nominee, for any job?"[50]

Nelle's closing statement argued that the "real" gender bias in this case was in the assumption that all women, deep down, really wanted to be mothers:

> …this automatic assumption that every woman wants to be the mother. There's the bigotry. Not all of us want to get pregnant. And what about the women willing to put in those 14-hour days? Should they concede advantages to their colleagues who chose motherhood? Is that fairness? The plaintiff isn't in here asking for equal treatment. She's asking for special consideration. And with all due respect to the women who want to give birth and start raising families, there are women like me who want to earn their partnerships under the same standards the men do. You (she turns to the plaintiff, Ms. Harper) chose to cut back your work to become a mother. You probably know joys I can't even imagine. I chose to concentrate on work in lieu of a family. (She turns to the jury.) Now, I suppose you could bestow upon her the same rewards and privileges at work that I enjoy. But you can't do it under the heading of fairness.

Tellingly, Nelle's argument did not identify one very important aspect of the feminist occupational crisis: the persistent inequity in family care-giving and household responsibilities—and thus, in the vast majority of cases, only women have to struggle with this choice at all. However, on *Ally McBeal,* the fictional Ms. Harper, unlike the real Ms. Baird, was not made to "atone for the sins of women who not only juggle private and public roles, but who also dare to suggest that those roles, and the gender-differentiated notions of caring which underlie them, are not separate."[51] Instead, she was awarded $642,000 in damages.

Another aspect of the occupational crisis of feminism addressed in *Ally McBeal* narratives is the difficulty the demands of their work life posed for professional women's, and men's, development and maintenance of satisfying romantic relationships. None of the associates at Cage & Fish have families. Of the nine main characters featured in the series' first two seasons, six are working women—Ally McBeal, Georgia Thomas, Renee Radick, Nelle Porter, Elaine Vassal, and Ling Woo—five of these six women are attorneys as are the three major male characters (Richard Fish, John Cage, Billy Thomas). During the first season, Judge Jennifer "Whipper" Cone was a regular, minor character. Of these, only Georgia and Billy, the married couple, had a stable and apparently satisfying relationship (for the first several seasons). However, only occasionally did these two leave the office at a reasonable dinner hour to dine together, attend the theatre, or a concert. Most of the time Georgia and Billy, like the other members of their firm, worked 14-hour days, caught a bite at the pub in their office building, and then relaxed by dancing with other young workaholic professionals who came to the pub after their 14-hour workdays.

One episode that reiterated this occupational dilemma was "The Green Monster." In it, Ally and Renee discussed over lunch whether or not they should use Ling's male escort service to try to attract men. When Renee admonished Ally to think logically, Ally exploded:

Ally: You want a little logic from me, Renee? We put in twelve-hour days working on our professional lives. We agree that a personal life is more important but we don't really work on that. I am going to apply myself, Renee. I'm going to apply a work ethic to my private life.

Renee: Does that include renting somebody?

Ally: I'm not excluding anything, and I'm not going to apologize for it. This isn't about me wanting a man, either. This is about me wanting a partner. Okay? A partner to go through life with. And since I happen to be heterosexual, that limits the field to me, at least if I want to have sex, and I do, I like sex. (Her voice starts to rise.) And if that makes me weak, tough, then I want to be weak. I want a partner. I want sex. I want a house, with furniture. I want to have a baby. I want to have all of it.

Despite Ally's best intentions and creative dating strategies, most episodes end with Ally slowly walking home down a nearly deserted street, alone but still convinced that she can simultaneously fulfill her feminine desires for interdependence, romantic love, fashion and sexual attractiveness and her feminist desires for individual career/occupational success, financial independence, and a raised social consciousness and awareness. For *Ally* feminists "'having it all' means not giving things up (the pleasures of feminine adornment and heterosexual romance) but struggling to reconcile...feminist desires with...feminine desires."[52] For fans of *Ally*, the series' attempt to negotiate the contradictions between feminist and feminine identities was exactly what made the series so engaging.

Third Wave feminist Leigh Shoemaker writes that frustration with the ongoing dualisms between professional and relational, public and private relationships have fueled the crisis of feminism for Gen X. As Shoemaker explained:

> This is a unique time in history.... Second Wave feminism made it possible for us, as women and as future feminists, to choose male 'role models' as examples of strength [just] as traditional ideas about masculinity—still entrenched—had made it apparent that we could not be both strong and female.... Feminists of my [third wave] generation learned at a young age that we were girls and that we could do anything the boys could do, but also that to achieve that goal, we could no longer be girls (thanks to 1980s conservatism). We could not admit to feminine qualities—to compete, we had to disavow "girly" emotions, responses, appearances. We had to be just as hard as the boys. We might have thought that we were making great strides for girls on the playground, but in fact, through valorizing masculinity and devaluing femininity, we were reaffirming the old, restrictive dualisms that we were trying so fiercely to rebel against.[53]

Shoemaker's complaint exemplifies Gen X feminisms' frustration with perceptions of an incompatibility between feminist and feminine identities and the consequences of this conflict for women's professional and personal lives. Linking back to one of our probative questions—is this good or bad for feminism?—we see that one of the most contentious arenas in which this has played out is that of sexuality and the Third Wavers claim to their empowerment as women through re-appropriation of the male gaze.

Generational Differences and Backlash Culture

> I am twenty-five years old. On my left upper arm I have a six-inch long tattoo of a voluptuous cowgirl. One of her hands rests jauntily on her jutting hip. The other is firing a gun. An earlier feminist might frown upon my cowgirl's fringed hot pants and halter top as promoting sexual exploitation, and might see her pistol as perpetuating male patterns of violence. Yet I see this image as distinctly feminist. Having a tattoo signifies a subculture that subverts traditional notions of feminine beauty. That this

tattoo is a pinup girl with a gun represents the appropriation and redefinition of sexuality, power and violence—ideas characteristic of third wave punk feminism.[54]

Born in the U.S. in 1971, Third Wave feminist Melissa Klein—like Ally McBeal—is part of a generation of women who grew up benefiting from the Second Wave's public political struggles and who have rejected some—though not all—of the sensibilities and narratives of Second Wave feminists. Like other members of this younger generation of feminists, Klein sees many Second Wave feminists as unwilling to acknowledge feminisms that don't look like 1970s feminism, a response that Diane Elam has called the "blind obedience" or "dutiful daughter" syndrome.[55] According to Klein, Third Wave feminism

> has moved away from a struggle for equality toward an engagement with difference, an assertion that girls can have the best of both worlds (that they, for example, can be both violently angry and vampily glamorous). This feminism owes much to the struggles of the Second Wave, yet it differs in many ways, especially in the way it is defined by contradiction.[56]

Many Second Wave feminists, as illustrated in the journalistic critiques of Ally McBeal described earlier in this chapter, have great difficulty in accepting Third Wavers' embrace of contradictions—including exuberant expressions of sexual desire and pleasure in wearing sexy, girlie fashions attire alongside anger over continuing public and domestic inequalities such as the Air Force Academy and Iraq War rapes and sexual harassment of female students and soldiers—as legitimate expressions of feminism. One focus of the contemporary crisis in feminism is Second Wave feminists' responses to Third Wavers' exuberant public expression of sexual desire. In contrast, Third Wavers see their choices in fashion and behavior as "seek[ing] to embrace sexual desire and expression, freeing it from the limits of patriarchy and heterosexuality as well as from what they perceive to be the antisex sensibilities of Second Wave feminism." In fact, many self-identified Third Wave feminists "describe the profound sense of empowerment they experience in defining themselves sexually, first and foremost, and thus reclaiming their sexuality."[57]

In contrast, many Second Wave feminists regard midriff-baring, micro-mini-wearing Third Wavers like Ally as patriarchal collaborators whose behaviors perpetuate the sexism Second Wavers struggled against. As evidenced by popular reviews of the series, to some Second Wave feminists these sartorial expressions of female libido are not an exercise of freedom, but rather an affirmation of the hegemonic masculine view that intelligent, successful professional women "deep down" really still just want to be "the thinking man's sex kitten."[58]

Cultural memory and historical embodiedness play into this criticism. The Second Wavers' trenchant criticism of Ally's miniskirts and other sexually revealing attire work rhetorically to construct a cultural memory of past struggles to de-colonize female sexuality from masculine interests. By the mid-1960s the pill had become widely available and AIDS was not on the horizon[59] and by the end of the 1960s miniskirts worn under ragged army jackets were a popular fashion statement on many college campuses, as was the mantra "Make love not war." Despite the momentum feminism's Second Wave (aka Women's Liberation Movement) gained during the 1970s, popular media countered these feminist political statements with updated fantasies from the patriarchal, hegemonic masculine imaginary: Remember the 007 girls (who could forget Pussy Galore) and *La Dolce Vita* as well as the sanitized sexuality of *Beach Blanket Bingo*—in sexualized attire (miniskirts and bikinis). Remember the sexist banter on *Laugh In* (1968–73), the most politically charged television programming in 1960s America. Remember how the "*Playboy* philosophy" appropriated the new sexual freedoms for women made possible by oral birth control. Remember how sexually independent women were disciplined (murdered) in *Looking for Mr. Goodbar* (1977) and *Dressed to Kill* (1980).

Second Wave journalists' and viewers' criticisms of Ally McBeal as antithetical to feminism express the frustration felt by those who remember having their consciousnesses awakened to the realization that they were not being treated as equal partners in the civil rights movement, the peace movement, or in their everyday lives. These feminists began a political and cultural revolution to eradicate inequities at work, at school, and in the courts, and their castigation of Ally McBeal, Madonna, and Courtney Love reflect their anger over the political legal backsliding of the 1980s and 1990s and their frustration at what they perceive as the apathy of the younger generation of feminists toward feminist political goals. For these feminist viewers and journalists, Ally's increasingly short skirts made her the antithesis of a feminist and a poor role model. They read Ally's adoption of the signifiers of sexualized feminine fashion as participating in the very sexism Second Wave feminism had struggled against and as legitimizing the hegemonic masculine view that all women are primarily and fundamentally objects of sexual desire. *The New Republic*'s Ruth Shalit, for example, labeled Ally "the mainstream apogee of what *Esquire* magazine called 'do-me feminists' and an 'avatar of female carnality.'"[60] According to Shalit, Ally represented "the dark side of do-me feminism": a woman who was

plucky, confident, upwardly mobile, and extremely horny. She is alert to the wounds of race and class and gender, but she knows that feminism is safe for women who love men and bubble baths and kittenish outfits; that the right ideology and the best sex are not mutually exclusive. She knows that she is as smart and as ambitious as a guy, but she's proud to be a girl and girlish. She is a little like Monica Lewinsky…. a slap in the face of the real-life working girl, a weekly insult to the woman who wants sexual freedom and gender equality, who can date and litigate in the same week without collapsing in a Vagisil heap.[61]

For Shalit, the *Ally McBeal* series was a classic example of "the packaging of prurience as an anthem of emancipation," whose narratives and representations were "nothing but a male producer's fantasy of feminism, which manages simultaneously to exploit and to deplore, to arouse and to moralize."[62]

On the other hand, however, some Second Wavers have fairly rigid expectations of what feminist political statements should look like; many have ignored how younger feminists have contributed to women's history and built on, not torn down, the foundation of the Second Wave. So, for example, these now middle-aged feminists have not recognized as feminist political action "the thousands of little girls with temporary tattoos on their arms, and Mia Hamm soccer jerseys on their backs, who own the bleachers at the Women's World Cup…. [or the feminist political] activism…in the twenty-nine-year-old woman's challenge to her doctor's blithe directive that she get a hysterectomy to deal with fibroids in her uterus."[63] Indeed, the contemporary crisis within feminism, argue these Third Wavers, is at least partly a function of a difference in generational perspectives.

The Third Wavers saw much of the prescriptions and proscriptions they resisted within the critiques leveled against *Ally McBeal* by feminist journalists and viewers. Implicit in their critiques was the

insist[ence] that junior feminists be good daughters, defending the same kind of feminism their mothers advocated. Questions and criticism are allowed, but only if they proceed from the approved brand of feminism. Daughters are not allowed to invent new ways of thinking and doing feminism for themselves; feminists' politics should take the same shape that it has always assumed. New agendas are regarded at best with suspicion on the part of seniors, at worst with outright hostility.[64]

Ally McBeal explicitly invited viewers to reflect humorously on the perceived generational binary between "old" and "new" feminisms. The episode "Love Unlimited" featured a caricature of Second Wave authoritarianism and Third Wave feminists' insistence on breaking away—leaving the Mothership, if you will. In this episode, as Ally walked out of a courtroom and into a crowded hallway, a loud, pushy woman named Laura Dipson, Executive Vice President of Women for Progress, accosted Ally and informed her that she had been named one of Women for Progress's 1999 professional role models. When Ally replied that she did not want to be a role model, Dipson retorted, "Well, that's very sweet, but I'm afraid you really have no choice." Dipson then lectured Ally about changes that Ally would need to make in the way she dressed, and topped off her grand pronouncement by saying, "I'd really like to fatten you up a bit. We do not want young girls glamorizing that thin thing."

At this point, a very disgruntled Ally demanded to know who in the world this presumptuous woman was. Dipson again introduced herself and continued her lecture about Ally's failures as a feminist: "Now, my sources tell me that you feel an emotional void without a man. You're really going to have to lose that if women are going to look up to you." Once more Ally indignantly averred that she did not want women to look up to her at all. As Ally started to walk away, Dipson grabbed Ally's arm and ordered her not to be "pissy": "You're a role model and you'll do exactly what we tell you to do. Yeah, and you can start by dropping that skinny whiny emotional slut thing and being exactly who we want you to be. Nothing more, nothing less, can you do that pinhead?"

In one of its most obdurately postfeminist moments, this scene illustrates the series' efforts to address the crisis in feminism caused by generational differences and experiences by effectively *fueling* them. The extreme rigidity and authoritarian tone adopted by Dipson represent the demonizing portrayals of feminism that mainstream media had begun to broadcast by the mid-1970s— and the *only* portrayals still given airtime. Second Wave Dipson was portrayed as a caricature, including her cold, insensitive and exceedingly brusque manner of speaking, dowdy clothes, and an arrogant, dictatorial demeanor. On the other hand, Ally was also portrayed as a caricature of a Third Wave feminist—micro-miniskirt, moony eyes, and selfish pouty rejection of any social responsibility to act as a role model for other young women and men (despite having been law review editor at the top law school in the country). In this interchange, Second Wave spokeswoman Dipson castigates Ally for her (and her generation's) embrace of fashion, popular culture and her overt (to the point of unprofessional) display of female sexual desire. Dipson's lecture clearly spanks Ally and other young feminists for ignoring the fact that most of them would not be experiencing the occupational and personal opportunities for fulfillment and expression had it not been for generations of previous feminists' struggles to achieve the legal protections ensuring their occupational and social rights.

Although the episode above critiques Ally's selfishness and apoliticism, it also supports her right to find her own way and to develop new expressions of feminism. While many Third Wave feminists—including Ally in various episodes—acknowledge that they are standing on the shoulders of previous generations of feminists,[65] they also reject some aspects of the feminism of the Second Wave, especially those which they see as reflecting "almost exclusively the perspectives and values of white, middle-class heterosexual women who define themselves primarily as oppressed victims of patriarchy."[66] One reason for this perception, as Third Wavers Heywood and Drake have explained, is that younger feminists like Ally have grown up influenced not only by Second Wave feminism, but also by the political and cultural backlash against feminism and political activism that has characterized the U.S. since the 1980s.

Susan Faludi has defined this backlash as a "powerful assault on women's rights, a backlash, an attempt to retract the handful of small and hard-won victories that the feminist movement did manage to win for women." Moreover, she argues, "just as Reaganism shifted political discourse far to the right and demonized liberalism, so the backlash convinced the public that women's 'liberation' was the true contemporary American scourge—the source of an endless laundry list of personal, social and economic problems."[67] This most recent episode of backlash, she explains, first appeared among the evangelical right in the late 1970s; by the early 1980s it had "shouldered its way into the White House," where, having found receptive political support, it soon also gained social acceptance as evidenced by its pervasiveness in journalism and popular print media[68] as well as film (e.g., *Fatal Attraction, Surrender*).

Part of *Ally McBeal*'s appeal for many viewers was her rejection of the messages of the 1980s backlash culture. As Leigh Shoemaker explained, "Second Wave feminism had taught me that, as a girl, I could do anything I wanted to do, but the backlash let me know that this was possible only as long as I wasn't a girl—as long as I wasn't soft and feminine and weak."[69] Ally rejected this backlash message and embraced the apparent contradictions between feminism and femininity: Ally and the other women in the series relished both the power expressed through their competent performances in the courtroom and contemporary signifiers of femininity—short skirts, obsession with girlie, sexy fashion and appearance, and the quest for romance. At the same time, they objected to male attempts to control their sexuality. For example, Ally verbally castigated Fish for his directives that Ally should use her sexual attractiveness to woo clients to the firm ("Compromising Positions") and to disarm opposing counsel through her presence as "window dressing" ("Let's Dance"). Concomitantly, however, Ally saw no problem with wearing miniskirts to gain the attention of attractive males. When Renee told her "men at court talk about your short skirts, and that's what you want them to do, right?" Ally smiled and replied, "No, I just want them to talk about my legs" ("They Eat Horses, Don't They").

The show could be very effective in dramatizing the contradictions and tensions faced by women and that contributed to the divide between Second and Third Wave feminist modalities. The "It's My Party" episode addressed directly the persistence and pervasiveness of chauvinistic attitudes toward female sexuality and its public expression in dress and behavior. Here the presiding judge found Ally in contempt of court for her short hemlines. Nelle defended Ally's right to wear short skirts, saying, "Nobody is denying the respect that should be afforded to you in this courtroom, and if she were in here in ripped clothing or tennis shoes, that would be one thing. But you're penalizing her basically because her attire is too sexually risqué, and that isn't right." And when the judge started to say, "If it undermines the credibility of this forum——," Nelle interrupted and argued this elegant explanation of Third Wave feminists' embrace of sexualized "feminine" fashion:

> Why should it [undermine the credibility of this forum]? That very assumption endorses the myth that a sexually attractive woman can't have credibility. That's a prejudice. It's bad enough the legal profession is still an old-boys club. Why should we have to come in here looking like old boys. [The judge interrupted to say that no one was asking Ally to look like a boy, to which Nelle retorted:] Every billboard and magazine cover tells us we should look like models. All the while, we have to fight the mindset, 'If she's beautiful, she must be stupid.' I fight it, too, and I bend to the prejudice. I don't have her courage. If I did, I might come in here and let my hair down once. [She took her long blond hair down from the bun in which it was wrapped]. If I didn't care about people automatically thinking I'm a bimbo, I might not always wear jackets. [She took off her jacket and tossed it toward John Cage; it ended up across his lap.] But people, men and women, draw unfair conclusions. We've come to expect a bias. [She looked directly at the judge.] But not from judges. What's most disappointing here: you saw this woman perform in court, you heard her argue, she won her case. And you're still judging her on hemlines. What do we have to do?

Nelle's summation directly challenged those critiques of Ally's vigorous assertion of individuality and freedom of expression through fashion as an insult to feminism. By visually and narratively asserting the series' and the title character's embrace of femininity, signified by Ally's wearing of miniskirts (and Renee's and Elaine's wearing cleavage-revealing dresses) *and* feminism, signified by Ally's lawyerly competence (and Renee's kickboxing defense of her right to say "no" to at any point in a date, and Elaine's sexual harassment lawsuit) *Ally McBeal* transgressed the binary structuration of Second Wave feminism.

Through the everyday lives of women as practicing attorneys, *Ally McBeal* both deconstructed and parodied the perceived contradiction between Second and Third Wave feminists' views of sexual expression and identity. Her actions and attire reflected the Third Wave feminists' simultaneous embrace of "elements of the Second Wave critique of beauty culture, sexual abuse and power structures while also acknowledging and making use of the pleasure, danger, and defining power of those structures."[70] Ally donned miniskirts and marched into male-dominated courtrooms where her successful legal performances, which were often concerned with gender discrimination, contested cultural gender scripts about appearance, sexuality, and competence.

The series' assertion that feminism and feminists can embrace, not merely accommodate, contradictions was a fundamental Third Wave tenet. Like their Second Wave predecessors, today's young feminists "take cultural production and sexual politics as key sites of struggle." However, they believe that unlike the foremothers, they "use desire and pleasures as well as anger to fuel struggles for justice."[71] Third Wave feminists agree that the personal is still, and always, political, but they also insist that feminism can take many forms. As Third Wavers Baumgardner and Reed put it,

> Today, the feminist movement has such a firm and organic hold in women's lives that walking down the street (talking back to street harassers), sitting in our offices (refusing to make the coffee), nursing the baby (defying people who quail at the sight), or watching TV shows (*Xena! Buffy!*) can all contain feminism in action. For women of the Third Wave—that is, women who were reared in the wake of the women's liberation movement of the seventies—a good dinner party (or any gathering of women) is just as likely to be a place to see politics at work as is a rally. It is a place to map a strategy for our continuing liberation, because, as with every wave of feminism, our politics emerge from our daily lives.[72]

Ally clearly shared both Second and Third Wave feminists' feelings that being the constant subject of controlling visual sexual appraisal is exasperating and degrading, but she also enjoyed feeling good about her body and expressing this in clothing that highlighted her physical features. Like Madonna, like Sarah Jessica Parker and the other fictional New York heroines of *Sex and the City*, Ally saw displaying her sexuality as empowering, as a form of re-appropriating her own body through her appearance. Contemporary young feminists who "want not to get rid of the trappings of traditional femininity or sexuality so much as to pair them with demonstrations of strength or power"[73] saw no irony in Ally wearing micro-miniskirts into court as she successfully sued sexual harassing and sexually discriminatory employers[74] and employees.[75] Melissa Klein notes, "[t]he dueling images of femininity and feminism…may initially seem confused or confusing. Yet these…forms of expression represent a mode of activism that is challenging rather than didactic and that leaves room for different and changing roles."[76] Put another way, Ally McBeal and company (Buffy, Courtney Love, Madonna, Cindy Lauper) left the Mothership of American feminism in search of new configurations of feminism and feminity. As Third Waver Jennifer Reed explains,

> If the Third Wave has learned nothing else from the work of the Second Wave of feminism, it has come to see the limits of the politics of purity. If we are trying to figure

out how to use differences dynamically, creating alternative families and connections, surviving a capitalist society without exploiting others, minimizing our own exploitation and that of other women and men, we can take our role models only from the audacity and tenacity we see modeled in a world that makes no room for us.[77]

The series we examine next, *Sex and the City*, strongly reflects this call for alternative families and communities, and does so in a way that realizes one of the earliest tenets of Second Wave feminism—sisterhood. That it does so at the cost of deliberating the social issues that Ally McBeal contends with is part of the contradiction that feminists from both generations strive to reconcile.

Sexual Pleasure, "Girlie" Culture and Playfulness

Sex and the City, as the name of the series implies, is about sexuality and desire. The four women characters—Carrie, Charlotte, Samantha, and Miranda—exist in a *mise-en-scene* in which the conditions that allow them to be economically independent and thus free to explore sexual desire are firmly in place. The series is similar to *Ally McBeal* in its portrayal of young professionals who have taken the gifts of Second Wave feminist activism and are flourishing as competent, autonomous, and amorous young women. It differs from Ally McBeal in that the political agenda of collective justice that anchors Second Wave feminist thinking is no longer in play at all.

The characters of *Sex and the City*, like many Generation X women born in the late 1960s and 1970s, have embraced the Third Wave subset that Baumgardner and Richards call "Girlies." "Girlies" are women who are in their twenties or thirties whose reaction to the "antifeminine, antijoy emphasis that they perceive as the legacy of Second Wave seriousness" is to reclaim "girl culture," including "such formerly disparaged girl things as knitting, the color pink, nail polish, fun…and their right to a cultural space once deemed the province of men; for example, rock 'n' roll…porn, and judgment free pleasure and sex."[78] According to Baumgardner and Richards,

We, and others, call this intersection of culture and feminism 'Girlie.' Girlie says we're not broken, and our desires aren't simply booby traps set by the patriarchy. Girlie encompasses the tabooed symbols of women's feminine enculturation—Barbie dolls, makeup, fashion magazines, high heels—and says using them isn't shorthand for 'we've been duped.' Using makeup isn't a sign of our sway to the marketplace and the male gaze; it can be sexy, campy, ironic, or simply decorating ourselves without the loaded issues (a la dye your hair with Jell-O!). Also, what we loved as girls was good and, because of feminism, we know how to make girl stuff work for us. Our Barbies had jobs and sex lives and friends.[79]

Central to Girlie culture is "a rebellion against the false impression that since women don't want to be sexually exploited, they don't want to be sexual."[80] *Sex and the City* is the latest television series to feature new "girlie" feminine feminists. Like *Ally McBeal*, *Sex and the City* is a woman-centered series that celebrates female sexuality.[81] While the four female protagonists search for sexually satisfying relationships drives the series' narratives, there is absolutely no mistaking these women are financially independent and tough-minded. Their successful careers—newspaper columnist, lawyer, public relations specialist, art gallery curator/manager—make them economically successful, autonomous professionals who can afford to own million-dollar apartments and buy $500 Manolo Blahnik shoes to complete their fashion ensembles. Their self-confidence leads them to conclude that being alone is far preferable to fake happiness with a man.[82] Like Ally, Nelle, Renee, and Elaine, the four friends of *Sex and the City* find achieving career success relatively painless compared to the difficulty of finding satisfying romantic relationships. The promo for the first seasons describes the series thusly: "Sexy, hip, smart and sassy, *Sex and the City* charts the lives and loves of four women and their quest to find the one thing that eludes them all—a real, satisfying and lasting relationship. Is such a thing possible in New York?"

Like *Ally McBeal*, *Sex and the City* used first person direct address to speak to viewers; however, in *Sex and the City* central protagonist Carrie Bradshaw's voice-overs not only commented on narrative events, they also introduced the weekly rhetorical question that the rest of the episode answers. This question, and the answer that the week's activities and reflections produced, provided the grist for Carrie's weekly newspaper column "Sex and the City." Among these questions/columns have been: Can women have sex like a man? Is motherhood a cult? Does size matter? Throughout its six seasons, series' narratives framed the four women's transgressions of bourgeois, heterosexual cultural expectations and traditional liberal Second Wave feminist expectations for female sexuality not as "unruly," but as normal, natural sexuality for contemporary post-Second Wave feminists. And apparently it succeeded in setting a number of viewers free to explore their own sexuality: Jane Arthurs noted, for example, that the series' highlighting of the foursome's use of vibrators to achieve sexual satisfaction resulted in a huge increase in their sales.[83]

Traditionally, Arthurs pointed out, "unbridled sexual appetites or loose speech are a mark not only of lower classes but of the unruly woman, who inverts the power relations of gender and has sex like a man."[84] Third Wavers Baumgardner and Richards explain their rebellion against those strictures:

Girlie doesn't so much identify different issues for young women as say that this generation of feminists wants its own institutions and a right to its own attitudes and interpretations…. The point is that cultural and social weapons that had been identified (rightly so) in the Second Wave as instruments of oppression—women as sex objects, fascist fashion, pornographic materials—are no longer being exclusively wielded against women and are sometimes wielded by women…. Girlie is replacing protective cultural "rules" with a kind of equality…. A lot of what Girlie radiates is the luxury of self-expression that most Second Wavers didn't feel they could or should indulge in.[85]

While *Sex and the City* rejected this double standard of sexual behavior associated with Second Wavers and resolutely celebrated the four protagonists' search for and enjoyment of sexual fulfillment, Arthurs noted, it also established that these contemporary feminists do have behavioral standards—but they are aesthetic not patriarchal standards for appropriate behavior. These four women do not have sex with just anyone: "Men who can't kiss very well, who smell, who are too short, or whose semen tastes peculiar are rejected [as sexual partners] on those grounds."[86] For Ally McBeal and the four protagonists of *Sex and the City*, sex is a source of great pleasure. Furthermore, being a sexually desiring and desirable lover is central to these women's identities. One of the ways the two series differ, however, is that *Ally McBeal* contains the potential transgressiveness of women's unbridled sexuality by sentimentalizing Ally's purely sexual liaisons (e.g., treating Ally's near-dalliance with an underage male client in "The Real Thing" as a nostalgic reliving of her adolescent romance with Billy) or by ridiculing her behavior (e.g., having sex in a car wash with a total stranger).[87]

However, as Arthurs pointed out, *Sex and the City* naturalized overt female sexuality and contained the threat women's sexual agency poses to hegemonic masculinity and capitalist power aesthetically—through the women's obsession with high fashion consumption. By reaffirming their acceptance of women's embrace of their roles as cultural consumers, *Sex and the City* argued that feminism's rejection of traditional gender power relations will not mean the death of capitalism:

> *Sex and the City* works through the problem of establishing the boundaries of respectability in a postfeminist culture where women share many of the same freedoms as men, but in which the residual effects of the double standard are still being felt…. Their transgression of bourgeois sexual decorum marks the foursome as…a challenge to patriarchal structures of power, but their adherence to the sleek control of the commodified body makes this compatible with capitalism.[88]

Another important difference between the two series concerns representations of sisterhood and female companionship. Feminist community was a tent pole of the Second Wave movement; consciousness-raising groups, as *Ms. Magazine*'s 1972 guide described them, were "intended to provide emotional refueling, companionship, and confidence building 'when we come back battered or ridiculed from trying to change our worlds'."[89] As Susan Douglas has explained, "the notion that all women were 'sisters,' bound together across ethnic, class, generational, and regional lines by their common experiences as an oppressed group was the most powerful, utopian, and therefore threatening concept feminists advanced in the 1970s.... [N]othing was more dangerous to the status quo than the concept of sisterhood. Hence, the absolute importance of the catfight to demonstrate as simply and vividly as possible that sisterhood was, in fact, a crock of shit."[90]

This radical conceptualization of sisterhood dissipated as women became part of the highly competitive, individualistic male-dominated "public sphere" and accepted the "patriarchal model of individualism"—the mantra of "power feminism": "stand tall and alone...to accept isolation as proof of survival, of strength, of the ability to persevere."[91] Power feminism, which Third Wavers Heywood and Drake aptly describe as "the voice of the father in his latest disguise,"[92] played a vital role in the 1980s backlash against feminism. It led many young women to buy "into the media demonization of 'sisterhood'.... letting ourselves, to use Susan Douglas's word, 'catfight' both with Second Wavers and across racial divides."[93] The concept of feminist sisterhood suffered further discredit from women-of-color feminists who began voicing their long-held critiques of the essentializing assumptions of the white middle-class feminists who dominated the Second Wave. Third Wavers acknowledged these critiques, and added their own challenges to earlier feminism's universalizing concepts of woman; they have begun to develop new alternatives— communities "imagined on different bases than that of the separatism of identity politics."[94] This alternative notion of sisterhood, as bell hooks has explained, envisions a community of women not "built 'in reaction to' what threatens us."[95] Rather, this notion of sisterhood envisions a feminist community based on what hooks characterizes as "commonality of feeling."[96] Tali Edut, Dyann Logwood and Ophira Edut described this sisterhood as what they wanted to express and nurture in their Third Wave women's magazine, *HUES*:

> Sisterhood to us meant having a support network strong enough that a woman could stand up for herself without feeling crazy or alone. It also meant having a greater sense of loyalty between women, so that, for example, we would believe each other if we said we were raped, not go after our best friend's boyfriend, stand up for the girl who gets called a slut, not feel threatened by someone we think is "prettier," and so on. Beyond that, we wanted to encourage a new style of communication among women that was [not] conflict-avoiding.... [we would be] able to accept each other's differences without feeling hostile or competitive because we had an in-your-face, no-holds-barred approach to communication. We wanted to see more women talk to each other instead of about each other.... We envisioned [it]...in terms of the old patchwork quilt cliché.

Each square would represent its own identity, but the pieces would be inextricably sewn together.[97]

Except for the pair of close friendships between Ally and Renee and Ling and Nelle, such sisterhood was largely absent from *Ally McBeal*. It was, however, the essence of Ally's direct descendant *Sex and the City*. Two years after Ally appeared on its cover, the four *Sex and the City* friends appeared on a *Time* magazine cover asking "Who needs a husband?"

While the series' title said the series was about sex and New York City, the series was primarily about love and friendship of women for each other. Indeed, in the penultimate episode of the series, Big told Carrie's three friends shortly before he jetted to Paris to ask her to return to New York and him, "You're the loves of her life. A guy's just lucky to come in fourth." Actually, the friendship shared by these four women was always the primary relationship for all of them, not just Carrie. They were there for each other through marriages (Miranda's one and Charlotte's two marriages), divorce (Charlotte's), pregnancy (Charlotte and Miranda), venereal disease (Miranda), infertility (Charlotte), the death of a parent (Miranda's mother), and breast cancer (Samantha). Their friendship, as Kushman noted, "is grown-up, layered, decidedly un-sitcomy. There were none of TV's usual misunderstandings and miscommunications, followed by a tearful makeup. These women stuck together, joked, listened and, on occasion fumed. Their friendship gave them comfort and strength and it defined their approach to almost everything, and everyone, else."[98] Amy Sohn agreed, "Carrie and her friends had changed the way people look at single women, at relationships, and at female friendships."[99]

These four women friends formed a support network of strong, independent women, transgressive in their affection for and commitment to each other. As Nelson described this new feminist family structure, "Like many single women before them, they became each other's surrogate mothers and sisters, fathers and husbands."[100] For example, "My Motherboard, My Self"[101] featured a touching scene in which Carrie arrived to walk down the aisle with Miranda at her mother's funeral after Miranda's sister and brother-in-law tried to strong-arm Miranda into "three-wheeling" down the aisle with them because, as Miranda angrily wailed, "God forbid I walk it alone, because that would be the real tragedy, right? A 35-year-old single woman is more awful than a coffin." In "Couda, Woulda, Shoulda"[102] when Charlotte learned that Miranda decided to carry her pregnancy full term rather than having an abortion, Charlotte yelled, "We're going to have a baby!" When Carrie faced eviction from her apartment when the building went condo, her on-again-off-again love of her life, Big, offered to loan her the down payment to buy it. Heeding Miranda's warning that "When a man gives you money you give him control," Carrie instead accepted Charlotte's loan—her Tiffany engagement ring from first husband Trey.[103] And when Samantha learns she has cancer shortly before Miranda's wedding in the park to Steve, Samantha, Carrie, and Charlotte try unsuccessfully to keep from spoiling Miranda's special day. They know each other so well, though, that keeping a secret is impossible, and with the reception swirling around them, the four friends sit at a table, hold hands, cry, and talk, talk, and talk.

Although the four central protagonists of *Sex and the City* did not overtly label themselves feminists, they modeled a form of contemporary feminism for viewers, and a central aspect of that contemporary feminism was their sisterhood: they were a community of women who were always there for each other—through the comings and goings of romantic relationships, birth of children, death and caretaking of older parents, agonizing decisions about abortion and cancer treatments. Their never-failing supportive friendship for each other enacted one of the thirteen points in the *Third Wave Manifesta*, the "acknowledg[ment] that, although feminists may have disparate values, we share the same goal of equality, and of supporting one another in our efforts to gain the power to make our own choices."[104]

At the end of the *Ally McBeal* series Ally left Boston (with her newfound daughter) and moved to New York to start a new life.[105] *Sex and the City* took up where Ally left off, and showed us the lives of four contemporary women who grappled anew with the feminist crises in occupational and personal fulfillment, expression of female sexual desire through behavior and fashion, and in empowerment and vulnerability. The characters of *Sex and the City*, as Sarah Jessica Parker noted, "and the actresses playing them, reap enormous benefits from the women's movement. The characters have sexual freedom, opportunity, and the ability to be successful. They have the ability to be leaders and to be strong, assertive, and confident. If you grow up with the right to choose, vote, dress how you want, sleep with whom you want, and have the kind of friendships you want, those things are the fabric of whom you are."[106] The women of *Sex and the City*, like feminism's Third Wave generation, grew up taking for granted that they could do anything and be anything they wanted. The only question for them was—what did they really want?

Unlike *Ally McBeal*, *Sex and the City* celebrated women's sexuality and sexualized appearance without criticizing it.[107] *Sex and the City* embraced girlie fashion culture and women's overt expressions of sexual desire as sources of empowerment. The series was transgressive in its rejection of the patriarchal whore/virgin mythic dichotomy, and in its articulation of a sexually explicit feminist discourse in the public sphere of action and media (Carrie's newspaper column). In *Sex and the City*, wealthy, white, heterosexual, professional women took back the streets. But the series rendered invisible women of color and women who were older, larger, differently abled, and less economically advantaged.

In *Sex and the City*, women have agency: Their actions drive the narratives. They hire maids and nannies to handle the domestic second shifts. The feminist crises of occupational fulfillment and balancing work life and home life that were ever-present verbally and narratively in *Ally McBeal* have largely disappeared for these women of means, though Miranda sometimes struggled as a single mother. They assumed that in relationships, men—as well as women— would need to adapt to make those relationships work. Sometimes the women were willing to adapt, sometimes they weren't; sometimes their male loves were willing to adapt, sometimes they were not. However, unlike the women in *Ally McBeal*, the women in *Sex and the City* were transgressive in their challenges to the patriarchal institution of marriage: Carrie, Samantha, Miranda—and even Charlotte (after her first marriage and her near-loss of Harry) wanted love, but not necessarily marriage. The series debunked the traditional masculine myth that "love and marriage go together like a horse and carriage." Indeed, the characters made it clear that such notions were as outdated as equine modes of transportation.

In these and many other ways, *Sex and the City* was a powerful feminist successor to *Ally McBeal*. According to many viewers, the series "very real and very honest depiction of friendships and love relationships" provided reflections of what women are really like. "I love the show's classiness and daring in terms of language, clothes, and graphic sex," said fan Rhyena Halpern. "It's a high-end version of our lives." For others, the protagonists provided role models. "I have learned so much: It's ok to hurt, cry, laugh, love and care. It's OK to be a woman. Even if you don't wear Jimmy Choos," explained one viewer.[108] Like *Ally McBeal*'s stories, *Sex and the City*'s narratives reiterated that both males and females feel vulnerable when they open themselves to loving and being loved by others.

Occupational success, free expression of sexual desire and attire, vulnerability, and power were indeed the fabric of the four protagonists of *Sex and the City*. Their actions showed viewers that feminism has made personal and occupational relationships more complicated only in the sense that men as well as women now must be willing to adapt. *Sex and the City* moved beyond Ally McBeal's mixed message of vulnerability and empowerment. For Carrie, Samantha, Miranda, and Charlotte, "the city isn't a place of danger and sin…it is a vibrant world of opportunity."[109] Their lives as single women provides an uplifting, if rose-colored addition, to the feminist cultural imaginary.

Sex and the City opened up spaces where women could and did tell *women's* stories, construct women's mythic spaces where women could speak openly and frankly about sexuality, sisterhood, relationships, and the ongoing crises with which contemporary feminists grapple. It articulated sexually explicit critical feminist discourse; it assumed and promoted a feminist ethos through the female-agent-centered narratives. Nowhere in its six years did the series use the female body and ethos to express a crisis of masculinity or to recuperate a masculine cultural imaginary. Furthermore, it successfully recuperated and reinvigorated one of the most politically threatening tools available to women—sisterhood. The series' portrayal of the power of a feminist community (even if it did not use that term) was one of the most transgressive aspects of *Sex and the City*.

Still, for the most part, *Sex and the City* lacked the probative self-consciousness of *Ally McBeal*. The larger project of feminism, that of economic, social, and political equity and rights for all, was the explicit subject of many of *Ally McBeal*'s narratives, while *Sex and the City*'s characters appeared unburdened by such collective matters. *Sex and the City*'s narratives reveled in the exuberant expression of women's sexual desire and sexualized appearance without subjecting the characters to critical scrutiny, and with only the lightest touch of critical self-reflection on the closet full of $450 shoes that made a stronger statement about narcissism and superficiality than feminist economic power. Far more than *Ally McBeal*, *Sex and the City* celebrated women's agency, but unlike *Ally*'s constant self-reflexivity, *Sex and the City* largely refused to critically interrogate its protagonists' choice to objectify themselves through their worship of consumer fashion.[110] As a result, Arthurs has argued, *Sex and the City* invited viewers to conflate these women's privileged lives of consumption and pleasure with real political power.[111]

The series also ignored any substantive divisiveness in feminism and avoided dealing with key feminist issues such as rape, sexual harassment, and job discrimination or addressing the ongoing efforts of conservative political and religious constituencies to erode women's rights and discipline working women. Arthurs' point about the way the series aestheticized consumerism and reinscribed the trivialization of feminine culture of gossip and shopping as contemporary professional women's métier is an important one. Ultimately, despite the series' potentially transgressive expressions of female sexuality, *Sex and the City* illustrated how the culture of consumerism can function to domesticate feminist political issues and nullify through commodification the threat that feminism poses to patriarchy.

Leaving the Mothership:
Feminism as Cultural Memory in Postmodern Culture

The pleasurable possibilities of *Ally McBeal* and *Sex and the City* are rich, indeed. Both series suggested to viewers that women can be strong *and* vulnerable, capable *and* flawed, "girlie" feminine *and* feminist savvy. Presumptive in both series was the worldview that women could be fully human, foibles and all: tough as nails professionally and still vulnerable as human beings; well rounded in the sense of balanced strengths and weaknesses. There were no super-women, no super-moms, no self-sacrificing heroines; there were no alpha-bitches, no scheming sluts, and no virtuous virgins; there were no dumb blondes, no jiggle jokes, and no laughably loonie chicks-next-door.

Ally McBeal dealt frankly with women's occupational, social and economic interests. The series invited viewers to fantasize about young urban women who actually took for granted their top drawer educational and career opportunities. At the same time, the series demonstrated that powerful men *still* regard competent, smart, and successful women as a threat and try to discipline them; viewers saw that young women could, in response, successfully thwart the efforts of powerful men to infantilize them. The series also demonstrated that older female feminists sometimes patronize or punish younger women; the narratives gave voice to a fresh generation of female spokespersons for women's liberation. The series was at its most poignant when narrativizing the emptiness and longing produced by the American tradition of a work-life *im*balance.

Sex and the City gave us the pleasures of woman-centered conversation, female friendships, and the profound love women have for each other. Female characters spoke frankly about their sexualities, an unprecedented event in American television. Who can forget the jaw-dropping episode when Charlotte called an emergency meeting of her friends to discuss the pros and cons of anal sex? Or Samantha's discursive rant on the displeasurable taste of "funky" semen? These fictional conversations were revelatory for American viewers. For male and female viewers alike, it was intensely pleasurable to watch women generating their own talk about a wide range of topics. Most important in the series, however, was the characterization of enduring friendship and love among women.

As we have seen in previous sections, there were some significant limita-tions to both series. Neither set of narratives dealt with the problems faced by working class women in American society; nor did either series deal with issues of race except for occasional stylized nods to political correctness or smirking ironic characterization (i.e., the assimilated Ling as stereotypical Asian "dragon lady"). Both series were hip to homosexuality, but none of the main characters did more than flirt with lesbianism. Because both series were comedies, they did not deal significantly with domestic violence or rape. In addition to these common problems, each series had its own particularized flaws.

Though *Ally McBeal* did address issues of equity central to feminisms's larger project, it infamously fingered Second Wave feminism for causing a work-life imbalance for women in American society. Feminism, of course, did not invent the imbalance; rather, as we and others have suggested, the capital economy never acceded to the demands placed on it when women joined the public work force. Additionally, Ally and her cohorts, characterized as Third Wavers, believed they could appropriate and harness the male gaze for their own amusement. Yet, there was no serious interrogation of whether desire and pleasure can be mobilized in support of the struggle for social justice—only the implicit claim that it ought to be so. Finally, the fictional Ally McBeal never wanted to be a leader (crusader) for women's rights, though she admitted to enjoying the benefits of liberation. As her male creator famously said, she did not want to sacrifice "personal happiness" to the cause of female liberation.

The characterized women of *Sex and the City* were notoriously white and privileged. They spoke a liberated discourse of female sexuality, but never addressed their privilege or the *institutional* powers that control female health: access to health insurance, legislation protecting reproductive health and control, and access to quality medical care. The characters constituted a strong community of friendship as individuals, but they did not voice commitments to a broader "sisterhood" of concerned women for female liberation. Finally, the sleek commodified bodies of the four female characters suggested that a "liberated" American woman micro-manages her own body pleasures in lieu of managing the national body politic.

At issue, of course, is how Third Wave feminism is *represented* in the two series. This issue brings us, finally, to the first of the three probative questions we posed in the introductory section of the chapter. Specifically, to what extent does representation of Third Wave feminism in these two series suggest a shift in public imagination about the logic and the ethos of feminism? Implicit in this question is a consideration of sign systems and the technologies that produce them. Simply put, how did television (and the web of entertainment publications) represent Third Wave feminism?

The ideological contours of the two series are constructed through a seamless interweaving of Third Wave feminism and postfeminism. As we have demonstrated, Third Wave feminism defines itself through playful embrace of popular culture, exuberant expression of sexual identity and desire, rejection of a feminist/feminine binary, and an individualistic understanding of choice. Postfeminism appropriates these ontological tenets for the benefit of capital culture, a practice commonly termed "commodity feminism" or "market-place feminism."[112] Angie Manzano describes free-market feminism as "focus[ing] on personal freedoms instead of women's rights, [on] personal maneuvering instead of structural oppression, and [on] personal choices instead of collective action."[113]

Here, we follow Sarah Projansky in defining postfeminism as "a *cultural response to feminism*, one that seeks to rework—to *steal* rather than to supersede—feminism."[114] Projansky identifies four distinct styles of postfeminism: (1) dead-feminism postfeminism reasons that feminism is no longer needed; (2) backlash postfeminism is both anti-feminism and anti-victimization; (3) equality postfeminism equates feminism with individual choice; and (4) pro-sex postfeminism is commodity feminism.[115] Of these four styles, we see one most clearly at work in the two series.

Pro-sex postfeminism is the common ideological link between *Ally McBeal* and *Sex and the City*. Pro-sex postfeminism centers on management and commodification of the heterosexual female body; in these fictional universes, straight white women and assimilated women of color do the managing. Characters find (mostly) guilt-free pleasure in shopping, accessorizing, grooming, preening and primping. Characters revel in popular culture: music, dance, nightclubs, fashion, restaurants, and so forth. Characters desire the male gaze and find power in manipulating it for social pleasure, but not for economic gain or survival. Hence, Ally wears short skirts and Samantha wears clothing that accentuates her "fabulous" breasts. Both sets of characters combine aggressive professionalism with exaggerated bodily display.[116] Ally is somewhat self-conscious about her urges to embrace "to-be-looked-at-ness" but her fictive sisters in New York never are. Finally, all the characters are very frank about their desire for satisfying heterosexual sex: They talk about sex, they fantasize about sex, they aggressively pursue male sexual partners, they have sex, and they talk about having had sex.

The articulation of Third Wave feminism in *Ally McBeal* positions historical feminisms as incompatible with contemporary signs of femininity. Playfulness, stylish self-adornment and unabashed sexual expression are juxtaposed against dour, joyless, frumpy, and sexually constraining older feminisms. In *Ally McBeal*, Third Wave Girls just want to have fun, and they can (mostly) because the equality thing has been worked out (almost). For the sisters in New York, feminism is reduced to *mise-en-scene*—at once constitutive to and artfully backgrounded in the series. In both series, individual choices for women are about style, sexual partners, management of the body and economic independence. Backlash postfeminism appears occasionally in *Ally McBeal* in the guise of contempt or distaste for "victimization" feminism. Ally may be vulnerable and uncertain, but she's no victim. Do these shifts in representational practices suggest changes in the logic of feminism?

The second question we posed in the introduction of this chapter concerns possible transformation in the rhetorical form of feminism: To what extent has the *form* of feminism changed since the populist inception of the Second Wave? The answer is both simple and very, very complicated.

Third Wave feminism has evolved from modern forms of populism to postmodern forms of play, from "the personal is political" to "the pleasurable is political." Antonio and Kellner explain that "a basic thrust of postmodern aestheticism upholds the vitalistic quest for experience and individualist flight from the disciplining, normalizing tentacles of rational culture."[117] Language play, language games and pastiche (a practice of decontextualization) create the possibilities for ceaseless, rebellious, creative play. Postmodern aesthetics create the possibilities for an ironic disconnect from commodification and normalized identity construction.[118] Proponents of postmodernity, such as Lyotard, believe that such play is potentially liberatory in that it imbues the individual with constitutive agency—we ceaselessly invent ourselves through playful embrace of contradiction, pastiche and pleasure.

Significant for our discussion, postmodern identity politics supplants the modern social movement and significantly alters the social space of emancipation. Second Wave feminists took the "personal" (normalized female oppression) to the rational public sphere of domestic policy, politicized women's experiences, and legislated more equality for women. Conversely, Third Wave feminists are more likely to occupy counter-public spheres (the Internet, postmodern art, radical magazines, the club scene, the localized music and dance scene, and female friendships) than the traditional spaces of public argument and legislative change. Within those counter-public spheres, Third Wave feminists politicize pleasure by appropriating the male gaze, embracing multiple identities, and re-claiming sexual pleasure.

Viewed from the perspective of ontological differences, generational conflicts may be regarded as less accusatory and intractable. What some Third Wave feminists regard as "feminist" activity and agency is unrecognizable to some Second Wave feminists who know and remember the logics of a populist movement. Conversely, some Third Wave feminists regard the logic of populism as flawed—specifically, the Us/Them binaries necessary for creating a symbolic oppressor and the hegemony that creeps into strategies for unifying the underdog group. In other words, Second and Third Wave feminists do not always *recognize* each other as participating in feminist practices. This inability to recognize each other has led to considerable divisiveness and strife. Misrecognition has produced intractable positions. At the risk of provoking claims that we, too, fail to recognize our Third Wave sisters and their contributions, we pose the third and final question: Has feminism been enriched or impoverished by contemporary challenges from a new generation of women?

Admittedly, the question looks to be one that will produce intractable outcomes. However, framed from Laclau's concept of "emptying the sign," the answer may be satisfying to both Waves. Recall that Laclau says that underdog groups must symbolically unify disparate lived experiences by constructing a chain of equivalencies. The greatest challenge for the group lies in *representing* the equivalency because the sign of equivalency must come from a *particular* set of experiences within the underdog group (we have already discussed the potential for hegemony). At the same time, the sign for the equivalential chain must be "emptied" (departicularized) to represent disparate or competing interests. Thus, Laclau explains, unifying signs are *both* enriched *and* impoverished through expansion. Equivalential chains are always already open to contestation and redefinition: What does it mean to *be* a feminist? The answer to the question has evolved over time and through social space, both strengthening and weakening the sign for unity. If we view feminism as ontological rather than ontic, then feminism must change over time in order to remain healthy and productive. But can philosophically different ontologies co-exist peacefully and productively?

The representational logics of modernity and postmodernity are thought by some to be incompatible.[119] More to the point, some question whether postmodern logics can produce emancipation and social justice.[120] These issues were at the forefront of feminist philosophy fifteen years ago. Susan Bordo argued that First and Second Wave feminists came to recognize themselves as the shadow sisters of the Enlightenment. Instead of the masculinist "view from nowhere"—disembodied, detached, abstract, universal—the shadow sisters spoke about the "view from here"—embodied, embedded, material, particular.[121] Paradoxically, even as the first two waves of feminism struggled to write themselves and women into the master narrative of American democracy, feminism as a social movement helped to rupture and dismantle the master narrative of manifest destiny and American superiority. At the same time, Bordo explains, the representational logic of postmodernity (produced in part by technology) constituted a "dream from everywhere" where human agents can fantasize about "the escape from human locatedness."[122] Bordo asks us to consider whether the fantasy of disembodied escape will be liberatory for women, a social group oppressed and persecuted through millennia for occupying unforgivable bodies. Donna Haraway argues that communication technologies and biotechnologies have become the "crucial tools recrafting our bodies."[123]

The crucial question for rapprochement between the two Waves, then, is this: Are emancipatory politics and postmodern play compatible? We hope so, though we share with other scholars significant misgivings about the way postmodern communication technologies are fundamentally grounded in capitalist economies.[124] At the same time, we are fascinated with the Third Wave cultural project to co-opt the male gaze. Margaret Miles once wrote that the female body could never be re-appropriated by women as a sign for women's lives and experiences: "[T]he female body which has played such a central historical role in the circulation of meaning in the Christian West is perhaps too assimilated to the male gaze to permit inscription with new meaning, with a female-defined sexuality and subjectivity."[125] Miles advised women to abandon the struggle to rehabilitate the female body as sign. Third Wave feminists have not taken her advice. Rather, they have boldly appropriated the signifiers of masculinist power for their own amusement. They have re-located the struggle for sexual agency and personal autonomy from male-dominated spaces to counter-public spaces; moreover, they have used their own bodies in the public spaces as signboards of contestation. Will this playful strategy promote social justice and equality, the goals of feminism?

Kenneth Burke's comic frame (perspective by incongruity) is instructive for answering this question.[126] Burke theorized the comic frame in the 1930s as a critical response to (a "therapeutic heckling" of) the twin empires of technology and capitalism.[127] Burke believed that comedy, conceived as social criticism, could serve as an instrument sharp enough for "discerning the play of economic factors."[128] Burke's notion of comedy requires a politicized, self-reflective recognition that unless capitalism and technology are ceaselessly interrogated, they will subvert the possibilities of civil democratic society.[129] Comedy, or perspective through incongruity, can help us de-naturalize that which has become normalized—provided we understand that comedy is not the same as humor: Humor merely deals with the symptoms of social malady; comedy reveals the causes. Humor sentimentalizes capitalism; comedy heckles it. Humor "dwarfs" the complexities of social situations; comedy discerns complication, paradox, and contradiction. Above all, Burke wrote, the comic frame "should enable people *to be observers of themselves, while acting*."[130]

The smirking irony of postmodernism and the teflon irony of postfeminism appeal to humor; they are strategically superficial, slick, and recyclable. Postfeminism of the sort we see in *Ally McBeal* and *Sex and the City* smirks precisely because characterized women in these stories do not have to worry about economic security, professional success, or political threat. Consumers of these programs and other popular culture texts are invited to skate on the surface of an endless supply of political incorrectness and hip, inside jokes. More to the point, young consumers are invited to sneer at American capitalism whilst simultaneously embracing technology and popular culture uncritically. Through humor, signification practices such as gender and race can be de-contextualized, de-historicized and de-politicized, rendering iconic sexism and racism playful through irony and pastiche. Politics give way to pleasure, pleasure is de-politicized, and capitalism goes unheckled. James Kastely puts it succinctly: "the current crisis arises not from any failure [on the part of feminism and cultural theory] but as the by-product of the unhealthy and imperial success of a symbolic order that has not been appropriately heckled."[131]

Meanwhile, we point out that in spite of the technological innovations and cultural upheavals that separate them, the Second and Third Waves have quite a bit in common. For example, Helen Gurley Brown, founder and editor of *Cosmopolitan Magazine*, offered the Second Wave generation a "liberatory" aesthetic that she called The Cosmo Girl; she was sexy and sexual, smartly attired, girlie feminine and feminist savvy. The Cosmo girl ceaselessly invented and re-invented herself; in fact, this was her primary project.[132] She popped up in film (e.g., Natalie Wood in *Sex and the Single Girl*), she appeared in television (e.g., Marlo Thomas in *That Girl*). She, too, fretted over combining work and family, profession and personal life. She liked to play and have fun. It is not a stretch to claim that The Cosmo girl is the forbear of the characterized Third Wave sisters in *Ally McBeal* and *Sex and the City*. Of the infamous Ally, Helen Gurley Brown says, "She's beautiful, she has a great job, and she's true to herself and all her inclinations…. She gets it all out; there's no hypocrisy…. Ally's a[n]…uninhibited, sexual young woman. She has me in her corner for virtually anything."[133] Our point is that history tends to repeat itself; but how would we know that without critical historiography of representational practices? Our concern about *representations* of Third Wave feminism, and about the self-expressed *sensibilities* of the Third Wave take the form of this final question: What happens to history, especially the history of oppression, in postmodern culture?

Emancipatory politics, as we have known it, requires the forging of a collective identity. Thus, an ontology of emancipation *requires* history—a narrative of oppression and the struggle against that oppression. Postfeminism and other hegemonic forces reduce feminist claims of a history of oppression to self-indulgent whining over "victimization." The rejection of victimization is a rejection of memory, a symbolic cleansing that crafts a future utterly dissociated from the past. Hegemonic representations play a significant role in this dissociation: since *Ally McBeal*, no prime-time show or Hollywood movies has addressed the feminist political project directly as its subject matter. We believe such representational practices resonate with neo-conservatisms which celebrate their privileged status and do not want to be obligated to the past or to memory of the past (i.e., Ann Coulter, Caitlin Flanagan, and Linda Hirshman). The burden of history is as crucial to women as it is to other historically oppressed groups. One can scarcely imagine Jews and Palestinians, African Americans, or homosexuals declaring that the history of oppression is a drag—though we acknowledge internecine strife over personal responsibility within these social groups.

As for the pleasures of technological and symbolic disconnection from the materiality and locatedness of human bodies, the "dream from nowhere," we offer a closing meditation. We often muse over the unwitting paradox in the introduction to *Sex and the City*. As the central character Carrie stands on a street corner in New York City, a bus emblazoned with a larger-than-life image of Carrie drives past, splashing the embodied Carrie with street water and debris. In that moment, the sign trumps the material; the embodied woman whose drive for perfection and perfectibility drives the narrative, is soaked by a force she cannot control. And so it goes.

Notes

[1] Benjamin Svetkey, "Kelley's Heroes," *Entertainment Weekly* 1998: 32–34m 37–38, 40.

[2] "TV: The Top 10," *Sacramento Bee* 6 May 1999: D7.

[3] "Ally McBeal," TV Guide online, 5–11 September 1998.

[4] Rachel Mosely and Jacinda Read, "Having it 'Ally': Popular Television (Post)feminism," *Feminist Media Studies* 2.2 (2002): 232.

[5] Veronica Chambers, "How Would Ally Do It? A Quirky Cult Hit Muses on Success, True Love, Unisex Bathrooms and (Eek!) Dancing Babies," *Newsweek*, 2 Mar. 1998: 58–60.

[6] Jon Katz, "Deconstructing Ally," *Hotwired* Online. 23 Sept. 1998: 1. http://www.hotwired.com/synapse/katz/98/11/katz1a_text.htm.

[7] Katz 2.

[8] Lonnae O'Neal Parker, "'Ally McBeal' Insecurity Blanket: Obsessed Fans of the Fox Show Say It's the Story of Their Lives," *Washington Post* 17 Feb. 1998, final edition: D1.

[9] Jeff Jarvis, "The Couch Critic: *Ally McBeal*," *TV Guide* Sept. 20–26 1998: n.p.

[10] Dinitia Smith, "Real-life Questions in an Upscale Fantasy," *The New York Times* 1 Feb. 2004, late final ed., sec. 13: 4.

[11] Kim McCabe and Janet Akass, eds., *Reading Sex and the City* (New York: I.B. Tauris, 2004).

[12] Ernesto Laclau, "Populism: What's in a Name?" *Populism and the Mirror of Democracy*, ed. Francisco Panizza (London: Verso, 2005), par. 1. http://www.cecs.nctu.edu.tw/record/ec11–4/POPULISM.doc.

[13] Karen Durbin, "Razor Thin, but Larger than Life," *The New York Times* 20 Dec. 1998: AR39, AR46.

[14] Durbin AR–46.

[15] Durbin AR–39.

[16] Steven Stark, "Lady's Night: *Ally McBeal*'s Quirky Appeal," *The New Republic* 29 Dec. 1997: 14.

[17] Stark 13–14.

[18] Olivia Goldsmith, "Word-perfect Women: Out of the Mouths of Babes," *The New York Times* 7 Dec. 1997, sec. 2: AR39.

[19] James Collins, "Woman of the Year: Confused and Loveable? Or a Simpering Drag? Taking Sides on Fox's Surprising New Hit," *TV Guide* 10 November 1997: 117.

[20] See Leslie Heywood and Jennifer Drake, eds., *Third Wave Agenda: Being Feminist, Doing Feminism* (Minneapolis: University of Minnesota Press, 1997); Helene A. Shugart, Catherine Egley Waggoner, and D. Lynn O'Brien Hallstein, "Mediating Third-Wave Feminism: Appropriation as Postmodern Media Practice," *Critical Studies in Media Communication* 18.2 (2001):194–210.

[21] Heywood and Drake 51.

[22] Mosely and Read 240.

[23] Brenda Cooper, "Unapologetic Women, "Comic Men," and Feminine Scholarship," *Critical Studies in Media Communication* 18 (2001): 416–435; Mosely and Read.

[24] Cooper 416.

[25] Mosely and Read 240, 245, 231.

[26] Mosely and Read 237.

[27] Qtd. in Gina G. Bellafante, "Feminism: It's All About Me!" *Time* 27 May 1998: 58.

[28] Collins.

[29] "Feminist Role Model or Ditsy Broad?" *Ottawa Citizen Online* 29 June 1998, italics ours. http://www.ottawacitizen.com/entertainment/980629/1820945.html.

[30] Qtd. in Matt Roush, Ileane Rudolph, Hilary de Vries, and Shawna Malcom, "What's Gotten into Ally?" *TV Guide* Dec. 18–24, 1999: 28, emphasis added.

[31] Maureen Dowd, "Liberties: Pass the Midol," *The New York Times* 15 April 1998: A-25. See also Maureen Dowd, "Liberties: She-TV: Feminism Narcissim, McBealism!" *The New York Times* 22 July 1998, op. ed., A19.

[32] Ruth Shalit, "Canny and Lacy: Ally, Dharma, Ronnie, and the Betrayal of Postfeminism," *The New Republic* 6 April 1998: 32.

[33] Bellafante 58.

[34] Chambers 58.

[35] See, e.g., Mary D.Vavrus, "Putting Ally on Trial: Contesting Postfeminism in Popular Culture," *Women's Studies in Communication* 23.3 (2000): 413–428.

[36] Shuggart, Waggoner, and Hallstein 196.

[37] Mosely and Read 235.

[38] Vavrus 413.

[39] Vavrus 425, 426, and 427 respectively.

[40] Mona Harrington, *Women Lawyers: Rewriting the Rules* (London: Routledge, 1993) 7.

[41] Harrington 3.

[42] Harrington 15, 104.

[43] Harrington notes that by the 1990s there were well over 300 law firms in the U.S. that had more than 50 lawyers, and a number that had over 1,000. One of these, the famous New York firm of Skadden Arps, Slate, Meagher and Flom, with over 1,000 lawyers, who grossed $400 million a year.

[44] Harrington 25.

[45] Harrington 26, 33.

[46] Harrington 16–17.

[47] The term "second shift" was developed by Arlie Hochschild, *The Second Shift: Working Parents and the Revolution at Home* (New York: Viking, 1989).

[48] Episode titled "Only the Lonely" which aired May 3, 1999.

[49] Harrington.

50 Anthony Lewis, "If It Were Mr. Baird," *The New York Times* 25 Jan. 1993: A17.

51 Patricia A. Sullivan and Lynn H. Turner, "The Zoe Baird Spectacle: Silences, Sins, and Status," *Western Journal of Communication* 63.4 (1999): 425.

52 Mosely and Read 238.

53 Leigh L. Shoemaker, "Part Animal, Part Machine: Self-definition, Rollins Style," *Third Wave Agenda: Being Feminist, Doing Feminism,* eds. Leslie Heywood and Jennifer Drake (Minneapolis: University of Minnesota Press, 1997) 104–105.

54 Melissa M. Klein, "Duality and Redefinition: Young Feminism and the Alternative Music Community," *Third Wave Agenda: Being Feminist, Doing Feminism,* eds. Leslie Heywood and Jennifer Drake (Minneapolis: University of Minnesota Press, 1997) 207.

55 See Jennifer Baumgardner and Amy Richards, *Manifesta: Young Women, Feminism, and the Future* (New York: Farrar, Straus and Giroux, 2000) 224.

56 Klein 207–208.

57 Shugart, Waggoner, and Hallstein 195.

58 Chambers 58.

59See Douglas 61–65.

60 Shalit 27.

61 Shalit 27, 32.

62 Shallit 30.

63Baumgardner and Richards 18 –19.

64 Baumgardner and Richards 224.

65 See Baumgardner and Richards; Heywood and Drake.

66 Shugart, Waggoner, and Hallstein 194–195.

67 Susan Faludi, *Backlash: The Undeclared War Against American Women* (New York: Crown, 1991) viii.

68 See, for example, Mona Charen, "The Feminist Mistake," *National Review* 23 March 1984: 24; Kay Ebeling, "The Failure of Feminism," *Newsweek* 19 November 1990: 9; Sylvia A. Hewlett, *A Lesser Life: The Myth of Women's Liberation in America* (New York: William Morrow, 1986); Megan Marshall, *The Cost of Loving: Women and the New Fear of Intimacy* (New York: G.P. Putnam's Sons, 1984).

69 Shoemaker 115.

70 Heywood and Drake 3.

71 Heywood and Drake 4.

72 Baumgardner and Reed 15.

73 Klein 223.

74 "Pilot" Sept. 8, 1997; "The Playing Field" March 16, 1998; "Let's Dance" April 26, 1999; "The Kiss" Sept. 22, 1997.

75 "You Never Can Tell" broadcast November 23, 1998.

76 Klein 225.

77 Reed 124.

78 Baumgardner and Richards 80.

79 Baumgardner and Richards 136.

80 Baumgardner and Richards 137.

81 See Jane Arthurs, "*Sex and the City* and Consumer Culture: Remediating Postfeminist Drama," *Feminist Media Studies* 3.1 (2003): 83–98.

82 For example, the episode titled "They Shoot Single People Don't They?" which aired Sept. 27, 1999.

83 Arthurs.

[84] Arthurs 92.

[85] Baumgardner and Richards 137–141, 161.

[86] Arthurs 93.

[87] In "Buried Pleasures" (Nov. 11, 1999) Ally and Ling kiss and go out on a date, and in "Two's a Crowd (Nov. 6, 2000) and "Without at Net" (Nov. 13, 2000) Ally dates two men simultaneously, only to discover that they are father and son.

[88] Arthurs 92.

[89] Faludi 351.

[90] Susan Douglas, *Where the Girls Are: Growing Up Female with the Mass Media* (New York: Random House/Time Books, 1995) 224.

[91] Douglas 119.

[92] Heywood and Drake 50.

[93] Heywood and Drake 49.

[94] Heywood and Drake 17.

[95] Shoemaker 118.

[96] Heywood and Drake 17. See bell hooks, *Outlaw Culture* (New York: Routledge, 1994) 217.

[97] Tali Edut, Dyann Logwood and Ophira Edut, "*HUES* Magazine: The Making of a Movement," *Third Wave Agenda: Being Feminist, Doing Feminism*, eds. Leslie Heywood and Jennifer Drake (Minneapolis: University of Minnesota Press, 1997) 91–93.

[98] Rick Kushman, "Cia, Friends: *Sex* Has Been More Than That," *Sacramento Bee* 20 Feb. 2004: E1.

[99] Amy Sohn, *Sex and the City: Kiss and Tell* (New York: Pocket Books, 2004) 160.

[100] Ashley Nelson, "Sister Carrie Meets Carrie Bradshaw: Exploring Progress, Politics, and the Single Woman in *Sex and the City*," *Reading Sex and the City*, eds. Kim Akass and Janet McCabe (New York: I.B. Tauris, 2004) 91.

[101] Season 4, episode 56.

[102] Season 4, episode 59.

[103] "Ring a Ding Ding," season 4, episode 16. In this episode, we learn that Carrie has done a poor job managing her finances. She cannot put together a down payment for the condo because she has spent too much of her considerable income on fashion.

[104] Baumgardner and Richards 280.

[105] Later in the series, Ally discovers that one of the eggs she donated while in college was used to produce an in vitro pregnancy and through a series of events, the daughter that was produced by this donation comes to live with Ally.

[106] Sohn 24.

[107] Arthurs 87.

[108] Qtd. in Cynthia Hubert, "Good-bye Girls: As *Sex and the City* Winds Down, What'll Become of the Foursome? Our Viewers Weigh In," *Sacramento Bee* 4 Feb. 2004: E1.

[109] Kushman E-5.

[110] See Rosalind Gill, "From Sexual Objectification to Sexual Subjectification: The Resexualisation of Women's Bodies in the Media," *Feminist Media Studies* 3.1 (2004): 100–105.

[111] Arthurs 88.

[112] See Robert Goldman, Deborah Heath, and Sharon L. Smith, "Commodity Feminism," *Critical Studies in Mass Communication* 8.3 (1991): 335–351; Shugart, Waggoner, and Hallstein.

[113] Angie Manzano, "'Charlie's Angels': Free-market Feminism," *Off Our Backs: A Women's Newsjournal* Dec. 2000: 10.

[114] Sarah Projansky, *Watching Rape: Film and Television in Postfeminist Culture* (New York: New York UP, 2001) 88. Emphasis original.

[115] Projansky 71–86.

[116] Projansky discusses the importance of bodily display in pro-sex postfeminism. See page 82.

[117] Robert J. Antonio and Douglas Kellner, "The Future of Social Theory and the Limits of Postmodern Critique," *Postmodernism and Social Inquiry*, eds. David R. Dickens and Andrea Fontana (New York: The Guilford Press, 1994) 140.

[118] Toby Young and Tom Vanderbilt, "The End of Irony?" *The Modern Review* 1.14 (1994): 6–7.

[119] Fredric Jameson, "Postmodernism, Or the Cultural Logic of Late Capitalism," *New Left Review* 146 (1984): 53–92.

[120] Christopher Lasch, *The Culture of Narcissism: American Life in an Age of Diminishing Expectations* (New York: Warner Books, 1979).

[121] Susan Bordo, "Feminism, Postmodernism, and Gender-Scepticism," *Feminism/Postmodernism*, ed. Linda J. Nicholson (New York: Routledge, 1990).

[122] Bordo 136.

[123] Donna Haraway, "A Manifesto for Cyborgs: Science, Technology, and Socialist Feminism in the 1980s," *Feminism/Postmodernism*, ed. Linda J. Nicholson (New York: Routledge, 1990) 205.

[124] See Shugart, Waggoner, and Hallstein; Eileen Meehan, *Why TV Is Not Our Fault: Television Programming, Viewers, and Who's Really in Control* (Lanham, MD.: Rowman & Littlefield, 2005); Angela McRobbie, "Post-feminism and Popular Culture," *Feminist Media Studies* 4.3 (2004): 255–264.

[125] Margaret R. Miles, *Carnal Knowing: Female Nakedness and Religious Meaning in the Christian West* (Boston: Beacon Press/BURNS & OATES, 1992) 176.

[126] Kenneth Burke, *Attitudes Toward History*, vol. 1(New York: The New Republic, 1937).

[127] James L. Kastely, "Kenneth Burke's Comic Rejoinder to the Cult of Empire," *College English* 58.3 (1996): 307–327. Retrieved from Proquest Dec. 7, 2004.

[128] Burke 214.

[129] See Kastely.

[130] Burke 220, italics in the original.

[131] Kastely par. 33.

[132] Moya Luckett, "A Moral Crisis in Prime Time: *Peyton Place* and the Rise of the Single Girl," *Television, History, and American Culture: Feminist Critical Essays*, eds. Mary Beth Haralovich and Lauren Rabinovitz (Durham: Duke UP, 1999) 80–83.

[133] Roush 28.

Chapter Four

Designing Women as Consumers...Again: Gender and the Myth of the Level Playing Field in the Information Age

Technology is a central factor in how cultures construct gender. Equally, cultural constructions of technology have been and continue to be gendered. The term *technology* encompasses a complex of artifacts, human practices, values, and cultures inextricable from the social contexts in which they are created and used. The proliferation of information and communication technology (ICT) throughout the fabric of daily life puts both men and women in frequent contact with computers and related systems. Though cultural discourses of gender have opposed femininity to technology historically, more contemporary constructions of femininity accommodate female interactions with machines. Yet, the discursive identification of technical expertise with idealized masculinity continues to support the male domination of information and communication technology innovation and design.

In the historic arc *Bad Girls* is traversing, starting with the first chapter's analyses of post-Vietnam cinematic narratives, we arrive at a juncture at which our investigations of textual fictions meet the material reality, where the fictional women we've encountered translate into real human beings confronting the conditions of everyday life. Chapter Two, "Hacking Women," looks at two of the very rare fictional representations of women who make technology their objects of desire. In those characterizations we observe the difficulty popular cultural forms had in imagining a whole and healthy woman devoted to technological expertise; moreover, development of these narrative roles in future cinematic and televisual portrayals failed to occur. The political, economic and cultural environment out of which such a paucity of imaginings is drawn is the subject of this chapter.

The information revolution, made possible by the dissemination of the personal computer beginning in the early 1980s, gave rise to often sweeping claims for its power to transform lives and societies. America's long-standing faith in technology as the foundation for social progress counts on the next technological fix to rectify failures to measure up to cultural ideals, and the computer revolution was no exception. Media representations of new technologies projected images of prosperity, connectedness, and liberation from social oppression. Women, addressed in terms of gender, as well as in their class and racialized positions in society, were to be particular beneficiaries of the information economy: the anonymity of cyberspace would eliminate gender bias.

Mainstream media representations, social commentaries, and educational curricula, discussed further below, often assume that gender neutrality is a natural component of computer technology design, and the opportunity for women's full participation in the new information economy unimpeded. That participation has failed to materialize: women's significant engagement with ICT educational fields and industry has not taken place. The U.S. and Europe publish numerous accounts of the coming shortage of skilled workers in technology and related science, mathematics, and engineering professions, and the lack of women in the educational tracks for these occupations.[1] Various strategies are being suggested to increase the interest of girls in computers and the participation of women in computer science degree programs, including same sex classrooms and interdisciplinary applied curricula.[2] Nevertheless, the number of girls and women engaged in the design of the technological future remains a fraction of the potential.[3] Girls, when pressed about taking computing classes in secondary schools or continuing on into computer science degree programs, used to claim lack of ability. They now claim lack of interest: "we can, but we don't want to."[4]

Numerous elements play into the absence of significant female participation, and this chapter reviews the most important of them. We examine research on how the social and cultural conditioning of young girls and boys affects experience with computing, the educational and corporate environments in which technological careers are advanced, and structural dimensions of society that maintain gendered differences in who and what assumptions shape the technologized future.

Our reading of the nature and place of transgressive women in cultural politics and media representations, however, offers a perspective that diverges from much of the current thinking on how to reverse women's lack of participation in shaping technological development. In viewing media representations as central elements in the production and reproduction of cultural politics and ideological discourses, we observe the impact of the marginalization of the feminist political agenda and the success of media and other institutional forces in silencing voices that point to gendered inequities. The kinds of messages that girls and women receive from public commentaries and popular media suggest that there are no external political or social structural barriers to their full participation in the computer-based information economy. The gendered meanings inscribed in computing are ignored; what women hear is that nothing limits their engagement in technological design and development other than their own individual degree of interest in combination with the intelligence and determination to succeed. Hegemonic discourses of freedom of choice successfully render women's participation in ICT research and invention a matter of personal predilection—just another lifestyle choice, or as Lawrence Summers would have it, further evidence that females lack the mental facility for math, science and technology.[5]

In concert with the trajectory of transgressive fictional women we are charting, what constitutes a productive transgressive position for a woman in the information economy? One approach to answering this question requires that women in both computer science and other disciplinary fields interrogate the realm of technology itself. When computer science, for example, is framed as immutable and objective, women must adapt themselves to an arena of human endeavor constituted by masculine attitudes, behaviors, and values. Mirroring the critical investigations of feminist scientists into how science is socially constructed,[6] countering the under-representation of women in computer science necessitates looking at the way that computer science and engineering are conceived and taught, to understand their construction through pedagogical canons, practices, and hierarchies, and through valorization of forms of research and application in both educational and commercial settings.

Christina Bjorkman, an engineer-computer scientist and feminist technoscience researcher, encourages women to occupy this transgressive stance. She argues that changing the ways of being in and "knowing" computer science are essential to involving women in technological fields *and* the transformation of the discipline itself: "This includes accommodating diversity: diversity among students, diversity in ways of knowing and learning (epistemological pluralism), diversity among practitioners of CS, and diversity of practices and approaches to knowledge in the discipline."[7] She draws on the concept of "world traveling,"[8] a form of boundary-crossing among professional and social roles that recognizes the necessity of feeling "at ease" in the norms, language, and social relations of the human realms in which we live and work. Feelings of *dis*-ease—of not being at home in the discipline, not quite accepted as a proven equal—wondering if the dis-ease itself is evidence of incompetence—typify the lived experience of Bjorkman and numerous women who enter computer science and engineering. Transforming the nature and culture of computer science to include diverse ways of being, learning, and doing computer science, educationally and professionally, thus becomes the work of the transgressive woman.

A significant dimension of this transgressive move is the examination of the "paradigmatic basis" for computer science, one that often reveals the very tight borders inscribed by hegemonic forces around what is considered "pure" computer science.[9] Bjorkman notes that feminist research on the relation of gender and technology has tended to focus on social relations rather than the technology in its technical dimensions, leaving feminist professional computer scientists and activists without the support of theoretical research into the construction and development of technology.

This tendency is compounded by the increasing "black-boxing" of technology, its architectures and algorithms known only to the very few who hold its code, while its users engage only with its inputs and outputs. As Bruno Latour argues in his work on morality and technology, "The more technological systems proliferate, the more they become opaque, so much so that the growth of the rationality of the means and ends...is manifested precisely by the successive accumulations of layers, each of which makes the preceding ones more obscure."[10] In consequence, the expert-user divide, noted by James Carey[11] and Carolyn Marvin[12] in their respective historical research on the telegraph and electricity, is reinforced; what this divide explicitly and tacitly maintains are the privileged forms of educational content, epistemological processes, and cultural practices that effectively exclude women.[13]

The success of political and social powers inimical to the feminist project is starkly evident in the widespread inability of women—once again—to name the source and nature of their own subordination.[14] Volumes have been generated on the complex of conditions by which educational and industrial technology environs are maintained as male enclaves, and the concomitant lack of confidence women express in their technical expertise. Nevertheless, hegemonic discourses of neutrality and equity dominate popular understanding of new technology, and both the recognition and the possibility of collective action against structural gender biases and injustice are subverted. The transgressive voices of women pointing to these barriers are once more relegated to faint cries from the borders as curricular reform and corporate efforts towards increasing representation in science and computing arenas are considered in isolation from the underlying fabric of inequity in which they exist.

We begin tracing the interwoven threads of how and why women remain peripheral to the design of the technological future by selecting a number of mainstream media expressions from the last decade that relate to ICT's impact on social biases, including those of gender.

Mixed Media Messages

MCI's 1997 television ad promoting Internet use employs rhetoric resonant with widely circulated expectations of the new computer-mediated information economy: "There is no race. There are no genders. There is no age. There are no infirmities. There are only minds. Utopia? No. The Internet." The promise?

A level playing field for both sexes, for all races, for all ages, and physical capacities, obliterating the social markers, structures, and boundaries that have established and maintained white masculine privilege for millennia.

A series of studies by the U.S. Department of Commerce found that by the year 2000, "The disparity in Internet usage between men and women has largely disappeared. In December 1998, 34.2% of men and 31.4% of women were using the Internet. By August 2000, 44.6% of men and a statistically indistinguishable 44.2% of women were Internet users" (October 2000). As measured by Internet use, the technology gender divide in the U.S. is considered closed.[15]

Fortune magazine's special issue in 2000, "The Future of the Internet," features 200 pages of stories on the top pioneer innovators and designers of the information age, all but one of whom are men.[16]

Thomas Friedman's 2005 bestselling *The World Is Flat* claims again that the playing field has been leveled—this time globally through economic and technological transformations.[17]

Harvard President Lawrence Summers addresses conference attendees in 2005 at Massachusetts Institute of Technology, informing them that women's inferior innate abilities are likely one reason why there are fewer women than men in top science jobs.[18]

The MCI ad of 1997 reflected a core and widely expressed assumption about the transformation of developed countries' economies by the computer revolution: social inequities, including gender divides, would be a thing of the past. Expansion of modes of communication through the Internet was seen as a motivating force in women's use of information technology.[19] If there were any genuine rationale in excluding women from technology-related occupations because of lesser physical strength than men, the nature of new computer technologies eliminated it. Even the inexorability of linking childrearing skills to the construction of femininity would not undermine the positive effects for women in the information society: telecommunications would allow women at home raising children to engage in professional careers and advanced education. Gender neutrality in information age social and economic opportunities had arrived.

Yet, the great body of evidence indicates that the loosening of masculine hegemony over technology has not taken place. The *Fortune* special issue of 2000 mirrors the absence of women in the technology fields that will define the future economy and culture. Thomas Friedman's claim in *The World Is Flat* for the level playing field ignores the political and social structures in the U.S. and around the world that sharply curtail women's full participation in the ICT revolution, and thus renders women's conditions invisible all over again. Harvard's President Summers' comments on the innate incapacity of women to excel in science reflect the intractability of assumptions about male superior intelligence and capability.

Early cyberfeminist enthusiasm for virtual environments that transcend the hierarchies assigning lesser value to women and minorities has been realized in the clear interest and competence demonstrated by women in their wide-ranging uses of ICTs and the Internet. At the same time, research by scholars such as Susan Herring[20] and Carol Adams[21] demonstrates the reproduction and magnification of traditional gendered interactions in online text-based environments. Other research, such as a study that brings together work on ICT-related employment and the relationship between gender and cyberculture, finds that deskilling of labor and women's teleworking are closely interrelated, and that the flexibility of working from home means that the employee rather than the employer must be flexible, often at the expense of the working woman.[22] The presence of children at home also means interruptions for women workers, and a failure to provide the focused and protected work conditions available to workers in a traditional office setting.[23] Women are significantly underrepresented in information technology jobs, systems analysis, software design, entrepreneurial roles, and programming.[24] As discussed in detail below, representative numbers of women do not occupy positions of prominence in the design and development of computer-based applications, nor in the educational realms from which future innovators and leaders emerge. ICT professionals have lower status and pay than do computer scientists, and women are more likely even within those ranks to occupy the lower rungs.[25] While in the U.S. and several other technologically developed countries women's use of the Internet rivals that of men,[26] women nevertheless retain the role of consumers rather than producers of the information economy.

Why does this matter? One of the most critical reasons can be gleaned from a talk given at a prestigious conference in software graphic arts. Danny Hillis, a pioneer in parallel computing architectures, gave the 2001 SIGGRAPH[27] keynote speech. He observed that computer graphic interfaces are increasingly the means by which reality is shaped, defined, and perceived. He concluded his talk by urging systems designers, software developers, and computer graphic artists to recognize the significant impact of their work on the world. There were about seven thousand attendees present, well over three-quarters of them male. The reality Hillis speaks of is overwhelmingly shaped and defined by men.

Computers have become ubiquitous, utilities in the same manner as electricity and telephone service. They are integrated into industrial and domestic functions in ways that at one time seemed pure fantasy: smart refrigerators, computerized running shoes, massive data storage on a device the size of a matchbook. The Human Genome project—wholly reliant on computer technology—has mapped the chromosomal content of DNA with the result that nanotechnology and bioinformatics are developing rapidly. The need for much broader diversity of insight into these developments requires, as feminist computer scientist Christina Bjorkman argues, that women become technically proficient in related areas as well as theoretically and sociologically sophisticated about their human implications.[28] As long as women continue to share little of the power and control over how these technological developments advance, their relevance and interest to women will remain remote.

Despite the rhetoric of social transformation that pervades talk about the information age, the boundaries that mark as masculine the domain of technical expertise remain firmly in place. Few women work in the technically demanding and inventive arenas of ICT; those women who do transgress these borders find themselves in a "chilly culture,"[29] a pervasive, masculinized hierarchy of educational and professional settings that discourages women who venture beyond sanctioned feminized roles in areas such as customer service and systems management. As Ruth Schwartz-Cowan remarked in delineating the binaries that continually place women subordinate to men, "We have trained our women to opt out of the technological order as much as we have trained our men to opt in."[30]

The failure of educational programs to recruit and retain women in science and engineering is discussed further below, but the trend toward fewer numbers of science and engineering students overall is part of a national pattern that has raised considerable concern. The need for students and workers in STEM fields—science, technology, engineering, and mathematics—is mobilizing national attention in the U.S. and abroad.

The STEM dilemma is by no means exclusively a result of gender inequities, but the lack of women in STEM fields is a component. The *SET Fair Report*, an extensive study in the United Kingdom, expresses the concerns of technologically advanced countries worldwide about the consequences of the absence of women in information technology-related fields: "The under-representation of women in science, engineering and technology threatens, above all, our global competitiveness. It is an issue for society, for organizations (as strategy and policy-setting agents), for employers, and the individual."[31]

The depletion of numbers of people educated and interested in pursuing STEM-related disciplines arises early in the educational pipeline. The problem is amplified by the fact that boys in significant numbers are falling behind in academic settings. They are diagnosed with learning disabilities and placed in special-education classes twice as much as girls; and their numbers have fallen on college campuses from 58 percent of the undergraduate population to 44 percent.[32]

At the same time, boys remain the principal focus of commercial and educational discourses about new technologies; their floundering means a future shortfall in men prepared to occupy technically advanced jobs. Meanwhile, girls continue to be brought up in cultural and educational environments that directly or indirectly reproduce technology as masculine. Consequently, schools have failed to frame ICT design and development as compelling career choices for girls, leaving half of the potential workers in ICT on the sidelines, along with their intelligence, creativity, values, and dreams.

The following sections of this chapter explore the relationship of women in technology, technology understood not only as tools but also as a "cultural product which is historically constituted by certain sorts of knowledge and social practices as well as other forms of representation" with direct impact on political, social, and economic power and control.[33] As discussed in Chapter Two, "Hacking Women," technology cannot be separated from the discourses in which it is embedded and through which it is defined. Our aim is to examine the interrelationship of discourses of gender and technology; we focus primarily on the communication elements at stake in the symbolic construction of technology. Much of what girls and women engage with fits the category of "technological," though it is often not recognized as such, and both material conditions and rhetorical forces function to maintain a playing field that, if leveling at all, is primarily leveling only for men. The study presents an overview of the statistical presence of women in computer-related educational programs and employment, the ideological and cultural processes that tie technology to constructions of gender, and the role of media in the production and reproduction of women and girls' continued marginal status as developers and designers of the information age. In conclusion, it looks at some of the interventions women are attempting to change their roles in the information economy.

The first section presents the current status of women's engagement with computer science and related educational disciplines, and of women's employment in technology fields. The section following provides an overview of historic and contemporary research on the maintenance of borders that construct women's place as outsiders in the information economy.

Women's Presence in Educational and Workforce ICT

Personal computers were widely disseminated in the early 1980s, as desktop computing transformed a vast range of human activity. Much of the rhetoric that accompanied this onset, often from advertisements like the MCI ad cited at the beginning of this chapter, anticipated the realization of social goals long equated with the impact of new technologies.[34] Building on the Second Wave of the feminist movement in the 1970s, a widely looked-for outcome of the impending information economy was the equalization of economic opportunity between the sexes. A television ad announcing the introduction of the Macintosh computer in 1984, for example, featured a *woman* throwing a hammer to shatter white male authority and control over technology.[35] Women's interest increased in computer science and engineering fields, and the numbers of women applicants rose in both educational and corporate institutions.

In the educational arena, enrollments of women began to grow in both undergraduate and graduate degree programs in computer science and computer engineering. The need for early education to promote math and science interest among girls became a focus, and by 1983, the percentage of women enrolled in computer science degree programs rose to thirty-seven percent.

The 1983 numbers, however, were the peak of women's enrollment. Gurer and Camp issued a 2001 NSF report on their research that found a dramatic decline in girls' enrollment in computer science from high school to graduate school, and a stunning twenty-eight percent decline in the number of undergraduate degrees awarded to women from 1983 to 1998.[36] Gurer and Camp's examination of the failure of the "pipeline" to lead women to positions of influence and prominence in ICT finds the following:

> Although women make up 50% of computer high school classes (Walker & Rodger, 1996), the percentage of bachelor's degrees awarded to women in CS [Computer Science] during the 1997–1998 academic year was only 26.7%…Not surprisingly the pipeline also shrinks through the academic ranks. According to the CRA Taulbee Survey, only 14% assistant professors, 13% associate professors, and 8% full professors were women in CS Ph.D.-granting departments during the academic year 2000–2001.[37]

Bikson cites further NSF research on the declining rate of Computer Science and Computer Engineering degrees awarded to women at both undergraduate and graduate degrees. Noting a three percent rise in doctoral degrees awarded to women in U.S. universities in 2001, Bikson remarks that the head of NSF's Computer and Information Science and Engineering Directorate ascribes this to an increase in the numbers of international women graduate students, which only further heightens the poor record of the U.S. in recruiting and keeping U.S. women in these programs.[38]

In 2001, the National Commission on Mathematics and Science Teaching for the 21st Century issued "Before It's Too Late: A Report to the Nation," warning that the level of math and science education of children in the U.S. is inadequate to the understanding and skills that will be needed to maintain a competitive edge in a global, information economy. The report forecasts an increase of five and a half million jobs by 2008 that will require substantial science and math skills, and quotes a Department of Labor estimate that current numbers of computer science graduates will have to quadruple to meet the demand.[39]

National Science Foundation's Committee on Equal Opportunity in Science and Engineering issued a report in 2004 on increasing the numbers of women in academic and professional technology-related fields. "Broadening Participation in America's Science and Engineering Workforce" presented findings from 1980–1992, and from 1993–2002.[40] The studies confirm that unequal higher education, research, and research grant opportunities continue to undermine women's advancement in scientific and technical fields. Comments from the findings of consecutive decades illuminate some of the reasons behind the lack of progress in recruiting and retaining women in technology-related fields in higher education:

> Higher Education, Training, and Research Grant Opportunity Findings (1980–1992): Gender bias apparently persists along the pre-college, undergraduate, and graduate school continuum. Women encounter far more barriers than men in accessing education opportunities, such as mentoring in science, mathematics, and engineering, research grants, fellowships, or research assistantships offered by NSF. Minority and disabled women encounter even greater barriers because of their additional diversity characteristics.[41]

> (1993–2002):
> Women scientists and engineers are underrepresented among principal investigators who receive NSF grants…Research experience for women and other underrepresented groups is lacking and is key for retaining students in STEM pathways. In the 1990s, women increased enrollment in graduate programs for science, but only low numbers of them attained degrees in engineering. There is a paucity of women with doctorates in STEM…Women are less likely to hold faculty positions in STEM in high school or college than men. Women with doctorates in STEM are paid less and are granted tenure less than their male peers.[42]

In addition, women are scarce in leadership positions related to technology in higher education. A 2004 Educause Center for Applied Research (ECar) study finds the overall ICT professional community to be predominantly white (ninety-three percent) and male (sixty-three percent), with men filling over seventy-eight percent of senior leadership positions.[43] The study reports that as of 2002 women ICT professionals in academic institutions earn twelve percent less on average than their male counterparts.

University programs in computer science and related fields provide learning and research environments important to the advancement of intellectual understanding and the development of innovative applications. While college degree programs are not the only routes available toward acquiring technical expertise, they do provide many of the best opportunities for people entering the highly innovative areas of technological invention and design. Consequent to the barriers created by gender bias in higher education, and the small numbers of those completing advanced degree programs, women in industry are significantly under-represented among those contributing to pioneer development work in advanced information technologies.[44]

Why Women Remain Peripheral to Technological Revolutions

Interest and ease in technology use have long been constitutive of the definition of masculinity, a definition dependent, as Cynthia Cockburn asserts, on a view of men "as strong, manually able and technologically endowed, and women as physically and technically incompetent."[45] A close affinity of men and machines is considered to be "natural," and the technical competence of the dominant cultural ideal of masculinity translates into actual or potential power of men over women.

One of the consequences of male control of technology manifests in what is defined *as* technology. Autumn Stanley's research into historical accounts revises conventional records of technical invention to include women's technological contributions.[46] Ruth Schwartz-Cowan's study of the U.S. housewife after WWII, *More Work for Mother*, finds that not only did the technological elimination of household chores forecast by marketers fail to materialize, but also that once domestic technologies were incorporated by women into routine housework, they lost the aura of *being* technology.[47]

In the early days of women's entry into office work, a similar re-categorization took place. Clerical workers were male until the age of suffrage brought young middle-class women into the workforce; once the women entered, clerical work was "deskilled" and office machines such as typewriters were no longer thought of as technology.[48] The reverse took place with the computer revolution. Computer programmers were initially women, as women were believed to possess the appropriate character traits necessary to a skill involving great attention to minute detail and an ability to withstand a fair amount of tedium. Once the computer began its ascendancy in market and domestic spheres, men claimed the programming jobs; perceptions both of programming's market value and technical expertise rose dramatically, as did the compensation.[49]

Carolyn Marvin's historical study sets the historical stage for the current marginalization of women in technology. Marvin regards the inventions of the electric light and the telephone introduced into U.S. society in the late nineteenth century as the new media predecessors of the mass electronic communication revolutions of the twentieth and twenty-first centuries. She argues that the introduction of new media disrupt social norms by providing new platforms by which "power, authority, representation, and knowledge with whatever resources are available"[50] are negotiated:

> New electric media were sources of endless fascination and fear, and provided constant fodder for social experimentation…media give shape to the imaginative boundaries of modern communities [and] the introduction of new media is a special historical occasion when patterns anchored in older media that have provided the stable currency of social exchange are reexamined, challenged and defended…the early history of electric media is less the evolution of technical efficiencies in communication than a series of arenas for negotiating issues crucial to the conduct of social life; among them, who is inside and outside, who may speak, who may not, and who has the authority and may be believed.[51]

Technical journals and popular media fantasies alike were active in extolling the potential for these new media. An essential element in the mass dissemination of the new technologies was what Marvin characterizes as the "invention of the expert," a class of men engaged in cultural production as much as technical dissemination. Class and race were factors in the claims by the elite group of men who sought control of the new media, but it was in discourses of gender that the expert class most clearly defined how and by whom electric communication technologies were to be used:

> Technical ignorance as a form of worldly ignorance was a virtue of "good" women, as they were invariably described in the professional literature.…Unlike men, women in the stories related by professional journals rarely learned from their mistakes in using technology, or corrected their misconceptions. They were sheltered from all such practical demands by an old and sturdy code of chivalry that required the protection of their ignorance by men. Beneath this habit of indulgence was the more important and even insistent point that women's use of men's technology would come to no good end.[52]

The technical and the popular media of the late nineteenth century were rife with narratives about women whose technical ineptitude, carefully constructed and maintained by rules of expertise that gave only men the training needed for technical competence, justified their exclusion from professional technology ranks and control over their communications. As the role of telephone operator, for example, quickly became the province of young women, the technical skills required for the job were ignored in press reports and fictional commentaries, and the moral reputation of the telephone girls was made fodder for speculation.

The professional electrical journals Marvin examines incorporate poetry and fabricated stories as filler that served to circulate "endless stories of women's unpreparedness and incapacity in a world of technical expertise" and reassure men that their dominant status and women's subordinate status would remain secure in the shifting social structures accompanying technological change.[53] Marvin reports on a 1889 business luncheon's keynote speech that reflects the conflation of women with technology, "woman the perfect telephone, the gift of gods to man," at the same time it clearly keeps in line women who may have attempted to claim technological prowess for themselves: "Both woman and the telephone were 'inventions' second only to man himself. Sent down to please man, both women and the telephone were mistaken for toys and turned out to be necessities."[54]

Over a hundred years later, the advent of the personal computer provoked a remarkably similar gendered discourse in *Wired*, a magazine very closely identified with the culture of the cyber-age in the 1990s. Melanie Stewart Millar's study identifies the construction of "hypermacho" man as central to digital discourse:

> More alone than ever before, it seems that the hypermacho man seeks to reassert masculine white privilege in an era of declining personal control over a rapidly changing world. He seeks to rebuild reality, entrench existing hierarchies, and escape the complexities of a diverse and unpredictable world. As a result…digital discourse is steeped in sexist language and racist assumptions.[55]

In relation to femininity, Millar finds a reassertion of traditional gender stereotypes mired in the virgin/whore dualism still core to representations of women. "Cyber-Barbies" were a staple of *Wired*'s verbal and visual depictions of women, a stylized 1950s and 1960s pop cultural image of an idealized, highly sexualized, yet motherly figure who uses hypermodern tools and language to serve male needs.[56] The cyber-femme fatale is cyber-Barbie's shadowy counterpart, a digital version of aggressive femininity scantily dressed in leather,[57] often found in graphic ads for computer games, and created to fuel male fantasies of a female cyber-warrior who secretly craves violent sexual domination.[58] As exemplified by *Wired* magazine, the digital discourse of new technology incorporates language of social revolution and unprecedented economic change at the same time it re-inscribes the sexual objectification fundamental to popular culture representations of women.

Ideological and Cultural Forces in the Information Economy

The symbolic association of technology with idealized masculinity contributes to the perception of technical culture as a male domain, and to the ongoing absence of women in technological design and development. Gender relations are inextricably bound up with technology relations; that is, technology constructs gender. Yet, understood as a discursive system, gender equally constructs technology.

Elisabeth Sundin's study in Sweden in 1997, drawing on earlier research such as that of Cynthia Cockburn and Sandra Harding,[59] further explores the symbolic construction of technology by discourses of gender. She begins with an investigation into the stereotypes of women and technology that fuel the cultural perception that women have a "problematic relationship" with technology, while men do not. Her goal, like many researchers into technology and gender, was to understand if the stereotypes and perception of this problematic relationship arose from empirical observations of women and machines, or if they had more to do with how technology is defined.

Sundin analyzes a 1980 Swedish public school curriculum devised to rectify earlier curricula that supported the view of technology as exclusively male. She compares her findings to how certain jobs are labeled as "technical" in heavily technologized occupations generally segregated by sex: truckers, engineer/technician and industrial sales (male occupations); nursing, retail sales, and office workers using computer-based hardware and applications (female). Her research finds that despite the effort to promote equality of the sexes in educational curricula on technology, activities of girls and female teachers involving machines and technical methods are nevertheless not classified as technical. In addition, both the men and women responsible for curricula redesign as well as the subjects in the workers group provided examples of what constitutes technology by correlating the gender of the user of an artifact or method with its technical status, reinforcing the symbolic content of technology as masculine. Both women and men expressed a similar impression: the machines and practices engaged in by women were not recognized as "technology."

Sundin concludes that, despite the gender-neutral definitions of technology that offer no rationale for the perception of a problematic relationship of women and technology, the symbolic dimensions of technology controlled by men create the perceived conflicts: "Technology per se is impossible to define. It can only be understood through the clarification of its symbolic manliness and of its close connection with organizing and power. Thus the problematic combination of women and technology seems to emanate from the side of technology. If we see this, the discussion around gender and technology might take a new and less problematic turn."[60]

The vast dissemination of computers and computer-based communications in the U.S. and Europe throughout the 1990s and into the present has helped change the perception of what constitutes technology. SIGIS, the Strategies of Inclusion: Gender and the Information Society project conducted in Europe in 2004, reports that, at least for older women, the "image" problem in which technology is symbolically associated with masculinity no longer accounts for the difficulties women face in information technology occupations. The SIGIS study finds far more daunting the lack of a critical mass of women workers in design and development positions, and the lack of confidence women have in their technical competency.[61]

Though many women currently in ICT educational programs and professions reject the notion that masculine associations with technology have a negative impact on their own self-perceptions and ambitions, nevertheless women's lack of confidence in their own technical expertise is often expressed in relation to their male colleagues' assessment of their own prowess. It is here that we can again observe the failure of adequate critical awareness of the impact of unequal gender relations in creating an alienating atmosphere for women. Karen Mahony and Brett Van Toen argue that the emphasis on "hard" areas such as mathematical formalism and abstraction in computer science curricula is one factor that aids in maintaining male dominance in computing fields, encouraging a "technical machismo" that women concerned with their own gender identity avoid.[62] The real-world, user-based focus that appeals to many women in ICT realms is regarded in academic as well as corporate settings as "soft," and therefore as professionally less serious and less valuable. Ironically, the reverse may be true: "more incorporation of arts-based skills and skills traditionally associated with women would actually result in a curriculum more likely to meet the needs of the computing and information technology industries."[63]

The ideological construction of the contemporary technological "expert" mirrors the invention of the expert reported in Carolyn Marvin's study of electricity in the late nineteen-hundreds, and serves in similar ways to control access to the top ranks of technology professions. The expert-user divide that results from the dichotomizing of the computer science field into abstract versus concrete disciplines not only marginalizes women's interactions with computers but also, as Linda Vigdor contends, closes down possible avenues in which technological education could be reformed to include broader perspectives and values.[64] A sociocultural understanding of technology allows for the incorporation of reflexive curricular elements such as the philosophy, history, and ethics of technology, subjects that are currently viewed as peripheral.

"The More Things Change, the More They Stay the Same: Gender Differences in Attitudes and Experiences Related to Computing"[65] compares self-reports of skill, comfort and engagement with computing between women in computer science majors and women in applied information technology disciplines such as instructional technology, information science, and informatics. Women have expressed greater interest in applying computing to the solution of social problems; the study aimed at measuring the validity of the assumption that women's experiences and attitudes about computing would improve in applied ICT programs. The study's findings contradict that assumption: women in applied programs expressed less confidence in their skills, comfort, and engagement with computing than did the men, and no more confidence than female computer science majors. Moreover, reports to the women concerning the persistence of conditions that favor more success for men in computing did not rouse the women to protest. The study's authors conclude that the subjects' internalization of society's lesser expectations for their performance in technical fields allows them to accept the unequal status quo.

Fiona Wilson's research on the reasons behind the continuing decline of women in computer science and related professions surveyed undergraduates in computer science and in a non-technical field. Her questions aimed at uncovering subjective beliefs about gender differences in computing performance and ability. One of the most significant elements in her findings is the depth of reluctance on the part of the young women, as well as the young men to acknowledge the cultural processes that worked against the women's success. Both women and men proved highly invested in rejecting any notion of gender inequality that might inhibit the equal chance given to women; they asserted that educational computing environments were gender neutral and offered the same opportunity to men and women. Male and female students asserted that their differences in personal capacity and ambition propelled the men rather than the women toward successful completion of computer science programs and commitment to future technical careers, and both sexes remained adamant that gender inequality and injustice do not exist in the educational system. Wilson interprets the women's collusion with male power as a manifestation of their adaptation to male-oriented organizational value systems.[66] The denial of structural inequities points to women's deep-seated lack of confidence in their innate capacity for computing expertise. The denial also demonstrates the fear of appearing to ask for special treatment, a fear that we argue resonates strongly with postfeminism and its claim that insistence on a political critique of structural inequities positions women as victims.

Juliet Webster,[67] among numerous feminist researchers,[68] focuses attention on management strategies, employment policies, organizational cultures, educational practices, and divisions of labor in the public and private sectors, as conditions contributing to the absence of women. In the workforce, women who attempt to advance in information technology professions frequently encounter workplace mores that undermine the advantage their technical skills would lend them:

> Their qualifications often count for less than adherence to a set of informal rules of the game for which their male counterparts are culturally far better prepared. Indeed, women in IT are on alien territory. The culture and practice of the computing profession is redolent with myriad forms of masculinity.... a culture which is not only alienating to many women, but incompatible with their lives. It is little wonder then, that women actively resist entering technological fields because of the cultural incompatibility with femininity. All this suggests that there are structural and cultural processes working to the exclusion of women from technology.[69]

Identifying the problem of women in technology as a simple one of exclusion from technological education and work ignores the structural barriers (for example, adequate childcare) and cultural conditions that underlie women's under-representation. Webster points out that attempts, therefore, to increase the number of women in technology by treating women merely as reluctant or ignorant of opportunities and in need only of information and encouragement are not sufficient. What is needed is far more attention to ways of transforming both the educational environment for women and the masculinist culture of information technology professions.

Years of gender-blind policy in managing the digital divide has exacerbated the situation for women. "Falling Through the Net," a series of four studies published over four years on the digital divide conducted by the U.S. National Telecommunications and Information Administration (NTIA), is an example. It added gender only in the fourth and last study to the list of variables that included race, income, age, and region. Educational institutions fail to encourage girls in computer science and engineering degree programs by ignoring that the teaching methods and values of mostly male faculty frequently alienate female students,[70] and that the few women students enrolled are often isolated by hostile behaviors of the primarily male students. Women who do complete degree programs in graduate-level studies are not met with the conditions that help them rise to the ranks of their male colleagues; the "leaky pipeline" of women experts for academic technology innovation often begins in inappropriate and discouraging educational environments.

The leaky pipeline phenomenon—recruiting women then failing to retain them—takes its toll in industry settings as well. A 2002 study by University of Pennsylvania's Annenberg Public Policy Centre of e-company executive boards found that only four percent of board members of the largest e-companies were women and only sixteen percent of large e-companies had women executives. Among those companies, Yahoo, RealNetworks, Ameritrade, Clear Channel,

CNET Networks, and Knight Trading Group had no women board members, while Alltel, Fox Entertainment Group, USA Networks, and WorldCom had no women executives.[71]

Harvard Business Review in 2003 presented the findings of a report on corporate leadership conducted by Catalyst, a research organization for women in business.[72] Their study found that women make up over half the managerial and professional labor pool, but account for only one percent of all Fortune 500 CEOs (and that number may have shrunk with the departure of CEO Carly Fiorina from Hewlett Packard in 2005). The women surveyed made it clear that their ambitions for senior leadership positions were as focused as those of their male counterparts who were getting those jobs; rather than lack of ambition, the majority of women respondents cited instead the obstacles to advancement created by exclusion from informal networks, stereotyping, lack of accountability on the part of senior leadership, shortage of role models, personal and family responsibilities, and limited visibility in the company. While CEOs stated different perceptions of the causes of women's failure to advance to the top—primarily citing women's ineffective leadership style and lack of skills—ninety percent of the CEOs and seventy-nine percent of the women agreed that lack of management or line experience was the primary barrier to women. The report terms "glass walls"—lateral barriers that stymie women's careers from the beginning—as potent a force as the glass ceiling in holding women back. Two-thirds of women and over half of the CEOs placed responsibility on senior leadership for failing to be accountable for women's advancement by ensuring them the management experience needed.

More attention is beginning to be focused on practices in both academic and corporate cultures that discourage women from pursuing careers in computer and science-related fields. A 2003 study found that research universities are losing female graduate student applicants to teaching institutions or non-academic jobs because academic advancement is structured to reward those who forego social and familial responsibilities.[73] A 2005 *Chronicle of Higher Education* article called attention to the same phenomenon, citing the need to revise family leave, childcare, and caretaker policies, as well as to move from rigid promotion and tenure requirements originally established for male academics whose family lives were provided and maintained by wives.[74]

The material and cultural realities of the new information economy tend to dispute the rhetoric of openness to women in IT corporate settings. The culture of technology companies plays a significant factor in women's underrepresentation, as professional practices and standards as well as values placed on work behavior privilege men in promotion and opportunity. A study conducted in Ireland's burgeoning IT industry on career advancement in a software production company tracked the paths of workers with similar training and skills; the "lads"—mostly single, young men who share a love of sports and the freedom to attend bars together after work—fed job information and inside company politics to each other. After a short period of time, this group of men was advancing rapidly through jobs that prepared them for senior leadership ranks in the industry. The few women workers in programming fields either were unable to participate in this informal affirmative action network, were recognized by superiors only for work that limited their potential in acquiring new skills, or were prevented by spousal considerations and childrearing from making the moves to the jobs needed to advance their careers. They stayed stuck in occupational levels that felt to them to be significantly lower than their interests and capabilities should have afforded them.[75]

Daniel Marshall's ethnographic study of a software company relates several variables in determining employee success that implicitly ensure that few women will be part of the design and development of new software.[76] He cites a "crash and burn" work ethic, particularly popular in new technology start-up ventures, that rewards designers who work thirty-six straight hours fueled by caffeine, junk food, and quick naps on the floors of their cubicles as necessary to break through to the "killer app." Though not mentioned in the study, the valorizations of this kind of self-abusive behavior and the lack of social and familial responsibility account in part for the proportional absence of women in such positions. Pregnancy and parental leave programs are part of the complexity of this aspect of women's reasons for avoiding or abandoning information technology careers: managers often steer women to lesser career opportunities in the belief that investing in their advancement won't pay off, and parental leaves are frequently not used because of the stigma attached to the part-time, "undedicated" worker.[77] The 2004 Oxford Internet Institute report states that the majority of women who have secured jobs in advanced levels of information technology design and development are childless.[78]

Systemic and cultural barriers exclude women and maintain male dominance in information technology. Evident in the research of Sundin and Webster, among others, is the need for a shift from a rhetoric of women's problems with technology to the recognition of the problems that men have with women in technology, of the exclusionary force of male control over the production of meanings in technology, and of the barriers women face in educational and workforce opportunities necessary to gaining requisite knowledge and experience.

Such findings lead us to re-consider an entrenched fixture in the naturalization of gender differences—the popular notion that women are less interested and therefore less proficient in interactions with machines. Technology must instead be understood within the context of the hierarchy of values that maintains middle-class, male hegemony and keeps gendered divisions relatively constant. If the focus shifts from the tool itself—a forklift, an automatic clothes dryer, a computer—to the context in which the technological artifact exists, then we can look differently at the outcome of technological change. We see that the more subtle but nevertheless ongoing reproduction of technology as masculine plays a key role in the maintenance of inequitable societal structures dominated by men. Comprehending the failure of the computer revolution to significantly alter the economic prospects of women or to dismantle the sexual divisions of labor that mark the under-representation of women in information technology design points away from women's technical alienation and directs us instead toward entrenched structural barriers.

Technology Culture and Girl Culture

Girls and young women display a greater confidence in their capacity to master technologies than do older women. The U.S. and Europe have awakened to the need for educational changes that draw girls into earlier engagement with computing and translate into high school and college enrollments in computer science programs. Women's inroads into other previously all-male professions such as medicine and law give weight to the notion that girls can and will enter into professions in the information economy that can play a critical role in shaping technological development.

Yet, the messages young women receive about computing careers are embedded in a cacophony of other mediated messages about identity, sexuality, femininity, and family that conflict with the gender-neutral rhetoric of ICTs. Girls and younger women are more likely than older women to be adversely affected by the computer industry culture's "geeky, nerdy, macho image that is so difficult to break down."[79] Gender identity is a source of greater confusion and conflict during adolescence, and constructions of "masculine" and "feminine" pursuits can be especially diminishing to girls whose pre-pubescent lives felt unconstrained by such limited horizons.[80] Advocates have been increasing for all-girls courses in computer science and women-only learning opportunities in reaction to the tendency for male-identified learning styles and individual versus cooperative activities to prevail in educational and corporate training settings.[81]

More mature women may claim alienation from computer technology because of the material conditions of unequal gender relations than because of its aura of masculinity, but girls carry a heightened awareness of cultural distinctions between masculinity and femininity. Magazines and a range of televisual and cinematic media project formulas for female success, economic stability, and identity that centrally locate heterosexual attractiveness in the equation. Girls at increasingly young ages are incorporated into consumer culture through mediated images such as those of super-thin fashion models and highly sexualized music videos, making them consumers of their own future sexual objectification.[82] While liberatory discourses of ICTs expound the opportunity for girls to develop and display excellence, popular media channels bombard them with celebrity images that highlight their own relative imperfections.

Discussions at the National Science Foundation Program for Women and Girls Awardee Meeting[83] highlighted issues from surveys on contemporary undergraduate attitudes towards gender equity in looking at the decrease of women in STEM-related degree programs. Their list included a growing backlash among young men looking for traditional home settings, the persistence of girls hiding their intellectual abilities from boys, evidence of girls and women more intimidated than a decade ago in competitive situations, worsening female stereotypes pervasive on MTV and similar media programming, and the ongoing denial by both sexes of the existence of systemic inequality. As is reflected in Chapter Two's analysis of the women hackers in *The Net* and *VR5,* sexual and social identity remain intractable factors when considering the potential of women in technological pursuits.

The computer gaming industry compounds these problems. As discussed in Chapter Two, male computer experts often move from their childhood fascination with computer games into the study of computer science. Critics have bemoaned the violence of the majority of computer games and the lack of appeal of many of them for girls. Current computer games are a compelling gateway to further interest in technical design and expertise; their gendered market focus both inhibits girls from following this route into technological pursuits, and creates a stark contrast between masculine and feminine technical interests. The gaming development world is dominated by a small group of males making games dictated by an equally narrow segment of male tastes, when what is needed are a wide range of multiple gendered expressions.

Educational software shares many of these same characteristics. An American Association of University Women commission found that a popular K-6 mathematics software game includes only twelve percent females in gender-identifiable roles and that the roles are passive.[84] In another survey of U.S. educational software, the commission found that eighty percent of adventure or leadership roles were male; that women appeared more than males only in the roles related to domestic and manual labor; and that multicultural and global themes were narrativized in terms of aggression, subjugation, colonization, and warfare.[85]

Early work by Sherry Turkle with MIT students uncovered strong feelings of alienation from the computer on the part of girls and young women in response to the kinds of identification and interactions with computers manifested by males.[86] Young women who had the mathematical skills and intellectual capacity to learn the inner workings of computers and advanced computational functions saw high interest in computers as the province of asocial, isolated males who create with the machine what they could not attain in human relationships. Turkle's subjects remarked on the close alliance of masculinity, constructed in terms of aggression and domination, with terminology applied to traditional discourses of computer system design, such as "kill," "crash," "abort," "execute." Such terms carry the implicit notion that "real" or "hard" computer science is done from a warrior mentality; for young women, adopting this jargon and thus aligning with this mentality makes for an uneasy alliance with masculine values and identity. These technically proficient young women were stymied by the conflict between cultural associations of technology with masculinity and those of being female.

The American Association of University Women report discussed above finds the persistence of a perceived conflict between notions of femininity and interest in computers reflected in girls' reservations about and their ways of participating in computer culture, as well as in their perceptions of ICT careers from an economic, educational, and cultural perspective. It notes that girls' perceptions of human interactions with computers are molded by stereotypes, often reinforced by media representations, that do not take into account the pervasiveness of computer technology across a wide spectrum of endeavors, leaving girls mired in a view of technology-related careers as a "waste of intelligence....materialistic and short-sighted."[87] The commission opposes the common "deficit" model that characterizes girls as computer-phobic and teachers as inadequate in secondary education of computing. Rather, it recommends that the valid and insightful nature of girls' views be used to change "the software, the way computer science is taught, and the goals we have for using computer technology."[88]

Jane Margolis and Allen Fisher's *Unlocking the Clubhouse* investigates ways in which girls' and young women's interest in computers is subverted by the cultural assumptions that have accompanied the rise of computer science as a discipline and profession. Having once been enthusiastic about computers, females too often encounter barriers to their continued interest: "Many once-enthusiastic female college students find themselves in a descending spiral of eroding interest through the corrosive effects of lack of confidence, negative comparisons to peers, poor pedagogy, and biased environments."[89] The authors found among their student interviewees at Carnegie Mellon perceptions that males "dream in code" while the women look for purpose and connection of computer science to wider interests and ideals. The image of the obsessed and already knowledgeable male pervades the normative values that girls and women use to measure both their own fit in the profession and their likelihood for success, a standard that frequently insures they will come up lacking. A paper written when its author was an MIT graduate student on the lack of women in computer science remarks on the hegemony of its masculinist values and cautions: "It is important to remember that women who do not throw themselves into the computer world might not be inferior to men, but that sacrificing everything to computers might not be something a psychologically healthy human being does. Perhaps men and women alike would be better off if some jobs and hacker cultures did not require giving up the rest of their lives."[90]

Girls complain that they do not regularly see women in the media who are engaged in computing research and careers.[91] A content analysis in 1998 of 351 television commercials featuring computer users sought to provide a benchmark of how women were portrayed.[92] Of the determinable sexes of roles portrayed, fifty percent of users were men and forty-six percent women, a significant increase of women compared to a 1985 study of magazine ads in which male computer users outnumbered women two-to-one. However, children and teenagers using computers were twice as likely to be boys, and overall computer users were likely to be young, especially in the case of women who substantially disappeared from the screen after 40 years of age. Women were predominantly cast in domestic or clerical roles, and almost never in roles as students, business professionals, or computer experts.[93] The researchers' hypothesis that women would be portrayed as less competent than male users was disproved, although female computer competency was associated with activities relevant to sanctioned female roles such as secretaries or telemarketers.

There are developments that have proved encouraging to girls and women's participation in the full range of ICTs. The National Council for Research on Women report (2001) "Where Are Women and Girls in Science, Technology and Engineering?" found that the opportunity to do research as undergraduates—an opportunity usually awarded to male undergraduates—helps motivate women students to move into and stay in STEM-related fields. Other interventions that appear most fruitful include the FIRST Robotics Competition, started in 1999 and sponsored by educational institutions and industry partners.[94] Middle and high school girls work in diverse teams to create robots and lego-artifacts for international competitions. Significantly positive results are being recorded in the increase in the girls' self-confidence and interest in STEM-related college curricula and professions.

In the information arena, the concept of the "blended librarian" holds promise for librarians of both sexes. The definition of the term, attributed to Steven Bell and John Shank, offered on the Blended Librarian website is: "An academic librarian who combines the traditional skill set of librarianship with the information technologist's hardware/software skills, and the instructional or educational designer's ability to apply technology appropriately in the teaching-learning process."[95] The ongoing development of the information society will require far more sophisticated means—both through professional expertise and through technological facilitation—to analyze and make sense of ever-increasing data streams. Given that the majority of librarians over the past many decades have been women, this is potentially a means for women to play a significant role in shaping our evolving reality and our relationship to it.

At the same time, close attention must be paid to this evolving field. In the past, such progressions in occupations have worked to inhibit women's advancement, rather than promote it, as discussed above in relation to the introduction of the typewriter in the early twentieth century, as well as the change in status of computer programming when men entered the previously female dominated field. If that particular historical pattern holds, we could see many more men becoming interested in and occupying the blended librarian roles. Once more women could be relegated to secondary roles, both in terms of technological expertise and in their ability to influence the progression of data management and analysis tools.

Conclusions

This chapter is concerned with delineating the position of women in the design and development of our technological future from a fairly broad communication perspective. In the wake of predictions that the computer-mediated world creates a leveled playing field of male and female possibility in work, family responsibility, and self-actualization, it is important to take a close look at the those arenas where change is expected. As is evident, the scope of transformation promised has failed to materialize.

Symbolic and social constructions of technology play a critical role in attracting or repelling the different sexes. The masculine hegemony that defines technology and maintains cultural barriers in order to control who designs our technological future is now failing to produce enough competent innovators and workers in the United States and Europe. The economic dominance of ICT by the U.S. has depended on the privileging of a particular group of males in American innovation and entrepreneurship. Since women now maintain a majority enrollment in undergraduate institutions, the failure to heed the gendered nature of engineering and computer science educational curricula and occupations, and the lack of sufficient societal institutions such as adequate child care that marginalizes women's full participation, is threatening the ability of the U.S. to stay economically competitive in the years ahead.

Symbolic masculinity and the gendered nature of technological culture have a substantial impact on males as well as females. The depletion in numbers of students of both sexes interested in science and technology at younger levels suggests that boys as well as girls are not being reached. The depiction of an aggressive and all-consumed technical innovator may not appeal to either sex as a satisfying life choice. Further research into how those careers are portrayed via interpersonal and mediated channels, how such careers are consequently perceived, and what sacrifices are associated with success in technology-related fields could further clarify the phenomenon of the leaky pipeline in computer science and engineering.

The president of the British Computer Society, Wendy Hall, looks to computing inspired by natural collective systems such as ant colonies, and neurological research that maps human cognitive associations as the direction for future software systems, a direction that would draw on women's skills much more organically:

> I suggest we stop trying to persuade women to be interested in careers based on computers as we know them today, when this is patently too difficult to do. Rather, we should look to future generations of computer systems and ensure that we seize this opportunity to change the image of our industry to one that women will be more interested to work in. The skills that will be required for such an industry are quite different from those required today. We will need people with backgrounds in biology or chemistry or medicine, and these are all subjects that attract women.[96]

We can add to that list of subjects the arts, humanities, social sciences, scientific visualization, environmental protection, government, business practices, and many more personal and professional endeavors that are being transformed in their performance and development by ICTs. Liberal arts studies in particular prepare students in critical thinking, awareness of epistemological foundations and historical precedents, ethical reasoning, written oral, and nonverbal artistic expressions and communication skills, and the ability to discover and synthesize a broad range of human endeavor needed for an enriched life, responsible citizenship, and effective work contributions in an information economy. The needs of a future society require imagination and creativity as much as technical mastery.[97] To perceive the evolution of an information society from this perspective indicates that both educational and communication modalities must incorporate a broader understanding of technology as a sociocultural phenomenon, rather than the reductive and instrumental view of technology as merely a set of tools. Designing curricula that integrate the arts and humanities into

STEM education could provide a more nuanced appreciation of the intersections of technology and culture, bringing much-needed critical thinking and awareness to computer science and engineering, and hands-on experience of technological design to humanities and social sciences. Involving girls and women in the invention and design of new technologies as a means of realizing their personal and professional interests could be what turns them from consumers to producers, engaged in defining the application and relevancy of computing for their own lives and others.

What continues to be avoided in the current culture, as discussed in the introduction to this book, is talk of pay inequities for equal labor and the responsibility women still bear for the domestic sphere. The structures of advancement in computing and engineering education and industry maintain the gendered divide between males as experts-producers vs. females as users-consumers by the economic inequities of gendered divisions of labor. Perhaps the most radical notion that is arising in the face of the growing shortage of qualified ICT innovators and highly skilled workers is that the nature of the technology industry, rather than women's relationship to the existing industry, must change.

The construction of discourses of masculinity and femininity in relation to technology must also broaden. The "Women and the New Economy" survey[98] notes that the rules for working women of an earlier generation were "iron-clad...that you had to give everything up in order to reach the glass ceiling; there were no alternatives."[99] The strategy prescribed by the survey is that women question societal demands and definitions that make the design of new technology off-limits to them, largely because their definitions of and commitments to a meaningful, balanced, and healthy life for themselves and others cannot be accommodated. The integration of computing into every aspect of human endeavor means that a range of ethical, social, economic, and political implications must be considered. Feminist anti-utopian arguments express important critical resistance to unexamined claims for new and emerging technologies. When such subjects as genetically engineered children and elongation of human life through integration with robotic bodies are bandied about by men who hold patents in bio- and nanotechnology realms,[100] clearly the design of technological systems is too critical a part of all our futures to be left in the hands of a narrow band of representatives of less than half the human population. It is our combined resources and capabilities that can provide the creativity, understanding, and experience needed to shape the evolution of information and communication technologies.

In "Hijacking Feminism" and "Hacking Women," the first and second chapters of this book, the transgressive woman is one who follows her passion, strength, skill, and dedication where no place has been made for her, but into which she pushes her way nonetheless. Several of the female characters we study in these chapters are adept with technology; yet, as we demonstrated, those characterizations of women did not become highly popularized. This chapter, "Designing Women," helps to explain the paucity of public imagination about female hackers by taking us out of the realm of fiction into the *realpolitik* of women's lives in an economy being transformed by the computer revolution. In engaging with new technology, women confront a realm of human endeavor constituted by rules that once again maneuver them into the margins. However, the rapid rate of technological development and innovation also offers an unknown future, one in which the need for creativity, ingenuity, and the synthesis of experience and wisdom from multiple roles in life could yet revolutionize the place women hold.

We move now into Chapter Five, "Oh, to Be Given a Sporting Chance: Televisual Representations of Women in the World of Sports News," in which we encounter two women producers of a television sports news show, who tackle technology, male talk, and sexual assault in their forays into the male bastion of prime-time sports. The series exposes the mythology of the level playing field by drawing attention to how perceptions of competence, leadership, and productive creativity are shaped by gender politics. In Chapter Six, "It's a Dick Thing: Ambivalent Coding of American Female Soldiers," we again encounter the myth of the leveling influence of technology on gender parity in American society. Chapter Six explores the *realpolitik* context within which female soldiers have moved into combat support units in the United States military. We argue that while computerized technologies of war have enabled women to participate in combat, sexist policy and practices in the military continue to undermine women's health, safety, mental health, and career goals.

Notes

1 See, among many: Wendy Faulkner (Principal Author), *SIGIS Strategies of Inclusion: Gender and the Information Society, Final Report* (University of Edinburgh, August 2004). Edinburgh: UK. 3 June 2005 http://www.rcss.ed.ac.uk/sigis/public/displaydoc/full/D08_Final_Public; Denise Gurer and Tracy Camp, *Investigating the Incredible Shrinking Pipeline for Women in Computer Science* (Final Report NSF 9812016, 2001). 31 May 2005 http://www.acm.org/women; AAUW Educational Foundation Commission on Technology, Gender, and Teacher Education, *Tech-Savvy: Educating Girls in the New Computer Age* (Washington, D.C., 2000); Oxford Internet Institute Policy Forum Position Papers, *Women in Computing Professions: Will the Internet Make a Difference?* (University of Oxford, June 17–18, 2004). 5 March 2005 http://www.oii.ox.ac.uk.

2 A number of reports suggest this as a possibility, including *SIGIS* (2004); also, Nikole Hannah-Jones, "Girls Get Own Class in Computer Science," *News and Observer,* 18 August 2005: 1A, ff.

3 See among others: *Falling Through the Net, Toward Digital Inclusion* (4th in Series from U.S. Dept of Commerce National Telecommunications & Information Administration, October 2000). 25 April 2004 http://www.ntia.doc.gov/ntiahome/digitaldivide/execsumfttn00.htm; Jane Margolis and Allen Fisher, *Unlocking the Clubhouse: Women in Computing*. (Cambridge, MA: MIT Press, 2002); Jan Peters, Nancy Lane, Teresa Rees, and Gill Samuels, *Set Fair: A Report On Women In Science, Engineering & Technology From The Baroness Susan Greenfield To The Secretary Of State For Trade And Industry* (UK: 2002). 3 June 2005 http://extra.shu.ac.uk/ nrc/section_2/publications/reports/R1182_SET_Fair_Report.pdf.

4 Gerda Siann. "We Can, We Don't Want To: Factors Influencing Women's Participation in Computing," *Women and Computing* (eds.) Rachel Lander and Alison Adam (Exeter: Intellect Books, 1997) 113–121.

5 Summers issued this statement as president of Harvard University.

6 See, among others, Sandra Harding, *The Science Question in Feminism* (Ithaca, NY: Cornell University Press, 1986); Evelyn Fox Keller and Helen E. Longino (eds.) *Feminism and Science* (Oxford and New York: Oxford University Press, 1996); Donna Haraway, "Situated Knowledges: The Science Question in Feminism and the Privilege of Partial Perspective," *Feminist Studies* 14, no. 3 (1988): 575–599.

7 Christina Bjorkman, Crossing Boundaries, Focusing Foundations, Trying Translations: Feminist Technoscience Strategies in Computer Science (Karlkrona: Blekinge Institute of Technology, BTH Dissertation Series No 2005:02, 2005) 12.

8 Maria Lugones, cited in Bjorkman 12.

9 Bjorkman 15.

10 Bruno Latour, "Morality and Technology: The End of Means," *Theory, Culture & Society* 19, no. 5/6 (2002): 251.

11 James Carey, "Technology and Ideology: The Case of the Telegraph," *Communication as Culture* (Boston: Unwin Hyman, 1989) 201–230.

12 Carolyn Marvin, *When Old Technologies Were New* (New York: Oxford University Press, 1988).

13 Linda Vigdor addresses the expert-user divide in her study of current technology curricula and the changes needed to transform its gendered discourse: "Education and Technology: A Prison of Enframement or a New Practice and Possibility of Being?" Paper presentation at European Computing and Philosophy 2006 Conference, Norwegian University of Science and Technology, Trondheim, Norway, 24 June 2006.

14 Fiona Wilson's research with college-aged men and women particularly uncovers the resistance in both sexes to tie the absence of women to conditions outside women's personal choice. Fiona Wilson, "Can Compute, Won't Compute: Women's Participation in the Culture of Computing," *New Technology, Work, and Employment* 18, no. 2 (2003): 127–142. Carolyn Heilbrun named this inability on the part of women to see and name the conditions that oppress them in her work from the 1970s: *Reinventing Womanhood* (New York and London: W.W. Norton, 1979).

15 U.S. Department of Commerce, National Telecommunication and Information, *Administration Falling Through the Net: Toward Digital Inclusion* (October 2000) 15. 13 November 2000. http://www.ntia.doc.gov/ntiahome/digitaldivide.

16 "The Future of the Internet," *Fortune Special Issue* 142.8 (9 October 2000).

17 Thomas Friedman, *The World Is Flat* (New York: Farrar, Strauss & Giroux, 2005).

18 Five months after these remarks and the controversy they created, Summers committed $50 million of Harvard's funds to changing the culture—through mentoring, childcare, late-night transport and so on—for women at Harvard (Pope, 2005). Summers has since left the presidency of Harvard.

19 Tora K. Bikson, "Yes, No, And Maybe: Answers To A Complex Question," in *Women in Computing Professions* (Oxford Internet Institute Policy Forum Position Papers, 2004) 4–7. 31 May 2005 http://www.oii.ox.ac.uk.

20 Susan Herring, "Posting In A Different Voice: Gender And Ethics In CMC," *Philosophical Perspectives on Computer-Mediated Communication* (ed.) Charles Ess (Albany, NY: State University of New York Press, 1996) 115–154.

21 Carol J. Adams, "'This is Not Our Father's Pornography': Sex, Lies, and Computers," In *Philosophical Perspectives on Computer-Mediated Communication* (ed.) Charles Ess (Albany, NY: State University of New York Press, 1996) 147–170.

22 Vicki Belt, Renald Richardson, and Juliet Webster. "Women's Work In The Information Economy." *Information, Communication & Society* 3, no. 3 (2000): 366–385.

23 Sarah Stein, "A Cyberroom of One's Own," In *Reload: Rethinking Women & Cyberculture* (eds.) Mary Flanagan and Austin Booth (Boston, MA: MIT Press, 2002) 148–157.

24 AAUW, *Tech Savvy* 19.

25 Sue Clegg, "Theorising the Machine: Gender, Education, and Computing," *Gender and Education* 13, no. 3 (2001): 307–324.

26 Ruby Roy Dholakia, Nikhilesh Dholakia, and Nir Kshetri, "Gender and Internet Usage," *The Internet Encyclopedia* (ed.) Hossein Bidgoli (Metuchen, NJ: John Wiley & Sons, 2004).

27 SIGGRAPH is the acronym for the Special Interest Group for Computer Graphic Designers, and its annual conference is the computing software industry's premiere event, attracting over fifty thousand attendees from around the world. The major computer game developers, Hollywood digital effects producers, medical and commercial applications designers, and representatives of all the computer design interfaces attend.

28 Christina Bjorkman, "Gender and IT Goes Second Millennium," Paper presentation at European Computing and Philosophy 2006 Conference, Norwegian University of Science and Technology, Trondheim, Norway, 24 June 2006.

29 *SIGIS*, 3.

30 Ruth Schwartz-Cowan, "From Virginia Dare To Virginia Slims: Woman And Technology In American Life," *Technology and Culture* 20 (January, 1979): 62.

31 Peters et al. 9.

32 Pat Tyre, "The Trouble with Boys," *Newsweek* (2006, January 30). 31 January 2006 http://msnbc.msn.com/id/10965522/site/newsweek/.

33 Wajcman, *Feminism Confronts Technology* 158.

34 Marvin, *When Old Technologies*.

35 Sarah Stein, "The '1984' Macintosh Ad: Cinematic Icons and Constitutive Rhetoric in the Launch of a New Machine," *Quarterly Journal of Speech* 8, no. 2 (2002): 169–192.

36 Gurer and Camp 3.

37 Gurer and Camp 3.

38 Bikson 5.

39 John Glenn, *Before It's Too Late: A Report to the Nation from the National Commission on Mathematics and Science Teaching for the 21st Century* (U.S. Department of Education, September, 2000) 10. 20 April 2004 http://www.ed.gov/americacounts/glenn.

40 National Science Foundation (NSF) Committee on Equal Opportunities in Science and Engineering, "Broadening Participation in America's Science and Engineering Workforce," (National Science Foundation CEOSE 04–01, December 2004). 9 July 2005 http://www.nsf.gov/od/oia/activities/ceose/reports/ceose2004report.pdf.

41 NSF, "Broadening Participation" 50.

42 NSF, "Broadening Participation" 61.

[43] Richard N. Katz and Gail Salaway, "Information Technology Leadership in Higher Education: The Condition of the Community" (Educause Center for Applied Research, January 2004) 7.

[44] Bikson 4–7.

[45] Cynthia Cockburn, *Machinery of Dominance: Women, Men and Technological Know-How* (London: Pluto Press, 1985) 203.

[46] Autumn Stanley, *Mothers and Daughters of Invention: Notes for a Revised History of Technology* (Metuchen, N.J.: The Scarecrow Press, 1993).

[47] Ruth Schwartz-Cowan, *More Work for Mother: The Ironies Of Household Technology From The Open Hearth To The Microwave* (New York: Basic Books, 1983).

[48] Margaret Davies, "Women Clerical Workers And The Typewriter: The Writing Machine," *Technology and Women's Voices* (ed.) Cheris Kramarae (New York: Routledge and Kegan Paul, 1988) 29–40.

[49] Wajcman; Anne Balsamo, *Technologies of the Gendered Body* (Durham: Duke University Press, 1996).

[50] Marvin 5.

[51] Marvin 4.

[52] Marvin 23.

[53] Marvin 30.

[54] Marvin 30.

[55] Melanie Stewart Millar, *Cracking the Gender Code: Who Rules the Wired World?* (Toronto, Ontario: Second Story Press, 1998) 51.

[56] Millar 102.

[57] Lara Croft is one such figure. She is played by Angelina Jolie in the film versions, based on a wildly popular computer game. The figure of Lara Croft is particularly noteworthy: having been designed to meet the fantasies of her adolescent male game-players, she has digitally enhanced breasts large enough to cause any real woman to topple over.

[58] Millar 105.

[59] Elisabeth Sundin "Gender and Technology—Mutually Constituting and Limiting," *Gendered Practices: Feminist Studies of Technology and Society* (ed.) Boel Berner (Department of Technology and Social Change, Linkoping University, 1997) 249–268; Cynthia Cockburn, *Machinery of Dominance: Women, Men and Technological Know-How* (Pluto Press: London, 1985); Sandra Harding, *The Science Question In Feminism* (Ithaca, NY: Cornell University Press, 1986).

[60] Sundin 262.

[61] Faulkner 27.

[62] Karen Mahony and Brett Van Toen, "Mathematical Formalism as a Means of Occupational Closure in Computing—Why 'Hard' Computing Tends Exclude Women," *Gender and Education* 2, no. 3 (1990): 321.

[63] Mahony and Van Toen 319.

[64] Vigdor, "Education and Technology."

[65] Christine Ogan, Susan Herring, Manju Ahuja, and Jean Robinson, "The More Things Change, the More They Stay the Same: Gender Differences in Attitudes and Experiences Related to Computing," Conference papers—International Communication Association annual convention, New York, N.Y., 2005. 20 March 2006 http://ella.slis.indiana.edu/~herring/ica.pdf.

[66] Wilson 138.

[67] Juliet Webster, "Information Technology, Women and Their Work," *Gendered Practices: Feminist Studies of Technology and Society* (ed.) Boel Berner (Department of Technology and Social Change, Linkoping University, 1997) 141–156.

[68] See Erik Arnold and Wendy Faulkner, "Smothered By Invention: The Masculinity of Technology," *Smothered by Invention: Technology in Women's Lives* (eds.) Wendy Faulkner and Erik Arnold (London: Pluto Press, 1985); Fergus Murray, "A Separate Reality: Science, Technology, and Masculinity," *Gendered By Design: Information Technology And Office Systems* (eds.) Eileen Green, Jenny Owen, Den Pain (Washington, D.C.: Taylor & Francis, 1993); Merete Lie "Technology and Masculinity: The Case of the Computer," *The European Journal of Women's Studies* 2 (1995): 379–394; Cynthia Cockburn and Susan Ormrod, *Gender and Technology in the Making* (Thousand Oaks, CA: Sage, 1993).

[69] Webster 152.

[70] An anecdotal example of this was given in recent conversation with a female PhD candidate in computer science. She related an experience early in the program that she recalls as a strong motivator in re-considering her choice of fields: in a computer graphics course, the male instructor chose to set up the programming assignments as in-class competitions, rewarding the student(s) who finished the fastest. As the female student explained, she was just focusing on learning how to program correctly—racing to beat others in the class was not an incentive for her, a response that was far outside the perceptual field of the instructor. She was one of only two women in the course. She has continued on, with top grades and at a level rivaling the best male students, to complete the doctorate, but throughout has never felt really comfortable in the department nor convinced that the academic computer science profession will be truly welcoming for her as a woman.

[71] Barbara Gengler, "Not Many Women at the Top of E-Companies," *Australian IT News* 3 September 2002. 5 September 2002 http://australianit.news.com.au/.

[72] Sheila Washington, Marcia Brumit Kropf, and Paulette R. Gerkovich, "What's Holding Women Back?" *Harvard Business Review,* June 2003, pp. 18–19.

[73] Anna L.W. Sears, "Image Problems Deplete the Number of Women in Academic Applicant Pools," *Journal of Women and Minorities in Science and Engineering* 9, no. 2 (2003): 169–181.

[74] Robin Wilson, "Rigid Tenure System Hurts Young Professors, Especially Women, Officials From Top Universities Say," *Chronicle of Higher Education* September 26, 2005. http://chronicle.com/daily/2005/09/2005092605n.htm.

[75] Margaret Tierney, "Negotiating a Software Career: Informal Work Practices and 'The Lads' in a Software Installation," *The Gender-Technology Relation* (eds.) Keith Grint, and Rosalind Gill (London: Taylor & Francis, 1995) 192–209.

[76] Daniel Marshall, "Internet Technologists as an Occupational Community: Ethnographic Evidence," *Information, Communication & Society / Special Issue: Work, Difference and the New Media Industries* 5, no. 1 (2002): 51–69.

[77] National Research Council (U.S.), "Women Scientists And Engineers Employed In Industry: Why So Few? A Report Based On A Conference." Ad Hoc Panel on Industry, Committee on Women in Science and Engineering, Office of Scientific and Engineering Personnel (National Research Council, 1994).

[78] Teresa Rees, "Women And Computing: Recruiting, Retaining, Promoting." *Women in Computing Professions* (Oxford Internet Institute Policy Forum Position Papers, 2004) 36–39. 5 March 2005. http://www.oii.ox.ac.uk.

[79] Wendy Hall, "Looking to the future: Vive la difference!" *Women in Computing Professions* (Oxford Internet Institute Policy Forum Position Papers, 2004) 16–17. 31 May 2005 http://www.oii.ox.ac.uk.

[80] Mary Pipher, *Reviving Ophelia: Saving the Selves of Adolescent Girls* (New York: Putnam, 1994); Peggy Orenstein, *Schoolgirls: Young Women, Self-Esteem, and the Confidence Gap* (New York: Doubleday, 1994).

[81] Nicole Hannah-Jones, "Girls Get Own Class in Computer Science," *News and Observer* 18 August 2005: 1A; *SIGIS* 32.

[82] Two documentary series that effectively demonstrate the sexually charged and degrading nature of ads and music videos are Jean Kilbourne's *Killing Us Softly 3* (2000) and Sut Jhally's *Dreamworld* series (1991, 1995, 2006) (Media Education Foundation http://www.mediaed.org/videos/index_html).

[83] National Science Foundation Program for Women and Girls Awardee Meeting, October 5–6, 1998. 3 June 2004 http://www.ehr.nsf.gov/EHR/HRD/ge/ge-index.htm.

[84] *Tech-Savvy: Educating Girls in the New Computer Age* Educational Foundation Commission on Technology, Gender, and Teacher Education (Washington, D.C.: American Association of University Women, 2000) 29.

[85] *Tech Savvy* 29.

[86] Sherry Turkle, "Computational Reticence: Why Women Fear The Intimate Machine," *Technology and women's voices* (ed.) Cheris Kramarae (New York: Routledge and Kegan Paul, 1988) 41–61.

[87] *Tech Savvy* 8.

[88] *Tech Savvy* ix.

[89] Margolis and Fisher, *Unlocking the Clubhouse* 76.

[90] Ellen Spertus, quoted in Margolis and Fisher 73.

[91] *Tech Savvy* 10.

[92] Candace White and Katherine N. Kinnick, "One Click Forward, Two Clicks Back: Portrayals of Women Using Computers in Television Commercials." *Women's Studies in Communication* 23, no. 3, 2000: 392–412.

[93] White and Kinnick 6.

[94] Alan Melchior, Tracy Cutter and Faye Cohen, *Evaluation of FIRST Lego® League Underserved Initiative* (Manchester, NH: U.S. FIRST, 2005). 5 September 2005 http://www.usfirst.org/jrobtcs/surveys/05FLL_Underserved_Full_Report.pdf.

[95] 10 September 2005 http://blendedlibrarian.org/FAQ.html.

[96] Hall 18.

[97] A recent *Fortune* article addresses this idea; see, Geoffrey Colvin, "The Imagination Economy," *Fortune Magazine* (5 July 2006). 5 July 2006 http://money.cnn.com/2006/07/05/magazines/fortune/imaginationeconomy.fortune/index.htm.

[98] Mindy L. Gewirtz and Ann Lindsey, "Women and the New Economy" (GLS Consulting, 2000). 28 May 2005 http://www.glsconsulting.com/womensurvey/womensurvey1.htm.

[99] Gewirtz and Lindsey http://www.glsconsulting.com/womensurvey/res-effects.htm.

[100] Bill McKibben, *Enough: Staying Human in an Engineered Age* (New York: Henry Holt, 2003).

Chapter Five

Oh, to Be Given a Sporting Chance…: Televisual Representations of Women in the World of Sports News

In television sports "men predominate in numbers and prevail in presence."[1] The Amateur Athletic Foundation sponsored studies in 1990, 1994, 1999, and 2004 examining television coverage of women's and men's sports, and all consistently found that men's sports receive 92–94% of media sports coverage. The Foundation's summary report looking back over media coverage of women's sports from 1989–2004 found "no 'evolutionary' growth in media coverage of women's sports that just happens….the proportion of coverage of women's sports on televised news…is absolutely flat."[2] Likewise, news is a largely male preserve. "Male domination of the news media begins, very simply," note Croteau and Hoynes, "with numerical superiority. The male presence in the news industry is immense and far-reaching."[3] While male dominance may be most obvious at the highest organizational levels—Lee and Soloman in 1990 reported that 94% of top management positions in U.S. news media are occupied by men, and 74% of all U.S. news directors and 87% of all television general station managers are men[4]—as the twentieth century ended, only 37% of all journalists, 29% of the correspondents on the three major national television networks, and 39% of all local news employees were women.[5]

When these two highly male-dominated worlds merge in sports news, both the storytellers and the stories told are predominantly male agent narratives that feed the masculine imaginary and buttress patriarchal ideology. Typically, explain Carter and Steiner, "The media function by either effectively erasing women's presence, by fundamentally denying their humanity, trivializing or mocking them, or by reducing them to a single 'feminine' characteristic, even if that characteristic could be regarded as 'positive' (like 'innocent,' 'nurturing,' or 'concerned for others')."[6] Given this generalization, the appearance in fall 1998 of *Sports Night*, ABC's half-hour fictionalized version of the backstage work lives of the sports news professionals at ESPN's *Sports Center,* is doubly transgressive, in featuring two strong, decisive, ethical, technologically competent, sports-knowledgeable yet feminine women as the Executive Producer and Senior Associate Producer of the cable network's flagship sports news program. Featuring such women in positions that women in real life do not typically hold is indeed deserving of further critical examination, especially as these fictional roles never reappear on television.

This chapter examines a prime time series' representation of two female transgressors in the male-dominated world of television sports news. In doing so, it reveals both liberatory and regressive aspects of this unique Emmy-award-winning series that conjoins technological competence, sports-knowledge, female-female mentoring, and female-male friendship, and that, according to ESPN Coordinating Producer Julie Mariash and ESPN Production Assistant Lisa Fenn, "has accurately depicted their lives as women in this male-dominated world."[7] That is, these women, even in the face of occasional, seemingly throwback actions or repercussions that rehearse their pre-revolution femininity, have laid siege on traditionally male domains carved out at the intersection of sports and televised news.

Foreshadowed in some of the episodes are two sorts of cultural transgression: not only the invasion of male idioms and action but also retaliatory actions by masculine representatives of the dominant culture. As border-crossing cultural warriors, the women characters of *Sports Night* are given the opportunity to demonstrate their significant abilities inside tightly policed male domains. At the same time, they are subject to narrative constructions that diminish them and undermine the challenge they represent to masculine hegemony. The dramatization of the two female leads reflects their containment inside one of the negotiations socialized early into girls: a show of personal power—intellectual, creative, physical, and so on—is attached to a display of incompetence. In other words, in a one-step forward two-back dance, women learn to pull their own punches to lessen the threat they pose to the male sense of entitlement and superiority. Further, male retaliations dramatized in the course of several episodes echo real-life attacks on women sports reporters, launched in order to sabotage their incursions on male turf. Narratively, they combine with some of the girlishness displayed by the two female leads to trace cultural boundaries around their new-found liberation and power. We note in this chapter suggestions of boundaries because they will loom much, much larger in the next chapter.

Our analysis will be organized in four major sections: (1) further investigation of sports media as a masculinist preserve; (2) an overview of *Sports Night*'s narrative universe and *raison d'être*; (3) the heart of the chapter, an examination of the women's transgressions by word and deed; and then (4) a look at the failures of the heroines so far as some tenets of Second-Wave feminism might be concerned. Our job is not to call technical fouls but, rather, to expand the understanding of cultural transgressions that become attached to powerful women in the stories of our time.

The Masculine Worlds of Television News, Sports, and Sports News

Forty-four years ago, women constituted 13% of the news workforce. Although the percentage of women in journalism nearly doubled between 1971 and 1998, as we noted earlier only around a third of all the journalism industry's professional and staff employees were women. Equally important, this increase in the number of women "does not translate into superior power and influence for women; instead, it has been translated to mean a decline in salaries and status for the field."[8] Typically, women in broadcast news tend to work in areas that are considered extensions of their domestic responsibilities, and regardless of differences in years of experience and education, women are paid less for the same work than are men.[9] Women dominate the low-salaried, entry-level positions that perform the mundane tasks of news production—as writers, producers and production assistants.[10] Furthermore, van Zoonen points out that the increased presence of women—albeit not in the top, decision-making positions—in news organizations has not resulted in "a more balanced and less sexist way of reporting."[11] Occupational socialization, she argues, results in "tension between 'femininity' and professionalism" that sees as binary opposites "feminine" and "professional" values. Female journalists, she explains, "believe that 'feminine' values such as compassion, kindness and humanity are at odds with qualities expected of journalists, such as a certain amount of directness, distrust, and toughness."[12]

Like news, sport is a male-dominated sphere. That sport is a central site for the production and reinforcement of male supremacy and hypermasculinity in society as well as in sports has been established by many feminist scholars.[13] News media use sports to attract male readers and cater to male tastes; despite large numbers of women who follow sports, Duncan and Messner explain that "sport has given men an arena in which to create and reinforce male superiority.... By excluding women from this arena and by making athleticism virtually synonymous with masculinity, sport provides opportunities for men to assert their dominance at a time when male hegemony is continually challenged and opposed in everyday life."[14] Lawrence Wenner further contends that sports is primarily the domain of men and that sports news functions "as socially sanctioned gossip sheets."[15] As can be observed in sports news as well as in the fictional *Sports Night*, sanctioned gossip appears to allow men's interest in the details of human relations, and the emotional and psychological inner states of other men, to be satisfied without a perceived threat to their heteronormative masculinity.

Melding such characteristics of journalism and sports today, we are left with a vision of a cultural institution that functions as a powerfully gendered social formation. The aggressive actions celebrated in both news and sports, the language of warfare so characteristic of TV news,[16] and commanding personae that rule through intimidation and subordination all mark sports news as a male preserve. Indeed, both journalism and sports, in many ways, are marked by what Walter Ong called "adversativeness." The reporter and the subjects of reports usually exist to one extent or another as adversaries, and certainly the same is true of the players of zero-sum games. Ong notes that "Adversativeness can be cultivated. In fact, deliberate cultivation of the adversative lies at the deepest roots of intellectual development, particularly in the West."[17] And the central theme of Ong's book is on distinguishing between the sexes, with adversativeness associated primarily with males across most species of animal life.

All of this is not to say that women cannot be aggressive and cannot manage sports news operations. The praying mantis female eats her male counterpart during copulation, and female managers in fact can manage, if transgressively, the masculinist domain of the sports room.

Sports Night: Plus çe change, Plus çe meme chose

Sports Night was a half-hour dramedy[18] that premiered on ABC September 22, 1998, and whose network run ended in May 2000. At the end of its first season it was the sixth highest-ranked new show of the season, though it was not a hit. According to many critics, this was because viewers (and the network) were never certain whether it was a comedy or a drama. "*Sports Night's* tough road is not entirely surprising," *TV Guide* critic Richard Furstman explained. "For starters, the show spends only about half its running time being funny, and just as often turns serious."[19] *New Yorker* television critic Nancy Franklin characterized *Sports Night* as a "casual and intense, obsessive and jaunty" show, reflecting its snappy writing crafted for characters with smart-mouths and sardonic wit. Among its pleasures she listed its "frequent rapid-fire exchanges that are meant to eliminate, but instead often create, confusion" and resemble "something out of 'David Mamet meets Abbott and Costello'."[20] Despite the humorous repartee, the show's underlying seriousness was the source of considerable conflict between series' creator and executive producer Aaron Sorkin and ABC, much of it over the use of a laugh-track: Sorkin did not want to use one, while ABC did. ABC won, except for one episode that is analyzed in detail later in this chapter.[21]

The "fastest half hour on network television"[22] had six regular main characters: Managing Editor Isaac Jaffee (Robert Guillaume), the "lovably gruff managing editor and authority figure;"[23] Executive Producer Dana Whitaker (Felicity Huffman); glib, wise-cracking *Sports Night* anchor buddies Casey McCall (Peter Krause), a recently divorced dad who with Dana Whitaker was half of "the show's most star-crossed noncouple," and slightly thin-skinned Dan Rydell (Josh Charles); " nerdy sports genius;"[24] Senior Associate Producer Natalie Hurley (Sabrina Lloyd); and Associate Producer Jeremy Goodwin (Joshua Malina). In the "Dear Louise" episode (Episode 7), as Jeremy starts to write his weekly letter to his hearing-impaired sister, his voiceover narrates his description of the people he works with in the "dream job" he has landed on *Sports Night*:

> Dana Whitaker is the Executive Producer of Sports Night, a great accomplishment for a woman her age. She got her love of sports from her father and six brothers, one of whom plays for the Denver Broncos. She got her education from a series of exclusive all-girls' schools that her mother insisted she attend so she wouldn't grow up to be like her father and six brothers. The result is an irresistible combination of brilliance inside the office and something of a little less than brilliance everywhere outside of it.

The series was rehearsed like a comedy on Mondays and Tuesdays, and then shot like a drama with multiple cameras over three 12-hour-plus days.[25] In March 2000, *TV Guide*'s cover and Matt Roush's cover story called it "the best show you're not watching."[26]

Aaron Sorkin said that the series "is not a sports show any more than ER is about surgery. It's about the lives of these people." Initially, the center of the show as Sorkin envisioned it was the friendship between the two anchors.[27] However, over its two years storylines developed each of the six main characters and the series itself evolved into an ensemble dramedy. Several aspects of the series invite social and political analysis; for example, its portrayal of an older African American gentle man who is not only the Managing Editor of this sports news program but also role model and mentor to the female Executive Producer he is grooming to take his place. As well, he was a nurturer and counselor of the entire program staff. Its portrayal of sensitive, verbal male-male friendship also deserves considerable commentary. But, this chapter focuses on the portrayal of the series' central female characters—Dana Whitaker and Natalie Hurley—in this innovative, male-dominated, self-reflexive television world.

Empowered Women in Charge:
Verbal-Behavioral Markers of Transgression

In myriad ways Dana and Natalie provide empowering twenty-first century counterpoints to both their timid, insecure, and highly competent but de-feminized television producer predecessors. Neither of these women is the 1970s' Mary Tyler Moore or the 1980s-90s' Murphy Brown. As ESPN staffer Julie Mariash explains, "You have to be pretty tough to fit in and take part in the goofing around in order to be accepted and succeed in your work, and I think both of the women in their show do that."[28]

Dana is extremely knowledgeable about sports and video technology, has a strong sense of professional and personal ethics, is interpersonally skilled, and is played as very attractive. Part of her job as Executive Producer is to run the daily meetings in which the news staff decides what stories they will cover, how important they are, and how much time and/or video to allocate to each. In handling this part of her job Dana is consultative yet decisively the person in charge of the daily sports news show. Her inclusive, informal run-down meetings foster a sense of involvement and ownership among the staff that good managers would envy and strive to achieve with their employees. She handles her two wise-cracking male anchors, as well as the rest of her staff, with humor, compassion and sometimes "tough love," though her rapid-fire control room directions and her gently delivered but starkly direct corrections and admonitions leave no doubt that she is in charge.

The central storyline in the first episode illustrates not only Dana's masculinist style but also her feminine compassion. That storyline concerns anchor Casey McCall, who is struggling emotionally with the divorce that he and his wife are going through. As a result he is testy with the people at work, including his anchor partner Dan Rydell, and his on-air persona lacks the charisma, energy, and well-timed witty repartee that always has marked his work. Aware of Casey's problems, Dana has been giving him some slack and has not confronted him about his attitude or poor performance. When Managing Editor Isaac Jaffee confronts her about the matter as they walk down the hall toward the morning run-down, she defends Casey in a rapid-fire conversation typical of the fast-paced verbal exchanges that characterize the series:

Isaac: I think the show is going to hell in a hand basket and I'm ready to fire the whole bunch of you.

Dana: Yes, but you won't because we're all family here, and I'm just like a daughter to you.

Isaac: No, this is a television show here, and you're very much like an employee to me.

Dana: I've got to give Casey some slack, Isaac.
Isaac: Why?
Dana: Why do I have to give him some slack?
Isaac: That's the question. If you can't tell me, I can't tell the network.
Dana: Isaac—
Isaac: Why? Is there something going on between the two of you?
Dana: Absolutely not!
Isaac: [louder] Then why?
Dana: Because I owe it to him, that's why. We *all* do. Now, he's having some personal problems—
Isaac: Oh, I know all about his problems. You know, the network knows all about his problems, too, at which point they become my problems, and I'm saying at the very *most* I want them to be *your* problems.
Dana: Got it.
Isaac: Do you?
Dana: Yes.
Isaac: [emphatically] Good!

This exchange is interesting on multiple levels. We see Dana taking and giving demands and judgments on an equal footing with her boss. We see the intertwining of family and workplace attributions, complicating relationships between Dana and both her charge Casey and her superior Isaac. We see her compassion expressed but within the demands of a workplace with bottom-line performance requirements. Those requirements are made even clearer later in the episode. After Casey has exploded in front of the network representative JJ and JJ has made it clear to Isaac and Dana that he's worried about Casey's on-air performances, Dana and Isaac debrief after the meeting, with Isaac telling Dana, "It's [the possible replacement of Casey] your call, Dana, but pretty soon it's going to be my call because—here's the thing—I can't let it be their call." Dana's feminine side is acknowledged indirectly but challenged even more directly; compassion has its place, but it's not the central virtue of characters-in-charge.

The central virtue is the competent management of the show by the woman who's the Executive Producer. Her competence is grounded not only in the directness of her confrontation of her star talent but even in her management of televisual discourse—the technotalk of this professionalized world. So, as she steps into Casey's office and sits down at his coffee table, the following conversation reviews his performance with personal concern yet with the markings of someone highly competent to offer that review:

Casey: Hi!

Dana: Casey—

Casey: Listen, I need you to give me 30 seconds off the NFL injury report and give it to me for the intro to the ACC recruiting violation.

Dana: Fine.

Casey: Thanks.

Dana: You're screwing up my show, Casey.

Casey: OK, keep the 30 seconds.

Dana: That's not what I meant.

Casey: I know, I was joking

Dana: I know you were joking.

Casey: I can tell by the way you're laughing.

Dana: That's 'cause I'm mad at you, and also it wasn't that funny.

Casey: Did you come in here to give me a pep talk? 'Cause if you came in here to give me a pep talk can we assume it's already happened and I'm peppy? [He stands up and starts to walk toward the door.]

Dana: [emphatically] Casey, sit down! Now, I know you think there are 250 other people in this place—

Casey: [interrupts and talks over her] No, I don't think there are 250 other people who could do the show.

Dana: Yes you do, but whether you're right or whether you're wrong. I'm the one who has the job, and I *love* it! I *love* producing *Sports Night*. I *live* from 11 to midnight, and the rush is so huge I don't come down until 3 o'clock in the morning. I *love* doing *Sports Night!* And you used to, too. [brief pause]. Now, hmmm, I came in to tell you that it looks like Cleveland's going to go to a four-man rotation for the stretch drive; I came in to tell you that it looks like segments 16–20 might have to get condensed for a possible story coming out of South Bend. [she continues with controlled anger in her quiet voice] But mostly I came in to tell you, 'You're screwing up my show!' [She rises and walks out of his office.] Natalie—!

Natalie: Yo!

Dana: Let's meet with your guy. [And they then proceed to do the interview with Jeremy discussed below.]

The key comment in this exchange, of course, is Dana's panegyric to the job. A few sentences capture her authority, sentimentality, sensitivity to others, professional competence, and willingness to manhandle those working for her. Moreover, her transgressive status is on display as she breaks with one of the more insistently socialized feminine tropes: her choice of words rejects the collaborative relationship aspect of running the show—"our" show—and vehemently aligns herself with the more typically masculine claim of individual ownership—"my" show.

In the "Shane" episode, Dana demonstrates both her competence and her compassion when she intervenes and refuses to allow Casey to violate his own (and the show's) journalistic integrity. Casey interviews Shane McArnold, a baseball player who just signed an $81 million contract with the New York Yankees, for a *SportsCenter* "Close-Up." Casey has not talked to McArnold since early in his career when McArnold gave Casey an interview when he really needed one. To Casey's surprise, McArnold has become a real jerk who badmouths New York, Yankee Stadium, and his teammates on camera. As they walk away from the interview, though he lacks the authority to do so, Casey promises Shane that he'll fix the interview by editing the tape, and meet him for a drink after the broadcast.

When Casey tells Dana he wants to re-edit the interview, Dana refuses to allow it. She leads him through a series of questions—did McArnold know he was on camera, did he know he was being taped, was there anything wrong with the tape?—and when Casey confirms that McArnold indeed did know that he was being taped on camera, she refuses to allow Casey to violate his journalistic ethics by doctoring the taped interview out of either celebrity blindness or misplaced loyalty. Casey then goes over Dana's head to Isaac, the Managing Editor. Sitting at his desk, Isaac allows Casey to paint himself into a corner by not telling Casey that Dana has walked into the room and is standing behind him. When Isaac asks whether Casey has talked about this with Dana, Casey tries to avoid both lying and admitting that Dana has denied the request by dissing Dana, saying "Oh, you know how unreliable Dana is, up one minute, down the next." As he says this, Isaac looks behind him and Casey realizes that Dana is there. Dana then walks Casey out of the room, upbraids him about going over her head, and reiterates that he is not to edit the tape to improve McArnold's image.

However, she does not just leave Casey hanging out there in the breeze. Knowing that it is going to be difficult for him to face McArnold after the interview airs on their broadcast, she and several other *Sports Night* staff members just "happen" to be at the bar where Casey planned to meet McArnold. When McArnold enters and speaks threateningly to Casey, Dana interjects support for Casey from behind him, and Elliott (who is a large guy) walks into the room. Casey then tells McArnold that he should not have promised that he could fix the interview because he did not have that kind of power, that he was just trying to impress McArnold, and that McArnold's astronomical salary is partly being paid for by New York baseball fans who work hard for their money and who deserve a little more respect. After McArnold utters a few more threats and leaves, Dana and the other *Sports Night* people assure Casey that they are proud of him for speaking up as he did, and Casey, too, is proud of himself for doing so.

Dana, in sum, is a man's man, a man's woman, and yet a woman's woman in the environment of late-night sporting news. She bobs and weaves through every conversation, intermixing professional sports argot, personal judgment, hard-boiled demands, and sympathetic understanding. She loves the people but has given herself to the job. All of these characteristics are summarized by Dan, following shortly upon the scene where Dana accused Casey of screwing up the show, when he reams out Casey for even thinking about leaving the show:

> Have you even noticed that Dana has been keeping JJ and the network away from you with a whip and a chair? Huh? Have you noticed that she's been risking her job for you every day? And do you really think, my friend, that is *that* much to do with your talent? These are people who like you, ok?

One more dimension of Dana's transgressiveness deserves commentary: she indeed does talk the talk—not just the technotalk of the studio, or the inside sports argot, but the talk of the brash, assertive boss. Consider the opening to Episode 26, "Cliff Gardner." Network brass are leaning on the show in the presence of a show-fixer, Sam Donovan (William Macy). The episode opens with *Sports Night* on-air, and Dana leading the control room chatter. Following are comments:

> Could the show be any stiffer tonight? ...
> I thought last night was as bad as it could get, but it turns out we had unexplored potential for stiffness....
> [After the floor director calls for two different tape shots:] Damn it, Dave get it together.... That's what we need, what we need is the control room to fall apart—that's just what the doctor ordered....

After a week, who cares? It took me two years to figure out how to run this show. He [the fixer] comes in here, he gets in our heads like a virus…we're so *stiff*…

[After the suggestion that the women in the control room should whisper in the ears of the anchors]: Why don't we just get them a lap dance?…

I'm afraid that from 11 to 12, this is *my* show, and I'll deal with things with the way I deal with things…

[At the break, Dana goes to the floor to talk with Casey and Dan]: I've seen better performances by inmates. Would you mind telling me what the hell's going on?…[Interrupting an explanation]: I don't want to hear about it! You guys sound like you're giving stock quotes—is there a reason I'm not aware of? [Interrupting another explanation]: Don't give me your excuses. We've got eighteen minutes of show left—what I'd like is for you guys to start earning your money. Anything you'd like to say? [Interrupting a third time]: Good!

In this sequence we see stereotypically male modes of confrontation: (1) sarcasm, (2) profanity-marked judgment, (3) wounded sense of fair play, (4) still more sarcasm in the lap-dance comment, (5) a reminder of the importance of hierarchy and authority, and (6) a series of interruptions that prevent explanation, thereby serving as hostile assessments and forceful demands. Not only sports but, generally speaking, sports talk is gendered—and that's certainly true of professional basketball, baseball, football, and hockey, the usual discourses of *Sports Night*. In this exchange with the sports journalism professionals, her two anchors, Dana beats them mercilessly with masculinist vocabulary and references: "Damn it, Dave, get it together," "lap dance," "this is *my* show," "what the hell's going on?" "I don't want to hear about it," "Don't give me your excuses," "what I'd like is for you guys to start earning your money."

Now of course these snippets of talk are not actually the province of one gender or the other; sex-based essentialism is not the point. Rather, the significance is this: Dana's aggressive mode in challenging sports-associated professionals, profanity, sexual allusion to lap dancing, refusal to permit accounts and explanations, and bottom-line reference to money all are markers of masculinist stereotypes. The symbolic world that not only constitutes the environment of *Sports Night* but also, in this case, informs the substance of every remark that Dana makes in her exchange with the boys are marked or signed as a man's lived experience. Dana not only has a man's job in a man's TV show; she has co-opted men's acculturated idiom as it has developed in locker rooms, bull sessions, bar rooms, and countless other environments where jock-talk defines identity or cultural membership. There is a Catch-22, however, as there so often is for women transgressing male-controlled borders: the cultural construction that opposes femininity to professionalism, noted by van Zoonen above, makes this kind of "ballsy" talk the *only* style associated with being a top studio producer. The backlash? Postfeminism pointing to portrayals such as this as reflective of a tough-talking, feminist bitch—that is, women to spurn.

Before we leave this topic, we should examine Dana's co-conspirator Natalie. Natalie is portrayed in softer, less experienced, and, yes, more feminine ways than Dana. She is, after all, the sidekick, not the hero, the aide, not the manager. We already have seen her engaging in nervous puttering when Dana is trying to see what job applicant Jeremy is made out of. "Small Town," Episode 13 of the first season, gives us a considerably larger dose of Natalie's professional commitments. Here, she is about to face her first night as director of the show, as Dana (and Casey) have the night off—as luck would have it, on a double date, Dana with Gordon and Casey with a blind date, Lisa. That conceit both separates Dana and Casey from the action yet allows them to watch and comment on Natalie/the show from a restaurant.

Natalie's strength-of-character, her abilities to walk the male walk and talk the male talk, are scattered through the show. First, she takes on anchor Dan's judgment as she figures out how to make up a minute-and-a-half of showtime. She begins by reviewing the show template:

Natalie: Bumpers in and out at 10. We'll tease Villanova for now, but that might change. Elliott, where are we on time?
Elliott: We need a buck-fifty back.
Natalie: What can we cut?
Dan: Formula 1.
Natalie: That's good film. Let's bump Oksana Baiul.
Dan: Oksana Baiul?
Natalie: Lose it.
Dan: The Ukrainian jewel, Oksana Baiul?
Natalie: Yes.
Dan: You can't cut Oksana Baiul!
Natalie: But look at how I just did.

This is followed by a second exchange with Dan over the evening's substitute anchor:

Dan:	I would never second-guess you, and I would certainly never question your choice of substitute anchor.
Natalie:	What's on your mind?
Dan:	I question your choice of substitute anchor.
Natalie:	She's fine.
Dan:	She's better than fine.
Natalie:	She's very good.
Dan:	She's very, very good.
Natalie:	So what's the problem?
Dan:	There's no problem!
Natalie:	It sounded like there was a problem.
Dan:	I'm not spreading ill will here. That should be clear. I'm not dropping a dime on anybody. Where I come from, we don't say things about people.
Natalie:	You come from Connecticut.
Dan:	That's right.
Natalie:	You don't say things about people in Connecticut?
Dan:	We do not.
Natalie:	What's the problem?
Dan:	Bobbi's a lunatic.
Natalie:	Dan—
Dan:	She's an off-the-charts lunatic.
Natalie:	Why don't you like her?
Dan:	I like her fine—Talented. Smart. Very professional.—But…total nut bar.
Natalie:	Got it.
Dan:	She's convinced that we slept together once and I never called her.
Natalie:	Did you?
Dan:	Did I sleep with her?
Natalie:	Did you call her?
Dan:	I didn't sleep with her.
Natalie:	Why does she think that you did?
Dan:	It's hard to say, but it could have something to do with the fact that she's psychotic.
Natalie:	It's going to be Bobbi.
Dan:	It's your decision.
Natalie:	Yes it is.
Dan:	Very exciting.
Natalie:	Thank you.

Natalie's next run-in is with Dana, who calls her from the restaurant just before the broadcast. Natalie at first won't take the call, then finally does after checking on video and sound levels in the studio:

Natalie: This is a comfortable chair [the director's chair].
Dana: You took your sweet time.
Natalie: Hey, could you put Casey on for a second?
Dana: But—
Natalie: —Just a second, then right back to you.
Dana (to Casey): She wants to talk to you.
Casey: Hey, Nat.
Natalie: Keep her off the phone.
Casey: —You bet. (Cuts off the phone call, then turns to the restaurant group): Hey, what do you know about the fennel salad here?

The next person to have a confrontative exchange with Natalie is program's Capo di Capo Isaac. Getting ready to come back to the program after commercial, Natalie calls for opening on segment 60 and then moving to segment 70. Isaac says to put in segment 68. Natalie says no. Isaac says yes. Natalie says no because "We blew off 68 in the 10:00 rundown," and tells Isaac to be quiet. He's shocked, questioning whether she actually asked him to be quiet. Natalie replies, "Right now you can fire me or you can stay quiet," to which Isaac replies, "You're good." Within minutes, her researcher-boy-friend Jeremy questions whether she can air a story of an eleventh-hour baseball trade as an "unconfirmed report." He pushes on her hard, until she says, "You want to leave the room?" "No," says Jeremy. "Then from time to time," she retorts, "allow for the fact that other people might be at least as smart as you are." Jeremy goes silent as Natalie telephones a housekeeping maid in a hotel to find out who's in a room; it turns out that two managers and some key players are. The trade has been witnessed, and a phone call to the Dodgers' General Manager confirms it. The episode ends with Jeremy and Natalie in the control room. As he watches her, she turns to him:

Natalie: What????
Jeremy: You're good, Natalie.
Natalie: Yeah.
Jeremy: I'm sorry.

Natalie:	What did you think I was here, Jeremy, some Gal Friday?
Jeremy:	No, I just didn't know that you were *that* good.
Natalie:	(rustling around, then going back to the opening of program where she bet Jeremy that there'd be no trade, with a five-dollar bill): You were right about the trade. (They kiss. Jeremy leaves during soft music. The music goes up-tempo as Natalie pumps her fist and leaves the control room. She has doubly impressed a man who is both her boyfriend and her subordinate.)

Overall, therefore, the softness, apparent vulnerability, and at-times deference of Natalie to her boss Dana mark dimensions of her femininity, but her zest for the job, her knowledge of both television production and the sporting world, and her forcefulness in command-when-in-charge all mark her as a worthy partner with Dana. Together they run the show. And in a sense the transgressiveness apparent in her behavior and language is all the more striking precisely because her discourse, demeanor, and bodily stances suggest her womanliness. But yet, as Mariah Burton Nelson's *The Stronger Women Get, the More Men Love Football* argues, the more women succeed, the more threatened men feel and the more they need to challenge these transgressors into masculine spheres.[29] Notwithstanding the little tests of her resolve, knowledge, and composure, however—tests that reflect underlying reservations about her ability to handle the job even offered by her co-workers—Natalie not only carries off the broadcast without a flaw, but she displays daring, inventiveness, self-confidence, and journalistic skill in securing a major sports information coup with this exclusive trade story.

The Transgressive Woman as Mentor

For all of Natalie's strength, however, when she does take over *Sports Night*, her actions and language echo those of Dana. Dana not only mentors Casey, Dan, and Jeremy, but most directly, Natalie. Traditionally, mentoring has involved interpersonal relationships in which the mentor, usually a more experienced colleague, provides to less experienced colleagues career support, direction, and feedback about their organizational performance, organizational barriers and pitfalls, and career growth opportunities. Recent scholarly work on mentorship has identified mentoring as including three components—career modeling, psychosocial modeling, and role modeling.[30] Career modeling by mentors involves coaching, protecting, sponsoring and providing challenging assignments that will help the mentee/protégé advance within the organization. Dana does this for Natalie when she takes her night off, putting Natalie in charge of producing the show ("Small Town"); for Jeremy, when she and Isaac send him out into the field to produce a show (Episode 3, "The Hungry and the Hunted"); and for Casey and Dan, when she lets them anchor their first boxing match (Episode 34, "The Cut Man Cometh," second season).

Psychosocial modeling by mentors enhances in the mentee "a sense of competence, clarity of identity, and effectiveness in a professional role"[31] while coaching mentor functions involve the senior professional suggesting "specific strategies for accomplishing work objectives, for achieving recognition, and for achieving career aspirations."[32] Dana serves as mentor for Natalie when she hires Natalie's top associate producer choice ("Pilot"), when she counsels and actively assists Natalie to find other job possibilities when it looks like her job at CSC might be slashed (Episode 42, "April Is the Cruelest Month," second season; Episode 43, "Bells and a Siren," second season). She defends and protects Casey when personal matters interfere with his ability to do his job ("Pilot") and encourages him to do what he knows is the journalistically right thing to do (Episode 29, "Shane," second season). She enacts psychosocial mentoring when she counsels and supports Jeremy after he is traumatized producing a hunting show (Episode 3, "The Hungry and the Hunted"), reassures him after his Y2K readiness plan crashes right before their show goes on the air (Episode 28, "Kafelnikov," second season), and helps him when he runs himself down trying to protect Natalie from hate mail and let her know he cares (Episode 6, "The Head Coach, Dinner, and the Morning Mail").

Consider in the "Pilot" episode, for example, Natalie's actions and verbal repartee in a hiring situation. She has narrowed down the candidates for an associate producer position, and she and Dana interview her top choice, Jeremy Goodwin (Joshua Malina). Notice her control of the situation, her handling of both the interviewee and her colleague, and the ease with which she manages the sports discourse that epitomizes sports news. We divide the interaction into three phrases:

I. Opening construction of the hierarchy

Natalie:	Jeremy, this is Dana Whitaker.
Dana:	We've met. [which they had earlier when a seated Jeremy volunteered an unasked explanation of Dana's sotto voce complaints about not getting a particular satellite feed]
Jeremy:	Yes.
Dana:	You have an impressive résumé. Let me ask you some questions.
Natalie:	[to Jeremy, who rises, and fumbles a little as he sits down] Are you ok?

Jeremy:	I'm ok.
Natalie:	Would you like a glass of water? A soft drink? We have Fresca—
Dana:	If you're taking orders, I'll have an angel hair pasta and a nice Merlot—
Natalie:	I'm just trying to—
Dana:	I know.
Natalie:	I'm just trying to make him comfortable.
Dana:	[turning to Natalie, says sotto voce to her] A little more professionalism is all I'm trying—
Jeremy:	[rising] I can come back later.

II. Female control of male interviewee

Dana:	[sits down, as does Natalie, and Jeremy also sits]. What are your favorite sports?
Jeremy:	I beg your pardon?
Dana:	What are your strongest sports?
Jeremy:	Oh, football.
Dana:	Good. Let's talk about basketball.
Jeremy:	I said football.
Dana:	I heard you. Let's talk about basketball.
Jeremy:	I can talk about baseball and hockey—
Dana:	Oh, you're pretty strong in baseball and hockey, are you?
Jeremy:	Not as strong as football.
Dana:	Great. Let's talk about the Knicks.
Jeremy:	I walked right into that one, didn't I?
Dana:	[writing on the paper on her slate] Well, I left the door wide open.
Natalie:	[seeing that this is not going well] Shot of bourbon?
Jeremy:	Please. [Natalie pops up out of her chair to get it]
Dana:	Sit! [second's pause]. I'm sorry, that was harsh; I hurt your feelings. [Natalie holds up both hands palms out to signal it's ok, and sits back down.] Name three things the Knicks need to do this season to make it to the finals.
Jeremy:	I couldn't get another question?
Dana:	You will, but not until I hear an answer to the first one.
Jeremy:	[he stands, rubs his head] What do the Knicks—
Dana:	Three things the Knicks have to do to contend.
Jeremy:	Ms. Whitaker. I have to tell you that I'd be great for this job…[he does a long rant that rehearses his qualifications, in-

dicates the level of detail he knows about sports statistics and asserts that he has watched every *Sports Night* telecast since it first went on the air and ends with] Does that make any sense?

Dana: [staring straight ahead at him]. I wasn't really listening.

Jeremy: Oh, god!

III. Female control of the situation and sports discourse

Dana: Jeremy, Jeremy. This is television. Things happen. If you want to work here you've got to not spontaneously wig out.

Natalie: Not 'til an hour before air time.

Jeremy: Right, right. The Knicks.

Dana: Name three things.

Jeremy: Improve their free throw percentage.

Dana: Yes!

Jeremy: Run the floor.

Dana: [encouragingly]. OK! One more!

Jeremy: Uhhm, tell Spike Lee to sit down and stay off the floor?

Dana: OK! Welcome to *Sports Night!* [She gives him a high five and walks away to address the next problem.]

In this brief interview Dana makes it eminently clear in her witty, charming, yet very firm manner, both to Jeremy and to Natalie, that Dana is knowledge-able, competent, and very much in charge. She needs to see how Jeremy responds under pressure because putting on a daily sports news program is a 12-hour pressure cooker job, so she asks him a question that requires him to think, in the area that he himself thinks he is weakest in, but one that is not at all impossible. Then she demonstrates her patience and compassion, as well as her firm professionalism, when she doesn't send him packing after he initially freezes and then wigs out a bit with his rant, but instead prompts him again to answer the question, encouraging him as he does. And yet, to keep him on task she ignores his call for emotional support and his recitation of his virtues: she needs to see them, not just hear about them. With Natalie, Dana's breezy, slightly sardonic comment lets Natalie know that she is acting more like Jeremy's agent than his supervisor and that she should be friendly while maintaining a modicum of professional distance during a job interview, even if she does think he's the best person for the job. And, Dana finishes by affirming her knowledge of basketball and the people who work for her by offering positive judgments about Jeremy's assessments of the Knicks. She manages both the people and the subject matter in thought, word, and deed. Dana's professional, firm, yet supportive managerial style and her loyalty and commitment to her employees are evident from the series' beginning. She can work a man's world on a man's show.

In performing these mentor functions, Dana mentors the other woman in her office as well as viewers, especially female viewers, by providing a role model of a capable, successful woman in the male-dominated world of sports news. Female role models are vitally important for enabling women—and men—to see women's options and choices. In concretely visualizing female sports news professionals, *Sports Night* affirms women's transgression into this male-dominated realm. Its narrative portrayals of Dana's and Natalie's gifted handling of news, sports, and media production technology challenge constricting gender stereotypes and assumptions about women's competence. To compensate for the threat that such female competence poses to the masculine worlds of sports, news and technology, however, the series occasionally claws back these culturally transgressive representations with narrative elements that contradict the female depictions and feminize, trivialize, and sexualize both Dana and Natalie. In doing so, these two women are bracketed as anomalies and the breach their presence wreaks on hegemonic masculinity in these male-dominated domains is threatened by containment.

Throughout the series and in the balance, however, Dana is presented as an excellent manager and mentor, and both she and Natalie are portrayed as technologically and organizationally competent producers who are very knowledgeable about many sports, and who are capable of juggling myriad bits of information and multi-tasking. The Executive Producer position is an exceedingly complex and difficult position, which Dana loves and is very, very good at. But being a woman in this position transgresses cultural norms for the masculine worlds of sports, news, and media technology, and narrative kernels[33] in many episodes representationally and discursively reaffirm that these are male domains.

The Transgressive Woman as Culturally Bounded

In "Rebecca" (Episode 14), for example, Dana talks with Casey about her concern that Gordon, the associated federal district attorney whom she has been dating, is going to break up with her because she is so involved with her job. Casey counsels her to talk to Gordon and to tell him the truth about how she feels, "You'd be amazed at how attractive the truth can be sometimes," he advises her. "Not for a woman," Dana responds. "The truth is I have a job that involves me, that stimulates and rewards me, and takes up a lot of my time. And I'm not willing to do my job just a little bit. I want to do all of it. It's part of me and I'm different without it. And that is who I am and that is who you need to love. Except it won't work." Casey assures her that it will work, and adds,

"Dana, any man who hears that doesn't say, 'For a woman like you, for a person like you, I will take whatever time you can give me and be grateful all my life'....is just taking up space for the rest of us." While Casey's response is indeed the sort of response a male feminist might make, Casey offers this comment at least as much because he is in love with Dana as he does as an assertion of his feminist beliefs in relational equality and respect for one's career commitment.

In terms of the show's narrative, Dana's response correctly reflects the attitude of Gordon, and, regrettably, many heterosexual males: the truth that a woman who loves her job as much as she loves her partner is not attractive to most men.[34] Gordon breaks his engagement with Dana, in part because of her devotion to her job, but also, he says, because he does not believe that Dana loves him; he thinks that she is in love with Casey but unaware of her feelings for him. Whatever is true in the symbolic world of *Sports Night*, transgression has its price.

Another strategy the series uses to reaffirm the limitations of Dana's womanhood is by undercutting her technological expertise. While on the one hand Dana is shown as very technologically competent in terms of satellite, studio and field video production, and simultaneously tracking and calling for multiple graphics, texts, in-studio camerawork, taped segments and live feeds, she is also portrayed as a hands-on technological klutz in "What Kind of Day Has It Been" (Episode 23, first season). In the previous episode, "Napoleon's Battle Plan," Dana discovers that her fiancé Gordon has been sleeping with Sally, the producer of another program on their cable network. To cope with her insomnia, she reads photography catalogs and decided to buy herself a very expensive single lens reflex camera, plus a lighting package. In "What Kind of Day Has It Been," Jeremy asks her, "Dana, do you have the first idea how to operate any of this equipment?" When Dana responds that she has read the owner's manual cover to cover, Jeremy retorted, "I read Dr. Zhivago cover to cover; that doesn't make me the czar." Shortly thereafter, Dan responded to the call to assemble for a photograph, and commented, "Dana, how much did you spend on this?" To which Dana replied that she was treating herself.

When everyone but Casey was present, Dana decides to take a practice picture. She starts to explain what is going to happen: "You are going to hear three beeps—Beep. Beep. Beep.—followed by a one and a half second pause. Then a flash from my Exeter 220–6 strobe with the 18-inch parabolic reflector. Ready?" The three beeps sounded, but the flash did not go off. As Dana walked toward the camera saying, "Well, it's a little timing problem," the strobe went off. Later, Dana gathers everyone for another picture. She has everyone hold still, sets the timer, runs over to sit with everyone. The three beeps go off, but the strobe does not flash. As she says, "All right. Everyone just stay where you are. This is nothing. This is a small timing problem," the film comes pouring out of the camera.

Trying to be positive, Natalie comments, "Well, at least the strobe didn't explode," which is the cue for the strobe to explode. At this point, Dana loses it, yelling, "OK, that's it. That is absolutely IT!" Then, in a move that brings the fact of Gordon's cutting off of their engagement, Dan suddenly asks her, "Hey, where are your rings?" and Casey responds "at the cleaners," Dana truly explodes and delivers this barely controlled hysterical outburst:

> It's not at the cleaners, you idiot. There's no such thing as an overnight ring cleaners. Gordon and I broke up, which is just the most recent in a series of humiliations. And I'm Ok with it. I can take it. But this, this is really the living end. I've seen enough to know that I have seen enough. Now I want something good to happen. I want something good to happen before the day is over, and I'll be the judge of what's good. One good thing before the day is over. I swear, that's all I want.

Then, suddenly we hear (before we see him) Isaac's voice [Isaac has been hospitalized because of a stroke]: "Hey, lady, are you thinking about getting my show on the air anytime soon?" And after greeting Isaac, and re-loading the film into the camera, Dana succeeds in taking a picture (though just as the shutter flashes, everyone's eyes turn to the side to follow Jeremy's voice and arm pointing to the television screen).

Although Dana eventually does learn to successfully operate her expensive new camera equipment, she is publicly subjected to ridicule as she struggles to learn to operate it, and she deals with her technological learning curve by having a public, hysterical outburst. This sequence of scenes suggests that while women, like Dana, may acquire technological expertise, such expertise is not "natural" for women. The accompanying hysteria likewise reaffirms her gender. Dana is far more sexually and relationally engaged than her technically proficient counterparts in *The Net* and *VR5*, but, despite her command of the exacting technical world of television production, Dana's emotional availability is counterbalanced by undermining her technological mastery. The inclusion of such reversals in a television series such as *Sports Night* appear to re-affirm masculine hegemony, as if the display of women's full power must be throttled back by acts that mitigate the challenge they pose. As we see in the next narrative arc of the series, retribution for that challenge can take the form of very real brutality.

Sports Night further contains and polices women's transgression into the masculine world of sports news by sexualizing them. The "Mary Pat Shelby" (Episode 5) and the following week's "The Head Coach, Dinner, and the

Morning Mail" provide powerful illustrations of this. In "Mary Pat Shelby," as we have noted, Dana and Isaac are elated when they negotiate an exclusive *Sports Night* on-air studio interview with Christian Patrick, an all-star football player who has just been convicted of felony assault for breaking his girlfriend's jaw and throwing her down a flight of stairs. They promote the upcoming interview nonstop, and Dana sends Natalie out to the Meadowlands locker room to do a pre-interview with Patrick. However, when Dana finally receives the interview guidelines from Patrick's agent and lawyer, guidelines which say that questions about Mary Pat Shelby's assault are totally off limits, Dan and Casey tell her that she got beat, and that she is doing a big thing badly. Dana responds that she doesn't need a civics lesson from them, she's aware of the moral questions posed by doing an interview in which the one topic that everyone wants to hear about isn't even raised, but promoting the interview will get people to tune in to their excellent, but third-place show, and she can't educate viewers to how good *Sports Night* and move it out of its third-place basement is unless they tune in: "I'll do anything short of a wet T-shirt contest to get us there, and these days, the wet T-shirt contest isn't looking too bad."

Natalie returns from the pre-interview rubbing her wrist, and tells Jeremy, who notices the huge bruise on it, that it got caught in a door. She stays in the editing room, editing the tape from the interview during the run-down meeting. In the middle of the run-down meeting, Isaac bursts in to say that there is a breaking story coming out of the Meadowlands: the custodian saw Christian Patrick exposing himself to someone, grabbing her wrist, and there was some kind of a struggle. Jeremy is the first to realize that the woman in the story is Natalie.

After Isaac, Dan, Casey, Jeremy, and Dana go talk to Natalie about what happened, Isaac tells Natalie that he has sent for a car to take her home. She asks if she's been fired, because if she isn't she says that as the Senior Associate Producer she would like to stay and do her job. Isaac assures her that she certainly can stay and do her job.

As Natalie, Casey, and Dan leave, Dana tells them that this is a whole new ballgame and they have an exclusive story that they need to promote because it's going to get told, anyway. And besides, she adds, Natalie deserves to have her story told. Dan and Casey agree that they cannot not report this story just because it happened to one of their news team, but Dan tells Dana that it seems to him that Natalie doesn't want her story to be told. And indeed, Natalie's initial reaction is not to tell her story. As she explains to Dan, she has a Master's degree in journalism from Northwestern and like every woman reporter in the world, she recalls vividly what happened to Lisa Olson, so she knows that if she files a complaint against Patrick the whole world will come crashing down on her head. And, she points out, even in the soundproofed editing room she is sitting in, she can already hear the nonstop ringing of telephones.

The "Lisa Olson incident" involved the real-life Lisa Olson, who on September 17, 1990, as a sportswriter for the Boston *Herald*, was humiliated, degraded, and in her words "mind raped" by Zeke Mowatt and several other New England Patriots football players when she entered the locker room to interview cornerback Maurice Hurst about his role in the team's victory. Several naked players walked up to her; one of them invited her to "take a bite" out of his penis, and others shouted "make her look" as they made a point to suggestively "model their genitals" as they walked by her to the showers. Olson could not finish her interview, left, and informed her supervisor at the *Herald*. They decided to handle the issue privately with the Patriots; however, five days later the Boston *Globe* broke the story. Subsequently the *Herald* ran a number of stories about the incident, including one that reported that Victor Kiam, then the owner of the Patriots, had called Olson a "classic bitch," although Kiam denied having made the comment.[35] Her apartment building had the words "classic bitch" spray-painted on its front; she received threatening telephone calls and letters, and even death threats.[36] The harassment she experienced from Patriot fans continued even after Olson accepted a reassignment in October to cover the Boston Celtics and Boston Bruins.[37] Eventually, in order to continue her sports reporting career, she moved to Australia.[38]

Dan assures Natalie that he has no problem with her going along with Dana and taking a pass on reporting the attempted sexual assault. He just came to tell her that whatever she decides would be fine because situations like this are what friends gear up for.

When Dana realizes that Natalie doesn't want to tell her story or to file a complaint, she goes to talk to Isaac. They, in turn, talk to Patrick's lawyer and agent, who—along with Patrick—has arrived at the studio for the live interview during the *Sports Night* broadcast. Dana tells them that she and Natalie are prepared to deny to the police and to the NFL that anything happened at the Meadowlands if her anchors can ask anything they want about Mary Pat Shelby. They mull it over and agree that she gets the interview about Mary Pat Shelby— and the ratings she had wanted.

As everyone waits for the broadcast, Dana sits in the dark in Isaac's office thinking about what has happened. Casey comes in to talk with Dana who is feeling really badly because, as she explains to Casey, she sent Natalie rather than Jeremy to the locker room thinking that Natalie could provoke a more newsworthy response. She asks Casey if he thinks that Natalie knows that she "sold her" [for ratings]. Casey tells her that of course Natalie knows because

Dana is the one who taught her, but that Natalie also knows that Dana tends to do the right thing.

In the next scene, Dana rushes out of the editing room where Natalie is into Isaac's office, tells him that they are doing a big thing badly, and asks him if it is OK for her to fix it. When he says, yes, she goes to the set where Christian Patrick, his agent, his lawyer, and the show's anchors are standing around, not talking, waiting for airtime, and cancels Patrick's on-air interview, telling them that all deals are off. In one of the creative storylines in *Sports Night* that often elevated the show above most series running, Dana enacts the full range of the transgressive woman. She follows the enculturated masculine practice of Ong's "adversativeness" by deliberately baiting Christian Patrick with Natalie's presence in his locker room, but then, empowered by the courage of her empathy and her commitment to sisterhood, she sacrifices her immediate career ambitions to make it right.

In the final scene, Natalie confronts Christian Patrick as he is leaving the studio. He tells her that maybe he came on a bit strong, but adds, "It's a lot of fuss about nothing, isn't it?" Natalie doesn't respond to that, but she reminds him that he told her about how much he wanted to play football from the time he was a little kid. She says that that's how much she has always wanted to be a sports reporter, and that tomorrow, everything is going to come crashing down on their heads because after the broadcast she is going down to the police station and swearing out a warrant for his arrest. He turns, slams down the football he's carrying, and walks out.

Episode 6, "The Head Coach, Dinner and the Morning Mail," continues this storyline and further reflects sports reporter Lisa Olson's experience. Here is an episode where Natalie's sexual identity and her professionally gendered role clash. She spends the early portions of the program in a dither, unable to find some needed Michigan State videotape, talking about fixing the air conditioning when the actual need is to increase the heat in the studio, and causing Dana to say, "Double-check any items you're getting from Natalie—she's been screwing up lately." As the episode wears on, Natalie forgets to load some substitute videotape for a new segment, forcing the anchors to have to fill fifteen seconds with mindless chat about Tony Orlando. Everyone is aware of her experience with Patrick, and thus tiptoes around and excuses her mistakes; yet she pleads: "I expect to be treated like a professional! I expect to be yelled at! I want to be treated like my job is important!" When Dana says they are supporting her and would do so for anyone else as well, Natalie stomps out saying, "I'm going home!" and strides out of the room toward her office. Although Dana intends her words to reassure Natalie, Natalie recognizes that Dana is actually responding to a change in Natalie's identity and status. Patrick's attempted assault has sexualized her, and, in the eyes of everyone around her, jarred her out of her professional status and into a position of weakness and helplessness. As a sexualized, feminized, "helpless" being, she is being treated with kid gloves and not as a competent professional.

This is further confirmed when she arrives at her office cubicle to find Jeremy asleep on the floor next to a cloth tablecloth with napkins, two dinner place settings, a bottle of wine, lit candles, and take out in boxes. When she awakens him and asks what he is doing, he explains that he wanted to do something nice for her because he cared about her. As they talk, her anger fades when she realizes that he is sleep-deprived because he has been staying up all night deleting the hate messages and death threats from her email so that she will be able to go about her job as usual. She sits down on the floor with him, and almost immediately he falls asleep with his head on her lap. He continues to sleep even while Natalie is recuperated into her professional status through the episode's ending dialogue with Dana, who has found her in her office:

Dana:	Natalie, you've been screwing up all week and it's got to stop. Got it?
Natalie:	(with a big smile) Yes ma'am.
Dana:	Good.
Natalie:	Thank you.
Dana:	You're welcome (with the song "Someone to Watch Over Me" playing in the background).

Both episodes about the locker room attempted sexual assault Natalie experiences are based on the real-life Lisa Olson case and like Olson's situation, the *Sports Night* episodes make it clear that "in the context not only of women's entrance into sports reporting but of the renegotiation of gender roles in society at large, the locker room becomes contested terrain. [And] if men are to reassert control of that terrain, the female sportswriter must be displaced from her position as critic of male performance and reassigned to the more 'appropriate' role of sexualized object."[39] In the case of both the Lisa Olson incident and Natalie's assault, male athletes respond to the threat posed by women sports journalists' power with sexual violence. It is not just women's presence in locker rooms that is threatening or problematic, as wives and girlfriends have been seen there after sports team title victories. Rather, it is the presence in locker rooms of women with the power to criticize male performance, like sports news reporters, which threatens traditional sexual hierarchy: "The most glorified sports in this society are those that emphasize physical domination and subjugation. In these sports, men's bodies, particularly as weapons of physical violence, become sites of power.... what makes Olson so threatening is the fact that she is clothed, both figuratively (by her professional status) and literally, in a domain where men, and their bodies are exposed and potentially vulnerable."[40]

Sports Night's fictionalized version of this real incident is, to be sure, a cautionary tale that reiterates the point we have made throughout this chapter—that women in sports news are eroding or even attacking dominant cultural practices and hence pose a threat to hegemonic masculinity. However, as a story-within-a-story this particular plot also enables the series to contain the cultural threat posed by representations of women's expert professional performance by recoding them as sexualized females. In part, the story of the attempted sexual assault of Natalie resexualizes her and recoups her femininity.

Perhaps where the real containment is most evident, however, is in the lack of narrative follow-through on the fallout from the assault on Natalie. The episode that followed raised the reality of the death threats and other violent acts male fans feel justified in making on women who challenge the sanctity of sports figures and their territory. It left the damage at that stage, however, with Natalie reconciled to her sleeping knight's attempts to protect her. Natalie's speech about why she did not want to press charges—that her career as a sports journalist would be severely imperiled—was unfortunately grounded in realism. Lisa Olson, the sports reporter whose story prompted this episode, ultimately fled to Australia. Fifteen years later in 2005, a professor at the University of Iowa critiqued the university athletic department's habit of painting the visiting team's locker room pink.[41] She protested that the color's association with girls, used to connote "sissy," both promoted homophobia by characterizing the opposing team as "weak, girly men" and also further marginalized women's sports by diminishing the stature of female athletes. She received numerous death threats from male fans.

Sports Night, as dramedy, is not required to present a realistic view of just how much backlash there is against women entering into positions of authority and control in regard to male sports, but the neat resolution of the plotline implies incorrectly that females crossing the locker room threshold is a problem resolved. Even as we view fictional and non-fictional women move into male-dominated professions, shows like *Sports Night* remind us that the potential for female subjugation through male physical force and sexual predation is always lurking in the background.

Conclusions

This analysis of the television series *Sports Night* illustrates the typically contradictory representations of transgressive women in television and American culture. The series' two female protagonists, Dana and Natalie, display technological, journalistic, and interpersonal competence in their positions of authority in the male-dominated world of sports news. Their love and knowledge of sports encode them, in contemporary American culture, as nonfeminine and, therefore, threatening to masculinized power, which defines sports, news, and technology as male domains. As a result, the narratives in which these protagonists live and move employ strategies of trivialization, sexualization, and infantilization to contain the threat that these professional women pose to hegemonic masculinity. Thus, the *Sports Night* text illustrates the difficulty that the cultural form/forum of television, and the culture which it reflects, still has in envisioning fully actualized, successfully professional, feminist yet feminine women, in positions of power and authority in the world of sports news.

Historically, sport and sports news have provided an arena for reaffirming male hegemony in the face of societal challenges and changes. As Messner, Duncan, and Jensen note, "in the 20th century, the institution of sport has provided men with a homosocial sphere of life through which they have bolstered the ideology of male superiority."[42] *Sports Night* challenges this ideology in several important ways, as the analysis in this chapter illustrates. It features two women who are knowledgeable about sports, sports journalism, and media technology, who generously but firmly mentor their colleagues, who fearlessly and determinedly pursue their lifelong occupational dreams of working in national sports journalism venues—producing the best, the highest quality, national television sports news show. And it features two women who do this in the face of friendly (and not-so-friendly) colleagues' doubts about their competence.

Through its narrative representations of these talented women's transgressions into the male-dominated spheres of sports and news, *Sports Night* speaks to viewers about larger cultural anxieties about women, power, and traditionally masculine domains. This analysis, while it focuses on *Sports Night*, reads the series as intimately related to the political and cultural contexts that surround it and that informed its creation. Its representations of these professional sports newswomen simultaneously pay homage to individual feminists' success in breaking into these masculine domains and contain the power and competence of these women by contradicting portrayals of their strength and power with infantilizing, sexualizing, and trivializing depictions. The latter narrative kernels allay male fears that the presence of women in these worlds remains the anomalous exception, not the norm. As perhaps even the show's narratological status as dramedy prohibits its messages of cultural transgression from being flagged too obviously, the serious messages are often about the trials of lives lived in a two-gendered world, while its hip humor deflects attention away from acts of gender violation.

Examining this series, with its fictional, though in many ways realistic, glimpse into the exhilarating pressure cooker of sports news,[43] is important political work because narrativized identities legitimate particular ideological formations. As Kristin Langellier explains, "in a most profound way, our stories tell us who we are and who we can—or cannot—be at both surface and deep level meaning.... a political function obtains for all narratives, whether or not they contain explicit political content."[44] The representations of Dana and Natalie are not neutral. They are at times empowering and affirming representations of the female agency feminist politics has struggled to enable. Yet these representations ultimately neither escape nor relegate the patriarchal imaginary to historical archives.

We tell stories in order to answer critical identity questions, including "Who can I be?"[45] *Sports Night* tells us that at the dawn of the twentieth-first century, in the masculine world of sports news as in other professional worlds, women remain "outsiders in the clubhouse."[46]

As we move into the analysis of women in combat in the next chapter, we can look again at one of the framing premises with which we began the analysis of *Sports Night*: that representations of women and women themselves frequently disarm the threat they pose to male dominance by undercutting their expressions of strength and competence with enactments of weakness and incompetence. This particular gendered negotiation of power is adamantly rejected by G.I. Jane, the cultural warrior we encounter in Chapter Six.

Notes

[1] Donald Sabo and Sue Curry Jansen, "Images of Men in Sports Media: The Social Reproduction of the Gender Order," *Men, Masculinity, and the Media* (ed.) Steve Craig (Newbury Park: Sage, 1992) 174.

[2] Margaret Carlisle Duncan and Michael A. Messner, "Gender in Televised Sports: News and Highlights Shows, 1989–2005" (ed.) Wayne Wilson (American Athletic Foundation of Los Angeles, 2005) 24. 20 July 2006 http://www.aafla.com/11pub/over_frmst.htm.

3 David Croteau and William Hoynes, "Men and the News Media; The Male Presence and Its Effect," *Men, Masculinity, and the Media* (ed.) Steve Craig (Newbury Park: Sage, 1992) 155.

4 Martin A. Lee and Norman Soloman, *Unreliable Sources: A Guide to Detecting Bias in News Media* (New York: Carol Publishing Group, 1990).

5 See Judith Marlane, *Women in Television News Revisited* (Austin: University of Texas Press, 1999); Robert Papper, and Michael Gerhard, "Mixed Results," *Communicator* (2002, July/August): 26–29; Robert Papper, "Women and Minorities: One Step Forward and Two Steps Back," *Communicator* (July/August 2003): 20–25; Liesbet van Zoonen, "One of the Girls: The Changing Gender of Journalism," *News, Gender and Power* (eds.) C. Carter, G. Branston, and S. Allan (New York: Routledge, 1998) 33–46.

⁶ Cynthia Carter and Linda Steiner, "Mapping the Contested Terrain of Media and Gender Research," *Critical Readings: Media and Gender* (eds.) Cynthia Carter & Linda Steiner (Maidenhead, Berkshire UK: Open University Press, 2004) 11–36.

⁷ Steve Weinstein, "*Sports Night* Aims and, For the Most Part, Hits Its Target," *Los Angeles Times*, (5 December 1998): F22.

⁸ Pamela J. Creedon (ed.), *Women in Mass Communications: Challenging Gender Values* (Newbury Park: Sage, 1989) 17.

⁹ Liesbet van Zoonen, *Feminist Media Studies* (London and Thousand Oaks, CA: Sage, 1994) 53.

¹⁰ Patricia F. Phalen, "'Pioneers, Girlfriends, and Wives': An Agenda for Research on Women and the Organizational Culture of Broadcasting," *Journal of Broadcasting and Electronic Media* (Spring 2000): 239.

¹¹ van Zoonen, 1994 7.

¹² van Zoonen, 1994 54.

¹³ See, e.g., Susan Birrell and Cheryl L. Cole (eds.), *Women, Sport, and Culture* (Champaign, IL: Human Kinetics, 1994); Mary Jo Kane and Helen Jefferson Lensky, "Media Treatment of Female Athletes: Issues of Gender and Sexualities," *MediaSport* (ed.) Lawrence A. Wenner (London: Routledge, 1998) 186–201; Michael A. Messner, Margaret Carlisle Duncan, and Kerry Jensen, "Separating the Men from the Girls: The Gendered Language of Televised Sports." *Gender and Society,* 7 (1993): 121–137; Michael A. Messner, Michelle Dunbar, and Darnell Hunt, "The Televised Sports Manhood Formula," *Critical Readings; Sport, Culture and the Media* (ed.) David Rowe (Maidenhead, Berkshire UK: Open University Press, 2004) 229–245.

¹⁴ Margaret Carlisle Duncan and Michael A. Messner, "The Media Image of Sport and Gender," *MediaSport* (ed.) Lawrence A. Wenner (London: Routledge, 1998) 170.

¹⁵ Lawrence A. Wenner (ed.), *MediaSport* (London: Routledge, 1998) 132.

¹⁶ Dennis K. Mumby and Carole Spitzack, "Ideology and Television News: A Metaphoric Analysis of Political Stories," *Central States Speech Journal* 34 (1983): 162–171.

¹⁷ Walter J. Ong, *Fighting for life: Contest, Sexuality, and Consciousness.* Paperback ed. (Amherst: University of Massachusetts Press, 1981/1989) 20.

¹⁸ Leah R. Vande Berg, "Dramedy: *Moonlighting* as an Emergent Generic Hybrid," *Communication Studies,* 40 (1989): 13–28.

¹⁹ Richard Furstman, "Their Championship Season: We Go Inside *Sports Night*—A Lightning-Fast Front-Runner for Rookie of the Year," *TV Guide*, 47.13 (27 March-2 April 1999): 16.

²⁰ Nancy Franklin, "The Sporting News: Embattled Networks Need to Give Themselves a Pep Talk," *The New Yorker*, 74.41 (11 January 1999): 93.

²¹ Tad Friend, "Laugh Riot: What Happens When a Newcomer Tries to Bend the Rules of the Most Venerable and Conservative of Cultural Forms—The American Sitcom?" *The New Yorker*, 73 (28 September 1998): 76–86.

²² Furstman 16.

²³ Matt Roush, "The Best Show You're Not Watching: This Year's Honoree is *Sports Night*, a Comedy that Continually Scores," *TV Guide*, 48.11 (11–17 March 2000): 15.

²⁴ Furstman 16.

²⁵ Rick Kushman, "What is Ahead for *Sports Night*?" *Sacramento Bee* (14 March 2000): G-1, G-5.

²⁶ Roush 14–21.

²⁷ Furstman 14–19.

²⁸ Weinstein F22.

²⁹ Mariah Burton Nelson, *The Stronger Women Get, The More Men Love Football* (New York: Harcourt Brace, 1994).

[30] Kathy E. Kram, *Mentoring at Work: Developmental Relationships in Organizational Life* (Glenview, IL: Scott Foresman, 1985); Terri A. Scandura and Belle Rose Ragins, "The Effects of Sex and Gender Role Orientation on Mentorship in Male-Dominated Occupations," *Journal of Vocational Behavior* 43.3 (1993): 251–265.

[31] Kram 22.

[32] Kram 28.

[33] See Seymour Chatman, *Story and Discourse: Narrative Structure in Fiction and Film* (Ithaca, N.Y.: Cornell University Press, 1978).

[34] Tamala M. Edwards, "Flying Solo: Single by Choice." *Time* (2000, 28 August: 47–53); Jane Ganahl, "Embracing a Contented Life: Single Women Pass on the Idea that Marriage Cures All." *San Francisco Chronicle*, Sec. E (Living), (2004, 4 January): E2, E10.

[35] Kevin Mannix, "Kiam: 'She's a Classic Bitch,'" *Boston Herald* (1990, September): 24, 74.

[36] Mary Jo Kane and Lisa J. Disch, "Sexual Violence and the Reproduction of Male Power in the Locker Room: The 'Lisa Olson Incident.'" *Sociology of Sport Journal*, 10.4 (1993): 332.

[37] Leigh Montville, "A Season of Torment," *Sports Illustrated* (1991, 13 May): 60–65.

[38] Cathy Henkel, "Listen Carefully to Olson's Side," *Association for Women in Sports Media (AWSM) Newsletter* (1993, February): 1–3.

[39] Kane and Disch 333.

[40] Kane and Disch 347.

[41] Piper Fogg, "Professor at U. of Iowa Draws Death Threats After Objecting to Pink Locker Room for Visiting Teams," *Chronicle of Higher Education* 26 September 2005. 6 September 2005 http://chronicle.com/daily/2005/09/2005092607n.htm.

[42] Messner, Duncan, and Jensen 121.

[43] Weinstein F22.

[44] Kristin M. Langellier, "Personal Narratives: Perspectives on Theory and Research," *Text & Performance Quarterly*, 9 (1989): 267.

[45] See, among others, Anthony Giddens, *Modernity and Self-Identity* (Cambridge: Polity Press, 1991); Kevin D. Murray, "The Construction of Identity in the Narratives of Romance and Comedy," *Texts of Identity* (eds.) John Shotter and Kenneth J. Gergen (London: Sage, 1989) 176–205.

[46] Todd W. Crosset, *Outsiders in the Clubhouse: The World of Women's Professional Golf* (Albany: SUNY Press, 1995).

Chapter Six

It's a Dick Thing:
Ambivalent Coding of American Female
Soldiers in Gulf War Narratives

Prologue: Thelma and Louise as Cultural Warriors

In 1991, director Ridley Scott and screenwriter Callie Khouri revamped the rape-revenge film narrative through the mythos of the classic American western film.[1] The wildly popular *Thelma and Louise* caused a noteworthy schism in popular reviews at the time of its release, and remains one of the more contested film narratives in feminist film criticism.[2] The film plot is driven by the action of two female characters. Early in the plot, Louise shoots to death a male sexual predator (Harlan) who has attacked her friend, Thelma. The women flee the scene of the shooting and head for the Mexican border with various law enforcement agencies in hot pursuit. On their journey together (in a 1966 Thunderbird convertible), the women discuss whether they should turn themselves in and plead for clemency. Thelma argues that they were justified in killing Harlan. "Who's gonna believe us?" says Louise. "We don't live in that kind of a world."

American viewing audiences know that Louise is probably right. In the story, Thelma carelessly accepted drinks and dances with a smooth-talking stranger (Harlan), against the advice of the more cautious Louise and the local cocktail waitress. Even more significant, Louise shot Harlan *after* the imminent danger of attack had passed. Enthusiastic viewers in the original screening audiences of 1991 cheered when Louise put a gun to Harlan's head, aggressively interrupting the sexual assault on Thelma in the bar parking lot. When she and a weeping Thelma are a safe distance from Harlan, Louise scolds him. This display of female power enrages Harlan and though he is fearful enough of Louise's gun to stay put, with his hands in the air, he taunts the women verbally: "I should 'a gone ahead and fucked her," he sneers. Louise's eyes narrow, and she hisses, "What did you say?" Mis-calculating the lethal situation, and not realizing (along with the audience) that he is facing a rape trauma victim with a loaded gun, Harlan enunciates his last three words on earth with all the contempt he can muster: "Suck my cock." Louise fires the gun, Harlan falls dead against a parked car, and Thelma gasps in disbelief, "Oh my god, Louise, you shot him!" As if in a trance, Louise lowers the gun and takes a step closer to Harlan's body. "You watch your mouth, mister," she mutters to the corpse.

Audiences in 1991 gasped aloud, along with Thelma. This is the breathtakingly transgressive moment in the film; an enraged female wielding a deadly weapon breaks a fundamental rule of masculine fair play, particularly in the context of the Hollywood western. She shoots a man "out of play"—as much for what he said, as for what he had done. In effect, harassing gender speech is met with lethal force. Astute viewers can predict with some confidence that Thelma and Louise cannot get away with this magnitude of genre and gender transgression. More hopeful viewers can give themselves up to the immediate pleasures of the unthinkable: Kill the bastard, because he is a rapist (physical assault) and a soul killer (verbal assault) and because this is (our) cinematic fantasy. Run away; break the rules; talk back, look back, shoot back, fight back, refuse all offers of rehabilitation and reconciliation. Drop us a note when you get to Mexico.

In the end, both sets of audience expectations are realized or dashed, depending on the point of view of the viewer. Cornered by the F.B.I. at the edge of the Grand Canyon, Thelma and Louise choose certain death over institutional incarceration. Holding hands, joyous in their decision, they drive off the ledge. As the vintage Thunderbird shoots out over the iconic chasm, the shot dissolves into freeze frame animation. Like the male characters Butch Cassidy and the Sundance Kid, the female protagonists escape realist death and transcend to the mythic status of folk hero(ines). Thelma and Louise never make it to Mexico, but they never hit the bottom of the canyon, either.

The marked ambivalence of the film ending is born out in polarizing popular and academic reviews, as exemplified by Peter Travers for *Rolling Stone*: "are they feminist martyrs or bitches from hell?"[3] The debate over the film spans nearly fifteen years and a wide range of issues. Early writing about the film almost always produced binary questions: Is this film feminist or anti-feminist? Is this film good for women or bad for women? Does this film represent men fairly or unfairly? Should women use violence to protect themselves? Express themselves? Can female characters occupy masculine roles without becoming "masculinist" or "phallic"? Is female masculinity a good thing or a bad thing? Cultural ambivalence about female characterization through gendered violence and the dualist criticism produced in response to it continue to this day. In a 2002 article about recent films where women under duress use lethal force, *Time* magazine's Richard Corliss asks, "Is playing victim-heroes a victory for women?"[4]

Argumentative Frame

Our interest in *Thelma and Louise* is threefold: First, we are struck by its ambivalent structure and the remarkably polarized responses it evoked. We view ambivalence as productive rather than reductive; in that sense, our perspective is Foucauldian. Ambivalent texts are structured through complex contradictions or incompatible possibilities. Hegemony cannot unite the narrative, but neither can resistance overcome hegemony. The text is not simply "polysemic," enabling a range of readings and argumentative claims.[5] Nor is it "polyvalent," enabling oppositional slippage while favoring the pleasures of dominant reading positions.[6] Rather, it is ambivalent—capable of sustaining incompatible readings and perspectives, and refusing to adjudicate for or against clear ideological choices. The realist rupture at the end of the film suspends Thelma and Louise in prolonged liminality; they hover, in fatal rebellion, over the yawning cavern.[7] At the same time, they never make it to "Mexico"—the imaginary space of liberty and autonomy. Audiences of *Thelma and Louise* are not offered the imaginary possibilities of a beautiful beach in a quaint fishing village where two transgressive Americans might live out their lives peacefully and productively, like male protagonists Andy and Red in *Shawshank Redemption*. Moreover, the text of *Thelma and Louise* offers no definitive answer to the central dualist question: Have the female transgressors been contained or liberated? One can argue, quite convincingly, to either conclusion. This ambivalence probably accounts, in part, for the binary patterns in reviews of the film. Seeking an alternative to dualist entrenchment in feminist media criticism, we propose that one of the rhetorical functions of ambivalence is to express or maintain the undecidability of complex cultural problems.

Our second point of interest in *Thelma and Louise* concerns its director, Ridley Scott, and his involvement with female character transgressors of mythic stature (*Alien* and *Thelma and Louise*). Six years after *Thelma and Louise*, he directed *G.I. Jane* (1997), one of three films produced about American female soldiers in combat or combat training. In *G.I. Jane*, a transgressive female soldier played by Demi Moore appropriates the sexually harassing speech of Thelma's male rapist. "*Suck my dick*," she says to the training officer who attempts and fails to break her spirit with sexual violence. We believe Scott's manipulation of this parallel fragment of sexual violence is significant, and we will explore this in some detail later in this chapter.

Third, we view *Thelma and Louise* as prefatory for examination of three fictional films about American female soldiers in combat or military training programs. *Courage Under Fire*, released in 1996, was the first film to address the issue of women in combat situations. *G.I. Jane* (1997) explores the problems and possibilities for including women in elite special operations units. *The General's*

Daughter (1999), released shortly after The Citadel was opened to female cadets, addresses the very real problem of sexual violence against women in military academies. The connection to *Thelma and Louise* is twofold: (1) the relationship between equality and the gendering of spheres and bodies; and (2) the relationship between westerns and war dramas.

Concerning equality and the public sphere, Thelma and Louise play out a fantasy of violent resistance to gender and sexual oppression. As fictional characters, they invade the sphere of the western film genre—a cultural space where fictional male protagonists traditionally have used justifiable violence to protect liberty and property.[8] Thelma and Louise are hyper-aware of the impediments of female embodiment, even as they appropriate the guns, speech acts, plot action, and self-determination of the western. The film implies that oppression and injustice *always* are gendered and sexed for female characters. In other words, *Thelma and Louise* demonstrates how American concepts of equality and justice are gender- and sex biased. Mythic suspension of the transgressive females over the Grand Canyon suggests uncertainty about solutions to the problem of gender and sex inequalities. Similarly, each of the three stories about women in the military are structured by and through issues of gender and sex inequalities and ambivalence about the possibilities of "equal" partnering in the field of combat.

Concerning the relationship between the western and war dramas, both story formats provide a symbolic-moral environment where inevitable confrontations are worked out through violence. The western examines the clash between nature and civilization. The military drama examines confrontations between and among nation states, attaching the possibility of virtue to violence. Women seldom play dominant agents in either of these story categories precisely because of the violence and death. Women have been represented, paradoxically, both as forces of nature (unruly, base, irrational) and as forceful purveyors of civilization (life givers and stabilizing influences). "She" needs to be controlled and protected; she is life-giver, civilizer, and the reason men fight wars. When women pick up the gun and engage in struggle, violence, and death, ambivalence is generated. In other words, ambivalence is endemic to any narrative vehicle that positions heroic women to struggle violently and face brutal death.

We find these elements of gender transgression in each of the three films about women in combat. Each film narrative tells the story of cultural trauma consequent to female invasion of that most masculine of spheres, the province of the combat soldier. Each film confronts the viewer with representations of heroic female violence, pain and death. We argue that each film presents a structured ambivalence about female soldiering, suggesting the "undecidability" of the issue. To facilitate this argument, we trace the articulation of cultural anxieties about the intersection of equality, bodies, and spheres across the three films. We begin, however, by tracing these issues through the *realpolitik* discussions about women in the military, focusing most specifically on women and the draft and American cultural ambivalence about gender and civic obligation.

Public Argument, Civic Obligation and Gender Ambivalence

The 1991 Persian Gulf War marked the first time significant numbers of American female soldiers (41,000) served near combat zones or in combat roles.[9] Military women served in Operation Desert Storm as gunship pilots and crew, and as ground forces support units in proximity to combat zones. The American public and the Congress were impressed with female performance in this limited engagement.[10] Women persevered with skill and courage in a situation where no clear demarcation existed between "combat" and "support."[11] Moreover, the dominant role of technology in this war dictated that brute strength was no longer the primary defining characteristic of a competent soldier.[12] In the wake of this demonstration of female competence, the Congress quickly acted to reconsider and overturn the 1948 prohibition against women in combat for female pilots.[13]

In 1993, the Defense Department lifted most restrictions imposed on female soldiers in aerial and naval combat, opening about 30,000 jobs for women. President Clinton asked the Congress to ban the law prohibiting women on surface warships; Congress complied. In 1994, the Clinton administration officially lifted the "risk rule," permitting women to serve in hostile zones. By mid-decade, approximately ninety percent of all military positions were opened to women. Restricted service for women was, and is, limited only to submarines, most infantry ground forces (armor and artillery divisions), and special operations forces.[14]

The apparent ease with which women moved into combat positions in the 1990s belies the tumult in the 1970s and early 1980s regarding women and the draft. The Equal Rights Amendment failed to achieve ratification in 1982 in large part because of fears about drafting women into the military.[15] The Moral Majority was founded in 1979 to advance a conservative political agenda, fueled in part by a determination to block the constitutional amendment which many Americans believed would conscript women into military service and ultimately into combat. Feminist activists and scholars were ambivalent over women and military service. Historian Linda Kerber notes that "[f]eminists and liberals...rarely supported either registration or the draft."[16] On the other hand, Judy Goldsmith, representing the National Organization for Women, testified before Congress in 1980 that military conscription should include women. She argued that women would not be viewed as first-class citizens until they shouldered the burden of military duty. She argued, too, that only with equal obligation would women in the military receive equal pay and equal opportunity for training, advancement and decision-making.[17] Goldsmith was not the only influential public voice to argue that equal rights implied equal obligation.

In his 1980 State of the Union address, Jimmy Carter argued in favor of a "universal mandatory draft registration."[18] In the Senate debates over this issue, Senator Nancy Kassebaum (R-Kansas) argued vigorously in favor of the president's proposal: "I believe it [universal registration] is to show a national determination. It should require that both young men and women register. It should be universal...It should be something we regard as a civic duty and part of the political process of this country."[19] Senator Jake Garn (R-Utah) articulated the anxiety undergirding the opposition to universal registration: "How ridiculous can we get when we cannot recognize anymore...that there are basic fundamental physical and biological differences between men and women?...How far do we carry this ridiculous game of equality, on the basis of equity?"[20] Ultimately, the Senate defeated Kassebaum's amendment 40–51 on June 10, 1980. But the issue was not dead. It would take a Supreme Court decision to put the matter to rest, at least for a time.

President Carter's interest in universal registration hinged on factors other than gender equity. In November of 1979, Muslim militants in Teheran, Iran, took fifty American citizens hostage and repelled Carter's efforts to rescue them. The specter of failure and disgrace lingering from the Vietnam War continued with the two-year Iran hostage crisis. In February of 1979, U.S. Ambassador Adolph Dubs was abducted and killed in Kabul, Afghanistan, by Soviet backed rebels. Soviet troops invaded Afghanistan in December of 1979. As the international crisis deepened, Carter assessed the All Volunteer Force military, set in place by Richard Nixon in 1973.[21] Dismayed by the numbers and fearing a middle-eastern confrontation with Russia, Carter asked the Congress to re-activate registration; Joint Resolution 521 passed and registration was set to begin on July 21, 1980. However, a three-judge panel in the Third Circuit ruled that a male-only draft violated the constitutional rights of American men, under the fifth and fourteenth amendments, and registration was halted abruptly. The Justice Department immediately filed for a stay. Reasoning that the Supreme Court likely would agree to hear arguments, Justice Brennan issued the stay and registration of males commenced the summer of 1980.

Rostker v. Goldberg (1981)[22] was the culmination of over a decade of arguments about the equity of male-only draft registration. Though Nixon had ended the draft in 1973, the legal wrangling continued for nearly a decade between the Justice Department and opponents to male-only draft registration.

President Carter's anxiety over international tensions and the All Volunteer Military revived the public argument in 1980. At the same time, Carter's goal of gender equity was not without significant precedent in American society. The 1970s had seen important Supreme Court action supporting gender neutrality under the law. *Reed v. Reed* (1971) established that state laws must not explicitly discriminate on the basis of gender.[23] *Taylor v. Louisiana* (1975) determined that women are equally obligated with men to serve on juries.[24] *Rostker v. Goldberg* addressed whether women were equally obligated with men to register for the draft. The case revolved around three questions: Is the male-only draft discriminatory? Are there good reasons for exempting women? Who should decide whether women should be required to register for the draft? The majority opinion reversed the Third Circuit ruling: "[W]e conclude that Congress acted well within its constitutional authority when it authorized the registration of men, and not women, under the Military Selective Service Act. The decision of the District Court holding otherwise is accordingly reversed."[25]

The majority opinion took the form of a classic rhetorical syllogism:

Major Premise: "Congress determined that any future draft...would be characterized by a need for combat troops."[26] *The purpose of the draft is to raise combat troops.*

Minor Premise: "The restrictions on the participation of women in combat...are statutory."[27] *Women may not participate in combat, as per the 1948 ban.*

Conclusion: "Men and women, because of the combat restrictions on women, are simply not similarly situated for purposes of a draft or registration for a draft."[28] *Therefore, women should not be drafted.*

The majority opinion explicitly and flatly sidestepped the issue of gender equity, arguing that the District Court's concern with constitutionality was "beside the point."[29] Moreover, they reasoned, drafting women would unduly burden the military by forcing the armed services to train soldiers "who could not be used in combat."[30] In sum, the majority opinion found that while the male-only draft discriminates, it is not unconstitutional.

Justices White, Marshall, and Brennan dissented. White questioned the legitimacy of the majority claim that the 80,000 positions filled by women could continue to be filled through volunteerism. Marshall and Brennan, joining in their dissent, articulated the issue they believe the majority sidestepped: "The Court today places its imprimatur on one of the most potent remaining public expressions of 'ancient canards about the proper role of women'...It upholds a statute that requires males but not females to register for the draft, and which thereby categorically excludes women from a fundamental civic obligation."[31]

The cultural ambivalence embedded in the public arguments about women and the draft tangles the interests and anxieties of three institutional groups. First, the Supreme Court decision codified sex-based discrimination based on essentialist presumptions about men and women. Second, most feminists and liberals appeared untroubled by the legal, civic and philosophical conundrum posed by the ruling. Third, within a decade, the Congress would reverse itself on the dangers of combat for women and the risks for the nation of using female soldiers in combat zones. But none of these institutional strongholds could have foreseen a catastrophic terror attack on the United States in September of 2001, nor the protracted war to follow. As of May 2006, approximately 60,000 female soldiers have had active duty roles in Iraq. Since the war began, fifty-two female soldiers have been killed, over 300 have been wounded, and three have been taken captive.[32] Two of the captives (Jessica Lynch and Shoshana Johnson) were released; Pfc. Lori Piestewa died in captivity. By comparison, five female soldiers died in the 1991 Gulf War and eight nurses died in the Vietnam War.

In the years since *Rostker v. Goldberg*, four critical questions have arisen in public debates on the issues: (1) Now that female soldiers have moved into combat zones, are men and women more "similarly situated"? (2) Have the biological differences between men and women been ameliorated by technology and combat training? (3) Have women moved smoothly and successfully into military academies and combat zones? (4) Does the American public accept the realities of female casualties in combat?

We believe the answer to all of these questions is a resounding "no." The fault, however, lies not with women and their capabilities, but rather with longstanding institutional sexism and misogyny in the American military. Data collected by the Congress and the American military (inspired by the pressures of investigative journalism) demonstrate that women face disturbing risks for sexual harassment and assault in the contemporary American military. The contemporary military is a hostile workplace for women, and in *that* sense, women and men are not "similarly situated." Moreover, there are clear indications of American cultural squeamishness about the injury and death of female personnel in war zones. We move first to an examination of male-to-female sexual misconduct in the military.

Storming the Last(ing) Bastions: Rape and Sexual Harassment

When flight surgeon Rhonda Cornum was captured, held eight days, and raped by Iraqis during Desert Storm, the American press was relatively quiet. Major Cornum received much more attention, however, when the press covered the captures of Jessica Lynch and Lori Piestewa in March of 2003. When asked what it was like to be *the* rape victim of the 1991 Gulf War, Cornum replied somewhat tersely, "It's just another bad thing that can happen to you." She pointed out that male soldiers also could be sexually assaulted.[33] Pfc. Lori Piestewa died in captivity, but the dramatically staged "rescue" of Pfc. Lynch and her subsequent national saga seemed to mesmerize the American public for months. Constructed narratives about Lynch epitomized the cultural anxieties Americans have about female vulnerability to sexual assault by "enemy" forces. However, data collected by military medical officers and the Department of Defense indicate that American female soldiers have more to fear from their male counterparts than from the male combatants of Iraq, Kuwait, and Afghanistan.[34]

In 2003, *The Denver Post* successfully exposed a decade of sexual abuse of female cadets at the Colorado Springs Air Force academy.[35] The newspaper's coverage prompted appointment of a congressional commission to investigate allegations of abuse. The results of the inquiry were breathtaking. The Fowler Commission reported 142 allegations of sexual harassment and/or assault at the academy over a ten-year period. Moreover, the commission estimated that eighty percent of sexual harassment and assaults were never reported. Cases that go unreported generally are the consequence of female fears of retaliation and career sabotage by fellow soldiers and commanders.[36] The commission also reported that twenty to twenty-five percent of all male cadets stated that they did not want women in the academy. Finally, the commission established the embarrassing fact that commanding officers and the Congress had known about the abuse allegations but had done nothing about them.[37]

In 2004, *The Denver Post* published a series of stories about American female soldiers returning from Iraq.[38] Between October 2002 and November 2003, roughly sixty thousand (59,742) women served in the Iraq theatre. Thirty-seven women returning from duty in Iraq and Kuwait during that time "sought sexual trauma counseling" as a result of American male sexual violence.[39] In total, there were 112 reports of male-to-female "sexual misconduct" over an eighteen-month period, with 86 of those reports coming from within the Army.[40] Donald Rumsfeld "ordered a senior-level inquiry" into the allegations and on February 25, 2004, "Senate Democrats and Republicans sharply questioned the Pentagon's top personnel official and four four-star officers."[41] The congressional inquiry revealed that female soldiers experiencing sexual assault were offered little or no medical attention, no rape kits, and no counseling. Investigations into allegations were said to be shoddy, the alleged aggressors were not prosecuted and some of the assault victims experienced retaliation.[42]

Donald Rumsfeld signaled his disapproval of such embarrassing information in a communication to David Chu, the Pentagon's Undersecretary for

Personnel and Readiness: "Sexual assault will not be tolerated in the Department of Defense."[43] In March 2005, the Department of Defense issued a new policy for dealing with sexual crimes in the military. Under the new policy, assault victims may seek confidential medical aid and counseling before the crime is reported to commanding officers and investigators.[44] The Pentagon released a report through their Office of the Inspector General verifying that over "half of all women and eleven percent of all men enrolled in military academies reported some form of sexual harassment."[45]

These incidences of male-to-female sexual assault did not spring from an historical vacuum. The sexual abuse scandals in the American military are cultural legends: the Navy Tailhook debacle in 1991; the Army drill sergeant scandal in 1996; the scandal at Sheppard Air Force Base in 2002; gender discrimination in disciplinary actions taken against males and females for committing adultery; sexual abuse and discrimination allegations in military academies from 1976 to present; and so forth. Some military women believe that the abuse stems from systematic bias built into military academy training. Captain Rosemary Mariner, U.S. Navy, retired, was the first woman to fly tactical jet fighter planes (though not in combat). Asked by National Public Radio in 2002 to offer perspective on the pattern of sexual discrimination and abuse in the American military, she replied:

> Back in the 70s and the early 80s, we often felt that young men went to the Navel Academy and were taught there not to respect women, that that was something they actually learned at the academy, that they didn't come into the institution like that.[46]

The American military is still a hostile workplace for women, and in that regard, women and men are not "similarly situated." Current research indicates that women in the American military are at double the civilian risk for rape. Women in the military are four times more likely to be raped if their commanding officer tolerates sexual harassment in any form.[47] Technology and combat training have made it possible for female soldiers to serve in forward support units, but the danger of sexual assault by American male military personnel puts them at double the risk of their male counterparts. Military academies are not yet successfully de-segregated, and cannot be so long as military leaders fail "to face the facts of full gender integration."[48]

Female Casualties and Public Panics

Sex discrimination and sexual violence against American women by American men are not the only disquieting elements of female soldiering. Female casualties, especially combat-related injuries and deaths, create anxiety and uncertainty. As of March 2006, fifty-three female soldiers have been killed in the Iraq

War, out of a total of over 2,000 American deaths. Lori Piestewa was the first female casualty on March of 2003. Kimberly Hampton was the first female pilot killed, in an OH-58 helicopter.[49] In June 2005, four female soldiers were killed in a single attack—another "first." 1st Lt. Dawn Halfaker and Specialist Danielle Green were two of the first female soldiers to lose limbs. Halfaker lost an arm and Green lost her hand and forearm. They were featured in a front-page story for the *New York Times* on April 10, 2005. Photographs featured Halfaker playing basketball with one arm and both women with their respective prosthetic devices. The story focused on both women's pre-military collegiate athletic careers and post-injury struggles to overcome pain and disability.[50] The *Washington Post* reported that as of May 2005 "tens of thousands of female troops have served in Iraq, with dozens killed, hundreds wounded and some decorated for valor under fire."[51]

As late as January 2004, aside from the Jessica Lynch saga, relatively little had been said in the American press about female casualties. "It doesn't seem to be a big deal," said Navy Capt. Lory Manning, head of Women's Research and Education Institute.[52] But by May of 2005, the House was embroiled in rancorous debate over the issue of women and combat. House Armed Services Committee Chair Duncan Hunter proposed a measure that would bar women from serving in forward support positions—estimated by the Army to be about 21,925 jobs.[53] Hunter and Republican members of the subcommittee proposing the measure claimed that the Pentagon had violated the 1994 statutory limits on women in combat. The limits stipulate that women may serve only in brigade-size units.[54] According to the subcommittee, the Army in January "sent to Iraq a reconfigured brigade of the 3rd Infantry Division that was smaller and more deployable…which included 31 women in combat-support jobs."[55] Moreover, according to the subcommittee, the Army failed to notify Congress about this change in job status for female soldiers, another violation of the 1994 law. The Army conceded that re-organization strategies indeed included mixed-sex "forward support companies" that were "designed to be located together with combat battalions so they could provide them directly with supplies, maintenance and other support."[56] However, high-ranking Army officials insisted that highly mobile forward support troops did not violate the "spirit" of the 1994 limitations and were necessary given falling recruitment, a protracted war, and the unconventional terms of engagement in the Iraq War.[57]

House debate and public responses to the issue fell along clear partisan lines. Conservative House Republicans, special interest groups and conservative media organizations argued that the Army had usurped the authority of the Congress and had dabbled in dangerous political correctness. Writing for *Human Events,* Elaine Donnelly claimed that "congressional feminists and their media allies became stereotypically hysterical" over Representative Hunter's efforts to rein in the Pentagon and protect female soldiers.[58] The *National Review* argued that the Army was guilty of "social engineering" which, columnist Mackubin Thomas Owens claimed, ultimately would weaken the effectiveness of the American military.[59] Owens's arguments echoed the 1970s and 1980s anxieties and fears about women and the draft: First, the presence of women undermines unit cohesion. Second, physical differences between males and females lead to unfair double standards. And, third, mixed-sex units lead to "unleash[ed] eros" among troops.[60] Owens's arguments are consistent with arguments published by The *National Review* in 2002, under the editorship of Kate O'Beirne, and in cooperation with Elaine Donnelly, President of the conservative Center for Military Readiness. O'Beirne and Donnelly argued at the beginning of the Iraq War that women should not be exposed to combat positions because they lack the physical capabilities for combat, they disrupt unit cohesion, and they are vulnerable to sexual assault by enemy forces. In response to this most recent flap, Donnelly maintained her conservative stance: "Women do not have an equal opportunity to survive or to help fellow soldiers survive in a close-combat environment."[61]

Support for women in combat support units came from the Army, male and female military veterans, a prominent special interest organization, House Democrats and two recognized newspapers. Supporters argued that women are already serving in combat conditions in Iraq, that military resources are stretched to the limit, that limitations on female jobs discourages women from joining the military and that limiting exposure to combat puts limits on female achievement.[62] Female spokespersons were especially adamant in their assertions. Air Force Brig. General Wilma Vaught put the matter bluntly: "If you're assigned to a job that requires that you deploy and be in harm's way, that's part of being in the military."[63] Representative Heather Wilson, Air Force veteran and, until 2005, member of the House Armed Services Committee, was equally blunt:

> I think it's offensive. We've got women thousands of miles from home doing danger-
> ous work and for the first time in history the Congress is going to pass a law restricting
> how the Army can assign its soldiers? But not all of its soldiers—just women. What are
> they thinking?[64]

In 2002, Wilson had responded angrily to Donnelly and O'Beirne:

> ...how far do they want to roll it [female job and rank] back? Lt. Col. as top rank? 2%
> [of the military]? If so there's no way that we currently can defend this country.[65]

Karen Johnson, Executive Vice-President of the National Organization for Women, dismissed the concerns of conservative voices: "it [is] ridiculous to think women in war should be shielded from danger."[66] "You are sending a message that women can't do this job," said House Representative Loretta Sanchez.[67]

The matter was resolved (more or less) when Representative Hunter withdrew language from the measure specifically banning female soldiers from smaller modular brigades. However, as part of a compromise with House Democrats, he and his supporters left in a three-part mandate: First, Secretary of Defense Rumsfeld must review the 1994 policy on women and combat. Second, the Pentagon must continue to study the matter and issue a report to Congress by March 2006. And third, the Pentagon must notify Congress sixty legislative days before changing the status of any job position for female soldiers.[68] Ultimately, Rumsfeld's opposition to the measure probably helped motivate Hunter to withdraw the ban. Significantly, however, on June 23, 2005, General George Casey, Jr., the top U.S. commander in Iraq, advised the House Armed Services Committee that American women should not be placed in more danger than they currently face. He recommended against moving American female soldiers into the infantry. This is a significant enforcement of the 1994 regulations, especially since failing recruitment figures and the continuing war in Iraq have stretched the American military to the limits of operation.[69]

The issue of American women in combat is far from settled. The *Washington Post* and *The New York Times* published editorials in response to the most recent flare-up suggesting that the time has come for gender and sexual equity in the burdens of military duty. The *Post* argued that it makes little sense to exclude women from forward support positions. More significantly, the editorial questioned whether excluding women from combat makes any sense:

> Even if the prohibition on women in combat still makes sense—*which isn't clear to us*— why apply that ban in a way that limits the military's flexibility when its ranks are already stretched? Why, when the services are having trouble recruiting, tell women that their options will narrow as the Army modernizes? Since female soldiers aren't being kept out of harm's way in any event, why not let them perform the jobs for which they trained?[70] (emphasis added)

The *New York Times* offered the following (incendiary) advice in its editorial:

> [R]ecruits should be attracted by allowing enlistees to fulfill their entire service obligation through four years of active duty and ending senseless and offensive restrictions on openly gay people serving in the military and on women serving in combat.[71]

Over a thirty-year period, *realpolitik* arguments about equal rights and responsibilities with regard to military duty have revolved around two seemingly intractable questions: When it comes to military service and combat duty, are men and women equal, despite their physical differences? Do we want them to be? When these *realpolitik* questions are mediated through the dreamscapes of popular American cinema, the political morphs into a spectacle of primal anxieties and desires. In popular cinema, the same irresolvable questions or issues emerge, albeit framed through melodrama, mystery, tragedy and pornography.

(1) Will women be viewed as "prey" in a fully integrated military? Conversely, will men take undue risks to protect their female comrades?
(2) Will male soldiers trust and/or follow their female comrades in the field of battle? Are doublestandards necessary? Permissible?
(3) What happens to the publicly imagined female body when she performs soldiering? Will she become grotesque? Mutilated? Undesirable?
(4) What will happen to gender identity if women talk, fight, command and die "like" men?

Our next section deals with the three films produced in the 1990s dealing explicitly with women and combat duty, and the way they pose and answer each of the four questions. Each film expresses cultural ambivalence about women and civic obligation, sexual equality, and gendered hierarchies in the military. In a broadly cultural sense, each film expresses anxieties about female bodies in the geo-political public sphere as soldiers engaged with male cohorts and enemies. In that sense, the films explore the fluid intersections of gendered performance space and embodied performance in the context of nation states and war. To varying extents, each film expresses deep cultural anxieties specific to changing gender norms and soldiering. We begin with *G.I. Jane* because it presents the only female characterization with substantial narrative agency. We emphasize the significance of the relative paucity of cinematic representation of female soldiers, let alone females in combat.

It's a Dick (and Jane) Thing

In 1997, six years after the operation Desert Storm in the Persian Gulf, Ridley Scott directed and produced *G.I. Jane*. The story line is driven by Naval intelligence officer Lt. Jordan O'Neill, who beats the odds to become the first female Navy SEAL. (The scenario is utterly fictional, of course, since American women may not serve in special operation units.) In the story, no one expects O'Neill to succeed. The washout rate for SEALS is sixty percent for males, let alone for women, and O'Neill insists that she be evaluated by the same performance standards as the men.[72] O'Neill literally is beset by every character in the film. The Master Chief tries to break her; her male cohorts despise and distrust her; her fiancé pulls back from supporting her; the female senator who brokered the opportunity betrays her for political gain; other females in the film cannot fathom her commitment to this punishing program. "Do you ask the men why they stay in the program?" she snaps at a female medic who is baffled by O'Neill's determination.

About two-thirds of the way through the story, O'Neill finally is able to change the attitudes of her male cohorts and commanding officers during a particularly brutal training exercise. The SEALS trainees are put through a mock exercise to test their endurance to torture. The point of the exercise is to learn how to refuse any sort of bargain with an enemy. Predictably, the Master Chief chooses to use O'Neill to "break" her male cohorts. He methodically beats her, inviting her cohorts to "stop this" by "surrendering." Mouth bloodied, eyes blackened, hands cuffed behind her back, O'Neill tells her cohorts to stand strong. But the Master Chief is determined to demonstrate that "her presence makes us all vulnerable." He bends a handcuffed O'Neill over a table and begins to unzip his trousers; his intent is clear. O'Neill is defiant: "Oh yeah, like the men aren't afraid of this, too."

O'Neill's cohorts are horrified and demoralized to see their commanding officer preparing to rape a trainee. Just as they are weakening in their resolve, O'Neill surprises the Master Chief by attacking him from a prone position. She renders him helpless, kicks him in the scrotum and dances around him waiting for more. The watching cohorts roar their approval. The Master Chief regains the upper hand, but O'Neill refuses to stay down. Each time he hits her, she struggles to her feet. "Choose life!" he warns her. Pulling herself up to her full stature, bleeding profusely, and hands tied behind her back she sneers at him, in measured words: "Suck my dick."

For our purposes, this is the pivotal scene in the film. O'Neill's utterance, in concert with her physical toughness, transforms her status and stature within the military unit. Her male peers accept her henceforth; the Master Chief abandons his efforts to break O'Neill. What accounts for this remarkably transformative moment? Certainly, O'Neill appropriates masculinist violence to defend herself; but this is neither new nor especially transgressive. Within the logic of her story, O'Neill clearly was provoked and justified in her actions. The appropriation of masculinist speech, however, is a different matter and leads to a profoundly transgressive moment. Consider how and why this is so.

First, O'Neill de-genders sexual assault by claiming that rape and/or sexual humiliation could happen to any soldier. In so doing, she refuses a material vulnerability long associated with and represented through the female body. Second, O'Neill interrupts the rape through her own physical power and mental toughness—with both hands tied behind her back (the visual pun is undeniable). Third, when she utters the three words that got Harlan killed, she appropriates phallic power from the would-be rapist. She has beaten him, bested him; even if he rapes her, kills her, she has won. The surrogate spectators in the scene, her male cohorts, drive the point home with raucous, rowdy approval of her words and deeds. The Master Chief reluctantly concedes the battle. The remainder of the film illustrates O'Neill's successful integration into the elite unit.

In *G.I. Jane*, the female body is the primary problem that needs "solving." The problems are played out in three overlapping ways. First, the female body is presented initially as weak and ineffectual. In the first half of the film, we see a feminized and feminine O'Neill repeatedly fail to "pull her own weight" after she joins the elite training program. Much to the disgust of the Master Chief, for example, she cannot pull herself into a life raft during a training exercise. Moreover, she is not required to meet the same physical standards for training as the men. (She will challenge and overcome this restriction later in the film.) This double standard poses a problem for her male cohorts: How can she pull them to safety if she can't "pull her own weight"? The Master Chief proclaims that she is a threat to the unit because her weakness endangers everyone. What if he and his men have to put themselves and the mission at risk during enemy engagement to protect "the woman"?

The second problem with the female body is pollution of the masculine sphere. When O'Neill first arrives at the training camp, she is segregated from the common living space of her male cohorts and training staff. This segregation creates scheduling turmoil since O'Neill cannot share the shower/bathroom with her cohorts. Determined to overcome all obstacles, O'Neill finally talks her way into the male barracks, much to the dismay of some of the trainees. "Is that a tampon!?" one male trainee shrieks in hysterical outrage, looking at the contents of O'Neill's spilled pack. The moment is framed as potentially humorous, as though the emotional outburst were that of an immature boy ranting about "girl cooties." The scene speaks to the lingering resonance of millennia of misogynist disgust for the female body. As Margaret Miles puts it, "[t]he association of the female body with materiality, sex, and reproduction makes it an essential—not an accidental—aspect of the grotesque."[73] Though the moment is brief, it skillfully articulates the pollution anxieties characteristic of social segregation. The "other" must be kept at bay or interacted with in clearly prescribed ways so as to prevent contamination.

Female genitalia "in the house," so to speak, is not the same as ritualized masculine talk about women or the glossy images of sexualized female bodies.

The third problem with the female body is fear of hybridization, the "random combination of disparate parts, without functional integrity."[74] O'Neill reacts strongly to claims that she is weak, given special privileges, and incapable of enduring the physically punishing SEAL training. She shaves her head, begins body-building in her segregated quarters, and pushes herself to excel in all categories. Viewing audiences are positioned as voyeurs to watch her sweaty, glistening body as she does one-handed pushups and power sit-ups. The camera inspects her body intimately, but what we see is a series of potentially jarring juxtapositions: a shaved head and a heart-shaped face; equally prominent breasts and muscles; thickly muscled thighs, tight buttocks, and a "rack" of radically "cut" abdominal muscles—all devoid of softening, feminine fat. The voyeuristic close-ups of O'Neill's body show us an angular body with few curves. We learn during a check-up session with a female medic that O'Neill no longer menstruates because her body fat ratio is extremely low (rendering the tampons only symbolically menacing). O'Neill's hybridized body positions her to be read as a stereotypically "butch" lesbian—a charge that nearly ends her military career. But perhaps the most striking portrayal of O'Neill's hybridized body appears at the end of the film where she and the Master Chief resolve their differences in an intimate interpersonal moment. O'Neill's face still is bruised and battered from the beating she took from the Master Chief earlier in the story. Her head still is bald. On her body-builder frame she wears a light blue mini-dress. The face is a woman's; the shaved head evokes illness or annihilation; the body could be a transvestite. The hybridized ensemble is stunning, potentially disconcerting. Amy Taubin observes aptly that O'Neill as "spectacle is a gender bender that scrambles the iconography of top and bottom, butch and femme, exploding male and female identities in the process."[75]

The structured ambivalence of the film is signified primarily through this hybrid body in the mini-dress. On the one hand, O'Neill has proven herself ably to her male cohorts and all other detractors. But her body bears the marks of her success—she is bruised, battered, muscle-bound, and bald. The visual impact of her image is borne out in the title of Phyllis Schlafly's review of the film in *Human Events*: "How to Abuse Women (And Get Away with It)."[76] Schlafly's concerns, and those of various real world lawmakers, are echoed in the words of the fictional female senator in the film, played as homage to Ann Richards by Anne Bancroft. Explaining why she felt she had to use any means necessary to pull O'Neill out of the SEALS, even though O'Neill appeared to be succeeding in the program, Senator DeHaven says presciently: "No politician can afford to have a woman come home in a body bag." The bruised, muscled body is at once proof of triumph *and* proof of what we fear.

A related ambivalence is structured in the relationship between O'Neill and the Master Chief. Ultimately, he succumbs to the very weakness he warned his trainees about: He takes unnecessary risks to protect O'Neill in the field, and he is nearly killed as a result. Ironically, or perhaps predictably, O'Neill pulls him to safety after he is shot—proving once and for all her physical stamina and emotional toughness. The motivation that triggers the Master Chief's decision to put himself and the mission at risk is both sexist and racist. He and O'Neill are deployed to Libya on a search and rescue mission to save American personnel stuck behind enemy lines after a daring effort to retrieve a downed satellite. From his vantage point in the field, the Master Chief can see that O'Neill will have to kill a large Middle Eastern male combatant with a knife, by herself; she cannot risk alerting other enemy forces by firing her weapon. In a series of increasingly terse cross-cuts between O'Neill and the Master Chief, we see that she is poised expectantly with her knife and that he is looking through the scope of a high-powered weapon. At the last possible moment, the Master Chief makes a decision: "He's a big boy—I'm taking him out." The Master Chief's utterance about the size of the Arab male is matched by a stereotypically unflattering visual representation of him—swarthy skin, nappy hair, unshaven face and sweat-stained clothing. The appeal to gender and racial bias is clear: O'Neill might be over-powered by the Arab male; as an embodied female soldier, she is equally vulnerable to capture and rape. Embodied male soldiers must protect their women from sexual contamination by the enemy.

On the one hand we see that the Master Chief does precisely what he warns his trainees against. He buckles under the pressure of undeniable gender (and racial) bias; one can scarcely imagine him saying "he's a big boy" to a male trainee in a similar situation. O'Neill's ability to rescue him suggests that she could pull *more* than her own weight and that the Master Chief's actions were unwarranted. On the other hand, the film refuses to imagine the possibilities of a female in hand-to-hand combat with a male combatant, or female death or capture. We are left with a convenient and internally unifying ending where the recovering Master Chief reconciles his differences with O'Neill in an intimate interpersonal exchange where he gives her his own medal for valor in combat.

The film scenario imagines, and then over-rides, this most anxiety-producing moment. Can we ever imagine "her" as a soldier in a deadly struggle with an over-powering enemy? Could she die like Mellish, the doomed Jew in Spielberg's *Saving Private Ryan*, who is penetrated slowly and sensuously by a knife-wielding member of the elite SS guard?[77] The ending of *G.I. Jane* leaves us symbolically hovering over a chasm of ambivalence, suspended like the vintage Thunderbird in a perpetually liminal space of undecidability.

Integration Is a Bitch

In *Courage Under Fire* and *The General's Daughter*, the central female characters are dead for all or most of the narrative. The deaths of these women serve as plot enablers; a memory of each woman is constructed through the agency of male leading characters who solicit information about the women from the men who knew them. In both stories, the dead female is an American soldier who has been murdered by American male military personnel. In each case, the women serve in a nearly all-male context where they have little or no contact with other women in the military. The male leads, Denzel Washigton and John Travolta, respectively, investigate the deaths of the women, and solve the problem by exposing the killers and facilitating punishment of all guilty parties.

Courage Under Fire is framed as memory work in the wake of the 1991 Gulf War, and, in particular, the emotional costs of remembering war trauma. The story unfolds through the experiences of Lt. Col. Nathaniel Sterling, played by Denzel Washington. Col. Sterling is assigned to investigate the combat death of Capt. Karen Walden, played by Meg Ryan. Capt. Walden is being considered for a posthumous Medal of Honor for combat, which viewers learn is a cheap ploy for political gain rather than genuine appreciation for Walden. During the course of his investigation, Sterling learns that Walden was shot and left for dead by male troops under her command. Sterling's own trauma in the Gulf War is revisited through a series of flashbacks where viewers learn that he accidentally fired upon his own troops, killing one of his best friends. Sterling is able to come to terms with his own trauma by piecing together the story of what happened to Karen Walden. The film ends with Sterling placing his own medal for combat valor on the grave marker of Walden and saluting the marker.

The General's Daughter is the story of Capt. Elizabeth Campbell, who was gang-raped by her male peers at West Point. Her father, a high-ranking military officer with political aspirations, participated in covering up the assault so as to avoid scandal and public censure for West Point. As the narrative begins, we see that Capt. Campbell is deeply disturbed, allegedly because of her inability to recover from the rape trauma and her father's betrayal. When she is discovered (presumably) raped and murdered on the training grounds of the base where she works, Warrant Officers Paul Brenner (Travolta) and Sarah Sunhill (Madelene Stowe) are called in to investigate the crime. In the course of the investigation, they expose the rapists at West Point, the murderer, and the moral failings of Capt. Campbell's father. The film ends with Brenner saluting the coffin of Campbell as it is loaded into a cargo plane for transport to burial.

The difference in degree of female character agency in the two films is worth noting. Karen Walden represents greater female power than Elisabeth Campbell, though both are tough, smart, and academy graduates. Walden is a combat soldier and commander in the field; Campbell teaches psychological warfare at a military base. Walden's men mutiny and abandon her for dead, but they never threaten her with sexual violence. She dies heroically by holding off enemy fire until the men in her command are safely aboard a rescue helicopter. Campbell is brutally beaten and gang-raped by her academy peers because, as one soldier put it, they hated that she was smarter and that "she squatted to piss." She dies a victim of parental betrayal and sexual violence. Walden's body is largely inaccessible to the camera; Campbell's nude, spread-eagled, bound body is available for voyeuristic inspection.

The similarities between the women are revealing, as well. Each woman's death is a mystery to be solved through the agency of male investigation and recollection. Each film ends with a scene of the investigating male saluting the grave marker or coffin of the dead woman. Each woman's death leaves a wake of devastation: suicides, murder, ruined careers and moral collapse. Each woman's embodied presence as a soldier triggers the primary problem to be solved—"she" disrupts the homosocial male bond between men that is and has been the foundation of the American military. The surface level of each film narrative condemns the individual actions of men who cannot get along with women. Yet, each film's assumptive ground affirms that *esprit de corps* is fractured by the presence of female soldiers.

Courage Under Gender Hierarchy

Popular critics were divided over the artfulness of a story about a dead female helicopter pilot, told from multiple points of view. Richard Schickel resists any comparison of *Courage Under Fire* with *Roshomon*: "[I]t's really just a crudely manipulated mystery story."[78] By contrast, the *Boston Globe* makes the comparison to *Roshomon*, praising the "film's determination to examine attitudes toward women in combat."[79] Whether artful or not, the film does pursue the "truth" about Walden's fitness for command through a series of interviews with the men in her command. In a series of competing recollections, Capt. Walden is revealed as a highly capable medivac helicopter pilot and commander of a rescue operation.[80] When her airship comes under fire in the course of a rescue operation, the men in her command begin to question her ability to lead them. Ultimately, a mutinous soldier shoots her. A wounded Walden warns the men that she will pursue disciplinary action against them, and then stays behind to cover them as they race across the desert to the rescue helicopter. The men tell the pilot that Walden is dead and leave her to be incinerated by the flames of an air-support strike. When Col. Sterling finally unravels the truth about what happened, the soldier who shot Walden kills himself. Walden receives the Medal of Honor posthumously for exceptional courage under fire.

The primary problematic under-riding the plot of *Courage Under Fire* is the cultural expectation that female officers will fail in their command—not necessarily because of incompetence, but because gender-mixing in combat upsets the delicate balance of *esprit de corps*. The constructed memory of Karen Walden portrays her as a highly dedicated officer, skillful and courageous pilot, and a loving single mother to a daughter. As an Army pilot, her body size and strength are of less significance than her ability to maneuver an airship under fire. As a medivac pilot, her mission is to protect and evacuate vulnerable American soldiers on the ground. The denouement of the film narrative affirms that she did so, even when she was seriously wounded. The film implies that Capt. Karen Walden had earned the Medal of Honor, even though the motivation for recognition was suspect. So why did the men in her command rebel and abandon her in the field? To answer this question, we must look at the structured parallels between Walden and Sterling.

Sterling's trauma stems from giving the order to fire on an American tank that his gunner mistakenly thought was Iraqi. His trauma deepens when the Army attempts to coverup the mistake. After he returns from the Gulf, Sterling begins to drink heavily and to come unstrung. The Army awards him a prestigious combat medal and grounds him with the assignment to investigate Walden's death. Musing over his predicament in a drunken stupor he says, "They gave me medals and then buried me." When he discovers discrepancies in accounts of Walden's death, Sterling is once again told by the Army to cover up the disturbing information and rubber stamp the award. Sterling refuses; discovering the truth about Walden is balm for the lies he has been forced to tell about his own mistake. "In order to honor her...we have to tell the truth about what happened over there...the whole hard truth," he says to his commanding officer. In the end, the Army is forced to admit an incident of friendly fire and the fragging of an officer in the field. Sterling recovers his spirit and the memory of Karen Walden is publicly sanctified as heroic.

The structured ambivalence of the narrative lies in the solution to the problem of females and *esprit de corps*. On the one hand Walden is exonerated of failure in the field and honored as a combat hero. On the other hand, the insurrection stems specifically from her sex and gender. "I'm not giving up my weapon, *cunt*," says the mutinous soldier Monfreiz, when she orders him to stand down and surrender his gun. The same soldier accuses her of feminine weakness: "Are you *crying*"? he asks in disgust. "It's just tension, asshole" Walden replies. When she is gut-shot by the mutinous soldier, she refuses to let any of her men check the wound. When they tell her she needs their help, she replies: "I gave birth to a nine-pound baby, assholes; I think I can handle it." Viewers are reminded repeatedly that the most significant thing about Walden is her femaleness. Sterling was startled to learn that the case he was investigating was a woman. Walden is the *only* female character in a combat role. She is to be the first woman ever to receive a Medal of Honor for combat. She is the only combat character we see nurturing a child (in a series of flashbacks). But how are gender and sex related to *esprit de corps*? Sterling's character supplies the answer.

In the film, Sterling embodies the consummate soldier and leader, albeit he suffers from traumatic stress. His ease and familiarity with other male soldiers is dramatized for the viewer throughout the film. Through a series of short speeches to Walden's surviving men, he defines the meaning of *esprit de corps*. Men under pressure in combat situations must stick together. They must be willing to die for each other. Commanding officers must mobilize their men, steady them, inspire them and lead them into death, if necessary. There can be no turning away from danger if another soldier's life is at stake. Through Sterling's eyes, we see that Karen Walden personified every element of *esprit de corps*, save one: She was a woman. And the only clue we have about why her crew abandoned her—literally and morally—was her embodied status as female.

The structured ambivalence is striking. On the one hand, we see that Walden died heroically as a combat soldier in the field. On the other hand, the lives of four male soldiers were shattered by their inability to bond with a female commander. Moreover, defending the honor of a woman is the *raison d'etre* for Col. Sterling's investigation and the path to his recovery. Most significant, when the story ends, wounded masculinity has been restored and there are no longer any women to pose problems for the male social bond. The female soldier has been acknowledged, sanctified, and removed. No solution is (or can be) imagined to obviate the cultural bias undergirding *esprit de corps*—the homosocial bond among men.

Even the General's Daughter Is Not Safe

Elisabeth Campbell is a respected psychology expert and West Point graduate working at a military base in Georgia. Early in the narrative, she is found dead in what appears to be a ritual rape and murder. Through a series of investigative interviews, we learn with military investigators Brenner and Sunhill that Campbell was involved in highly risky sexual activities with the men in her father's command. The film gradually reveals that she uses her sex to punish her father for his moral and political betrayal of her. In one of the final flashback sequences, we see that Campbell (with help from a gay male friend) staged the final rape scene where she was killed. Naked and staked out on the ground, she summons her father to come and witness what happened to her years ago. Her father arrives, they exchange heated words, and the father walks away in disgust, leaving Campbell staked to the ground. "I don't give a damn about…what happened to you seven years ago," he tells her. She pleads with him, "Daddy, come back." Alone and helpless, Campbell is strangled to death by a spurned lover who had been stalking her. Like Monfreiz, Campbell's stalker kills himself when he is exposed as the murderer. The film ends with Campbell's father facing the prospect of a court-martial for his action to coverup criminal activity at West Point and on his base.

The fear that women will be viewed as "prey" in a fully integrated military drives the plot of *The General's Daughter*. The character of Elisabeth Campbell as a young academy cadet represents the female body at risk. Her very presence in an integrated military program triggers a predatory response from her male peers, and she is brutally raped. The film implies that military training hones the predatory instinct in male soldiers; a strong male commander is necessary to discipline and deploy predation in the interests of the nation state. Campbell's father, "fighting Joe Campbell," is just such an authority figure. He is revered for his ability to inspire and lead men. The film opens with his address to the men on his military base. In the speech, he describes the glue that holds any unit together—a sacred bond among men. Even Brenner, a hard-nosed detective for the Army's Criminal Investigation Division, expresses his admiration for General Campbell. Before he learns of the general's misconduct, Brenner pays tribute to "fighting Joe's" ability to steady men in Vietnam. Brenner confesses that his courage and determination had flagged until Campbell inspired him to carry on. When confronted about the details of his daughter's death, General Campbell asks Brenner, "Are you a soldier or a policeman?" In this investigation, Brenner (like Sterling) will have to choose between the truth and the Army.

The film's denouement demonstrates the problems that embodied females, such as Elisabeth Campbell, pose for the military. Gender integrated military training and combat deployment creates the potential for male confusion, resentment, and fear. Moreover, females are presumed to lack the instinct for predation and are thus always at risk in a masculinist organization where predation of the feminine (the weak) is evoked and practiced. We learn later in the film that Elisabeth Campbell "got separated" from her unit during a training exercise, and was set upon by a group of resentful male cadets. The scene is dark and claustrophobic; the camera peers down on a small and anxious woman. She is suddenly attacked by a group of wild young men with painted faces and dreadlock camouflage on their heads. In an ominous over-the-shoulder shot, we see one male pull the woman's panties down across her shapely thighs and legs. They tie her hands and feet to tent stakes, pinioning her body to the ground, while she cries out weakly for help. The scene evokes contemporary media constructions of male "wildings" with signifiers of frenzied brutality and animalistic behavior. (The dreadlock camouflage works as a racist signifier of bestial sexuality.)

Viewers learn of this incident from a kindly Army psychologist who tells investigators Brenner and Sunhill that "they raped her nearly to death." From the point of view of the psychologist, Elisabeth fell victim to a social experiment gone awry. Near the end of the film we learn that Elisabeth's father met with Army officials before he visited her in the hospital. In the meeting, General Campbell decided that "the best interests" of West Point would be better served by covering up the assault. "Close your eyes," he whispers to a battered and bruised daughter, "this never happened."

The post-rape character of Capt. Elisabeth Campbell represents the destructive and irresistible power of the pornographic female body. The film suggests that after the gang rape, Campbell became sexually deviant in an effort to prey on powerful males (and to embarrass her father). After her death, Brenner and Sunhill find a secret room in the basement of Capt. Campbell's residence. There, they find S&M sex toys and equipment, a hidden video camera, and videotapes of Capt. Campbell in black leather dominating male sex partners.

Capt. Campbell's appropriation of the pornographic as a way to prey on powerful men demonstrates two things within the logic of the narrative. First, Capt. Campbell understands the power relationship between sex and gender. Denied justice by her father and the Army, she performs predation in an unauthorized manner that ultimately destroys her and the men she "lured" into her "lair." Second, Capt. Campbell's predation is mythically feminine, not masculine. Unlike Capt. Walden, Capt. Campbell does not fight like a man. Rather, she uses the tools of the trade, so to speak, to destroy the men who have harmed her. Disciplined military predation exists to protect good girls; the nation is feminine and women embody the material interests of the nation. Bad girls and transgressive girls "feed" the predatory instinct; enemy states and female soldiers are pussies and cunts. The American military cannot guarantee protection for women who wander into the sphere of male predation, either by accident or choice.

The ambivalent structuring of the film is complex and disturbing. On the one hand, the film exposes masculinist cultural assumptions about militarism, masculinity, and predation. Men and women cannot serve together in the military, particularly in combat or leadership roles, because undisciplined men will hurt women. The pornographic lens of the film exposes the sado-masochism of gender relationships in military training and deployment.[81] At the heart of *esprit de corps* is a homosocial male bond built on a masochistic willing-ness to die and a sadistic will to consume the enemy (the feminine). Elisabeth Campbell was gang-raped because of inadequately supervised gender mixing in the corps. She was so distorted by her victimization that she became "per-verted"—and she died because of her father's political ambitions and lack of moral courage. The relationship between Brenner and Sunhill suggest that men and women can work together cooperatively, safely and productively. Sunhill's ability to resist the predators and to discover the facts with which to solve the case favors a reading position that critiques masculinist assumptions and practices in the military. The agency of Brenner supports a reading that mascu-line predation is necessary and morally defensible, but only if appropriately disciplined and focused.

On the other hand, the film endorses masculinist assumptions about gender and sex relations. Elisabeth Campbell is victimized, infantilized, pathologized, and destroyed by her attempts to perform as a soldier. Sunhill's role as an embodied female Army co-investigator offers the perspective that no woman is safe from male predation. Taken together, the roles of the two female charac-ters suggest that there is no way to guarantee the safety of female soldiers. Sunhill, a C.I.D. investigator, is threatened twice and assaulted once during the course of the investigation. During the assault, her masked assailant invites Sunhill to imagine what it would be like to be raped. He then instructs her to tell her partner Brenner that "you don't shit on your brothers." Though Sunhill has equal rank with Brenner, she is neither part of the brotherhood nor is she a substantial threat. Rather, she is a pawn and potential victim in a power struggle among men. The visual and narrative structures of the film expose the sado-masochism and predation of military rules of conduct, even as the film posi-tions viewers as voyeurs to enjoy the pleasures of pornographic fantasies: Girls who willingly participate in deviant sex. Girls who attempt to lure their fathers into looking at their sexualized bodies. Girls who are at once beautiful, smart, tough talking and sexually available. Girls who are strangled with their own panties. Finally, the film suggests that rape trauma transforms women into revenge-hungry sluts who play dirty tricks and who cause "brothers" to fight one another instead of bonding to fight a common enemy.

The ambivalence of both films is structured by and through the possibility and threat of women desegregating the masculine spaces of the war zone. Like Lt. Jordan, Capts. Walden and Campbell are intelligent, capable, tough and articulate. Both film narratives imply that the woman could have made it on merit, had they not been set upon by male predation. Unlike Jordan, they are not able to appropriate the talk or the walk of *esprit de corps.* Each woman is destroyed, but so too are her destroyers. At the end of the story, audiences are once again left hovering over the cultural chasm of undecidability and angst.

Post-9/11 Military and the *Realpolitik* of Sexual Abuse

In a broader sense, these films about women in combat participate in an ongoing cultural argument about the democratization of the public spheres. Tom Englehardt observes that generalized anxiety over the Vietnam War, in conjunction with gender, race and sexual upheaval, has eroded what he calls "victory culture."[82] Vietnam and Watergate, together with the Civil Rights, Women's Rights, and Gay Rights movements, seriously eroded the social realities of dominant masculine prowess, white privilege, and heteronormative presumption. Post-Vietnam war films, in particular, represent the trauma of lost privilege for white males.[83] In the three films about female soldiers we see the resonances of eroded victory culture, a mournful tale of lost glory and the collapse of moral superiority.

All of these memory traces in the three films emerge from the cultural rubble of the Vietnam War and its deleterious effect on American national identity. In effect, the three stories about female soldiers are embedded in a cultural diegesis generated through masculine and male experiences. In that sense, the presence of women in combat is simply another anxiety-provoking element in the "post-adjustment" narratives of American dominant masculinity: post-feminism, post-civil rights, post-Stonewall riots.

Only one of the three films about female soldiers identifies dominant masculine culture as the generative source of sexual harassment and abuse of women in the military, albeit briefly. In *G.I. Jane,* the Master Chief and his support staff discuss the ethical limits of what they have done to Lt. O'Neill during the simulated torture scenario. One of the staff comments that the sexualized violence against O'Neill was "out of line" and he warns his superior, "It ain't gonna happen again." The Master Chief painfully straightens the broken nose O'Neill has given him, and then turns to his male staffer and says, sincerely and thoughtfully: "Yeah it will [happen again]. Maybe not with you, or these guys, or with me. She's not the problem...we are."

A backward look at *Courage Under Fire, G.I. Jane,* and *The General's Daughter* sheds light on the post-September 11, 2001, collision between gender politics and pragmatic national interests: Only sufficient numbers of women in the military support American wars abroad and offset or delay the re-institution of the male-only draft. As we pointed out earlier, Representative Heather Wilson put the matter bluntly as early as 2002, claiming that "[T]here's no way that we currently can defend this country" if the number of women in combat zones is rolled back.[84] As we have noted, public knowledge about the failures of the Vietnam War helped to bring about the end of the induction draft by 1973. But, sustaining an all-volunteer military meant de-segregating military schools and permitting women equal opportunity for advancement. Linda Kerber tells us that post-Vietnam military recruiters "were desperate for women."[85] Yet, as evinced in scandal after scandal, the masculine segregationist *oeuvre* of the American military has thwarted military and government officials and created danger and frustration for women.

Currently, a protracted war in Iraq has strained the all-volunteer military, giving rise to fears that the induction draft will be re-instated.[86] Aggressive nationalism abroad has necessitated unprecedented deployment of National Guard units (the "back door" draft) and gender bending in the front lines of the war. Should current all-volunteer recruiting strategies continue to fail to meet set goals, re-introduction of the draft could conceivably become a reality. Such a move surely will give rise to incendiary public debate over privilege and deferment. It is plausible to speculate that the debate will include the issue of sex equity. Since women now serve in combat zones, albeit in limited capacity, the logic of *Rostker v. Goldberg* no longer holds as defined by the Supreme Court justices.

Were Justices Marshall and Brennan right? Do American women have a fundamental civic obligation to bear the burden of military service? We would frame the question differently. We would ask: *Should women be forced to serve in an organization where their chances of being raped are twice that of their risks in civilian life?*[87] The logic of our syllogism would look like this:

Major Premise: The military constitutes a hostile work environment for women.

Minor Premise: In that sense, women are not "similarly situated" with men

Conclusion: Therefore, women should not be burdened with involuntary induction unless and until said hostile environment is radically altered.

The presence of women in Congress has helped bring national attention to the sexual harassment and abuse of women in the military, suggesting the possibility of social change. Representative Heather Wilson, R-NM (Air Force Academy, 1982), is the first female veteran to serve in Congress and on the House Armed Services Committee. She was instrumental in appointing an independent commission to investigate allegations of abuse at Colorado Springs. Senator Susan Collins, R-ME, and Senator Kay Bailey Hutchison, R-TX, pressured the Pentagon to investigate and respond to allegations of male-to-female rape in Iraq and Kuwait. Their actions helped bring about the first

(2004) and second (2005) annual Sexual Assault Reports to Congress by the Department of Defense.[88]

On May 15, 2006, Representative Louise Slaughter, D-New York, introduced H.R. 5212: The Military Domestic and Sexual Violence Response Act.[89] The proposed bill codifies and extends significantly the 2005 Department of Defense Sexual Assault Report.[90] Rep. Rosa L. DeLauro, D-Connecticut, one of the nineteen co-sponsors of the bill, offered a pointed statement about the purpose of the proposed legislation:

> [W]hile the [Department of Defense] has been making efforts to improve its prevention and response to domestic and sexual violence, services remain incomplete and inconsistent among the various branches...DoD policies are not codified and do not offer the same protections afforded to civilian victims.[91]

The proposed legislation establishes an office of Victims Advocate within the Department of Defense, creates "comprehensive confidentiality protocols to protect the rights of victims," and codifies "policies for preventing, responding, treating, and prosecuting cases of family violence, domestic violence, sexual assault and stalking within the military and among military families."[92]

The material circumstances of the thousands of women who currently served in the armed forces go well beyond the dramatics of public narratives about women in combat. Here, we include high profile stories about Jessica Lynch and Lynndie England, as well as fictional film narratives about female soldiers. Ironically, or perhaps perversely, the American armed services provide substantial work and professional opportunities for a disproportionately minority and poor population, hence garnering the popular phrase "the poverty draft."[93] The journal *Military Medicine* reports:

> Women in the military today are younger, more ethnically diverse, and have fewer socioeconomic resources than previous cohorts...[W]omen younger than 35 years of age in the military had less education, earned lower incomes and are more likely to rely on Medicaid than middle-aged military women.[94]

Half of all women serving in the military are members of a racial minority: African American women comprise 32%; Hispanic American women comprise 10.2%; Native American women comprise 4.1%; and Asian American women comprise 0.2%.[95] For working class women (and men), careers in the military provide otherwise inaccessible training in technology and communications, health benefits, retirement benefits, and career networks after the military. Young men and women across the racial spectrum frequently join the military for educational benefits, job skills, and health care. For women, the issue of combat duty may be of less significance than day-to-day encounters with institutional sexism and the harsh realities of sexual violence. The paucity of public imagination about these women and their stories is telling. The three films we reviewed for this chapter do not address issues of race or economic class at all. All three lead females are characterized as white, middle-class, and heterosexual; all three are highly trained officers. Lt. O'Neill and Capt. Campbell are characterized as socially privileged. There is no sense at all in these narratives that the female characters chose their careers in the military because they had few other options. Moreover, the films do not address the historical fact that the 1973 suspension of the induction draft has been borne on the backs of women, especially those women disadvantaged by race and social class.

Public arguments about women in combat express long standing cultural anxieties about shifting gender practices. Predictably, these arguments unfold along stridently ideological fault lines. The films we examine in this chapter are primary examples of those fault lines. Our examination of these films in their cultural context leads us to conclude that the issue of "women in combat," and all the ambivalences generated therein, may distract citizens and scholars from the equally pressing matter of studying and reforming the military as a safe and productive workplace for women. We believe it is the business of feminism to examine the way the burden of military service is borne on the backs of the least privileged and sometimes most vulnerable members of our society. The No Child Left Behind Act, for example, stipulates that high schools must provide the phone numbers of their students to military recruiters.[96] The Army currently accepts thousands of recruits "without high school diplomas."[97]

We conclude by addressing candidly our position that feminism should go where the women are. All three of us are steadfastly anti-war, pro-peace, and non-violence advocates. Yet, thirty years of feminist scholarship, teaching, and activism have taught us that feminism is for all women—not just the ones who happen to share our ideological viewpoints. Thus, we call upon feminist men and women in the arts, humanities, social sciences, and natural sciences to use their intellect, artistic talent, political acumen, and citizenship rights to study, explore, represent, and improve the lives of women in the American military.[98] The public imagination that produces iconic binaries such as Jessica Lynch and Lynndie England as *realpolitik* soldiers, and fictional binaries like the ones we see in the three films about female combat soldiers, perpetuates ambivalences that work to protect privilege and conceal exploitation. Thelma and Louise's turquoise convertible hovering over the canyon served its purpose in the public imagination of the 1990s; now, we must make our choices, keep our commitments, and move ahead.

Moving ahead means acknowledging and generating public talk (and/or art) about two challenges to feminism that flow from contemporary conditions involving women and the military. First, feminism must move beyond ideologically driven schisms that ignore or conceal the material realities faced by women who choose to join the military. Feminism can and should play an important role in the ongoing assessment and eradication of the dangers women face because of institutional sexism and misogyny in the American military. This means that feminism must push the limits of what counts *as* feminist concerns and commitments; our commitments as scholars, teachers, and activists should not be viewed as incommensurate with the lives and welfare of women in military service. At the same time, many of us will continue our commitments to anti-war, peace movements (such as Cindy Sheehan). We should not permit our philosophies and practices to be ensnared in either/or fallacies; surely feminism is complex enough to embrace complication and paradox.

Second, and closely related, feminism must confront the history of class and race dynamics that helped create the policy for an all-volunteer military. Neither Second nor Third Wave arguments adequately address the burden of national service women have assumed since Nixon set aside the induction draft in 1973. Post-9/11 seismic shifts in the domestic and geo-political scene mean that the female and male children of the least advantaged citizens (and illegal aliens) disproportionately serve and die in protracted wars abroad. Nor does either of the Waves adequately acknowledge the technological, educational, and professional opportunities offered by the military as incentives for poor and minority women (and men). Economic policies that necessitate war abroad, in collusion with a consumer culture that embraces comfort, have contributed to the deeply felt ambivalence many Americans have about military service. Feminism as philosophy and practice can disrupt the stultifying rhetorical effects of this cultural ambivalence and push us to examine the disturbing consequences of the impasse we have come to embrace.

Notes

[1] Ann Putnam, "The Bearer of the Gaze in Ridley Scott's *Thelma and Louise*," *Western American Literature* 27.4 (1993): 291–302.

[2] Marita Sturken, *Thelma and Louise* (London: British Film Institute, 2000).

[3] Peter Travers, "Women on the Verge," *Rolling Stone* 18 April 1991. Many popular and academic reviewers simply hated the film. See, for example: John Leo, "Toxic Feminism on the Big Screen," *U.S. News and World Report* 10 June 1991; Pat Dowell, "The Impotence of Women," *Cineaste* 18.4 (1991). Other writers were ambivalent. See, for example, Laura Shapiro, "Women Who Kill Too Much: Is *Thelma and Louise* Feminism or Fascism?" *Newsweek* 17 June 1991. The film continues to be a popular subject for academic work. See, for example: Tiina Vares,

"Framing 'Killer Women' films: Audience Use of Genres," *Feminist Media Studies* 2.2 (2002): 214–229; Patty Meyers and Susan Willhauck, "*Thelma and Louise* Do Religious Education: A Dialogue from the Edge for Leading with Hope," *Religious Education* 98.3 (2003): 382–399. The film has been appropriated by a number of special interest groups, for a variety of reasons. See, for example, the queer appropriation of the film in B. Ruby Rich, "Two for the Road," *Advocate* 18 February 2003.

4 Richard Corliss, "Girls Just Wanna Have Guns," *Time* 22 April 2002: 58–60.

5 John Fiske, *Television Culture* (New York: Routledge, 1987); John Fiske, *Understanding Popular Culture* (Boston: Unwin Hyman, 1989).

6 Celeste Michelle Condit, "The Rhetorical Limits of Polysemy," *Critical Studies in Mass Communication* 6.2 (1989): 103–122; Brian Ott, "(Re)Locating Pleasure in Media Studies: Toward an Erotics of Reading," *Communication and Critical/Cultural Studies* 1.2: (2004): 194–212.

7 We take the term "liminality" from Victor Turner, "Process, System, and Symbol: A New Anthropological Synthesis," *Daedalus* (Summer 1977): 68.

8 Judith Hess Wright, "Genre Films and the Status Quo," *Film Genre Reader III*, ed. Barry Keith Grant. (Austin: University of Texas Press, 2003) 42–50.

9 Bob Deans, "Women's Combat Role on Front Burner," *The Atlanta Journal-Constitution* 26 June 2005: 7A; *Cong. Rec.* 31 July 1991 http://web.lexis-nexis.com/congcomp/doc. 21 July 2004.

10 *Cong. Rec.* 31 July 1991 http://web.lexis-nexis.com/congcomp/doc. 21 July 2004.

11 Matt Kelley, "Little Reaction in Washington as American Women Fight and Die in Iraq," *The Associated Press* 16 Jan. 2004.

12 See *Cong. Rec.* 31 July 1991. See also Chris Hables Gray, *Postmodern War: The New Politics of Conflict* (New York: The Guilford Press, 1997) esp. Chapter 2 "Computers at War: Kuwait 1991."

13 *Cong. Rec.* 31 July 1991.

14 David Zucchino, "The Nation: Equal Right to Fight," *Los Angeles Times* 10 April 2004: A1.

15 Linda K. Kerber, *No Constitutional Right to Be Ladies: Women and the Obligations of Citizenship* (New York: Hill and Wang, 1998).

16 Kerber 284.

17 Cited in Kerber.

18 Cited in Kerber 278.

19 *Cong. Rec.* 10 June 1980: 13890.

20 *Cong. Rec.* 10 June 1980: 13889.

21 Thomas D. Boettcher, *Vietnam: The Valor and the Sorrow* (Boston: Little, Brown and Company, 1984) 426.

22 Herma Hill Kay and Kenneth M. Davidson, "Appendix A: *Rostker v. Goldberg*," *Text, Cases, and Materials on Sex-Based Discrimination* 2nd ed. (St. Paul, MN: West Publishing Co., 1981) 1015–1039.

23 Kenneth M. Davidson, Ruth Bader Ginsburg, and Herma Hill Kay, *Sex-Based Discrimination: Text, Cases and Materials* (St. Paul, MN: West Publishing Co., 1980).

24 The 1972 Supreme Court case *Frontiero v. Richarson* established that male spouses of female military personnel shall receive the same benefits as female spouses of male military personnel. The 1976 U.S. Court of Appeals case *Crawford v. Cushman* ruled that pregnant soldiers may not be discharged because of their pregnancy. See "Military Women: Who They Are, What They Do, and Why It Matter," *Women's Review of Books* 21.5 (2004): 7.

25 Kay and Davidson, "Appendix A: *Rostker v. Goldberg*," 1026.

26 Kay and Davidson 1021.

27 Kay and Davidson 1021.

[28] Kay and Davidson 1023.

[29] Kay and Davidson 1023.

[30] Kay and Davidson 1024.

[31] Kay and Davidson 1027.

[32] United States Dept. of Defense, Military Casualty Information, 16 May 2006 http://www.defenselink.mil/search/.

[33] Gretchen Cook (for WomensEnews), "U.S.: Controversy Arising Over Female Combat Veterans," *IPS-Inter Press Service* 11 November 2003.

[34] Diane Richard, "Rape in the Ranks: Reducing Risk in the Workplace, Barracks and Beyond," *Contemporary Sexuality* 37.7 (2003): 1, 4–6.

[35] Amy Herdy, "Betrayal in the Ranks," *Denver Post* 16 Nov. 2003: B4; Miles Moffeit and Amy Herdy, "Betrayal in the Ranks," *Denver Post* 17 November 2003: A18; Mike Soraghan and Erin Emery, "Air Force Brass 'Well Aware' of Assaults: Commission Assigns Blame, Names Those Who Ignored Academy Scandal," *Denver Post* 23 September (2003): A1.

[36] "Trials Rare After Charges of Sex Assault At Annapolis," *The New York Times* 19 March 2006, National sec.: 20.

[37] Former Rep. Tillie Fowler (Florida) chaired the investigating commission. She cited these facts in a radio broadcast with NPR: Tillie Fowler, "Congressional Report on Sexual Misconduct at the Air Force Academy," *Talk of the Nation*. Anchor, Neal Conan. National Public Radio, 23 September 2003.

[38] Miles Moffeit and Amy Herdy, "Female GIs Report Rapes in Iraq War: 37 Seek Aid After Allegations of Assaults by U.S. Soldiers," *Denver Post* 25 January 2004: A1; Miles Moffeit,"Pentagon Stalls Rape Legislation," *Denver Post* 11May 2004: A6; Miles Moffeit, "Bill Urges Victim Rights with Military," *Denver Post* 13 May 2004: A9; Miles Moffeit, "Rape Report Cites Failings: Pentagon Panel Urges Change," *Denver Post* 14 May 2004: A1; Miles Moffeit, "Military Sex-Assault Reforms Slow in Advancing," *Denver Post* 16 May 2004: A5; Miles Moffeit, "Pentagon to Address Sex Assaults," *Denver Post* 2 June 2004: A3.

[39] Miles Moffeit and Amy Herdy, "Sexual Assault by Peers a Risk for Military Women," *Houston Chronicle* 25 January 2004: A12.

[40] Eric Schmitt, "Military Women Reporting Rapes by U.S. Soldier," *The New York Times* 26 February 2004: A1.

[41] Schmitt.

[42] Schmitt.

[43] Lynette Clemetson, "Officer Testifies of Her Two Sexual Assaults in the Army" *The New York Times* 1 April 2004: A19.

[44] Pamela Martineau and Steve Wiegand, "New Rules Would Let Cases Stay Confidential," *Tacoma News Tribune* 21 March 2005: A4.

[45] Martineau and Wiegand.

[46] Rosemary Mariner, interview with Melinda Penkava, "Role of Women in the Military" *Talk of the Nation*, Natl. Public Radio, 27 May 2002.

[47] Diane Richard. Figures cited on p. 5.

[48] "Special Report: Women at War," *Sacramento Bee* 6 March 2005: Al.

[49] "U.S. Women in Combat," *The Herald* (Rock Hill, S.C.) 22 January 2004: 2E.

[50] Juliet Macur, "Two Women Bound by Sports, War and Injuries," *The New York Times* 10 April 2005, sec.1: 1.

[51] Ann Scott Tyson, "Bid to Limit Women in Combat Withdrawn," *The Washington Post* 26 May 2005: A1. See also a similar story that ran one year earlier: Darryl Fears, "Families Mourn

Daughters: 20 Female Service Members Have Been Killed in Iraq," *The Washington Post* 26 May 2004: A1.

52 Qtd. in Matt Kelley, "Little Reaction in Washington as American Women Fight and Die in Iraq," *Associated Press* 15 January 2004, 28 April 2004 LexisNexis.

53 Ann Scott Tyson, "More Objections to Women-in-Combat Ban: Army Says 22,000 Jobs Would Be Affected," *The Washington Post* 18 May 2005: A5; Thom Shanker, "House Bill Would Preserve, and Limit, the Role of Women in Combat Zones," *The New York Times* 20 May 2005: A20.

54 Ann Scott Tyson, "Panel Votes to Ban Women from Combat: Army Leaders Strongly Oppose House Subcommittee's Action," *The Washington Post* 12 May 2005: A8.

55 Andrea Stone, "Panel's Decision Reheats Women-in-Combat Debate," *USA Today* 20 May 2005: News, 07A.

56 Ann Scott Tyson, "Panel Votes to Ban Women from Combat: Army Leaders Strongly Oppose House Subcommittee's Action," *The Washington Post* 12 May 2005: A8.

57 Tyson.

58 Elaine Donnelly, "Hunter Admonishes Army on Women in Combat," *Human Events* 30 May 2005: 393.

59 Mackubin Thomas Owens, "GI Jane, Again: The Army Tries to Sneak Women Into Combat, and Some Congressmen Try to Stop it," *National Review* 6 June 2005: 23–24.

60 Mackubin 24.

61 Eric Tucker, "Women in Combat? It's Here," *Tacoma News Tribune* 3 July 2005: A5.

62 Zucchino A1.

63 Tucker A5.

64 Ruth Marcus, "The Woman Warrior," *The Washington Post* 24 May 2005: A-17.

65 "Pentagon Considers Ways to Make Military Service More Attractive to Women," *All Things Considered*, Anchor, John Ydstie, Reporter, Emily Harris. Natl. Public Radio, 2 August 2002.

66 Tucker A5.

67 Tyson A8.

68 Ann Scott Tyson, "Bid to Limit Women in Combat Withdrawn," *The Washington Post* 26 May 2005: A1.

69 "Defending America," *The New York Times* 10 July 2005, sec. 4: 11.

70 "Women at War," *The Washington Post* 18 May 2005: A16.

71 "Defending America."

72 Women are not required to be as fast or strong as men in performance trials.

73 Margaret R. Miles, *Carnal Knowing: Female Nakedness and Religious Meaning in the Christian West* (New York: Vintage Books, 1991) 150.

74 Miles 61.

75 Amy Taubin, "Dicks and Jane," rev. of *G.I. Jane*, by Ridley Scott, *Village Voice* 26 August 1997: 73.

76 Phyllis Schlafly, "How to Abuse Women (and Get Away with It), rev. of *G.I. Jane*, by Ridley Scott, *Human Events* 3 October 1997: 10.

77 Peter Ehrenhaus, "Why We Fought: Holocaust Memory in Spielberg's *Saving Pvt. Ryan*," *Critical Studies in Media Communication* 18.3 (2001): 321–337.

78 Richard Schickel, "Courage Underdone," rev. of *Courage Under Fire*, by Edward Zwick, *Time* 22 July 1996: 94.

79 Jay Carr, "'G.I. Jane': She's Demi-Tough," *Boston Globe* 12 July 1996: F-1.

80 Pat Dowell, "A Gulf War *Roshomon*: An Interview with Edward Zwick" *Cineaste* 22.3 (1996): 11–13.

[81] A. Susan Owen and Peter Ehrenhaus, "Animating a Critical Rhetoric: On the Feeding Habits of American Empire," *Western Journal of Communication* 57.2 (1993): 169–177.

[82] Tom Englehardt, *The End of Victory Culture: Cold War America and the Disillusioning of a Generation* (New York: Basic Books, 1995).

[83] Susan Jeffords, *The Remasculinization of America: Gender and the Vietnam War* (Bloomington: Indiana University Press, 1989).

[84] Emily Harris, National Public Radio, 2 August 2002.

[85] Kerber 266.

[86] "A Misguided View of a Draft, U.S. Military" *Morning Call* (Allentown, Pennsylvannia) 6 April 2006, 5th ed.: A6; Richard Lardner, "Rumors Persist About reinstatement of Draft," *Winston-Salem Journal* 9 June 2004, Metro ed.: A1; Michael Stetz, "Rumor of Military Draft Sparks Official Denials," *San Diego Union-Tribune* 3 July 2004, news: A1.

[87] See Manning.

[88] United States Dept. of Defense, "DoD Release Sexual Assault Report for 2005," 16 March 2006 http://www.defenselink.mil/releases/20060316–12651.html.

[89] H.R. 5212: Military Domestic and Sexual Violence response Act, *GovTrack.us* http://www.govtrack.us/congress/bill.xpd?bill=h109–5212 and *TheOrator.com News and Information* http://www.theorator.com/bills109/hr5212.html

[90] The Department of Defense report to Congress is 10 pages long; the proposed legislation is 68 pages long.

[91] "Rep. DeLauro Seeks Additional Resources," *US Fed News* 26 April 2006 http://web.lexis-nexis.com/universe/document 16 May 2006.

[92] *US Fed News* 26 April 2006.

[93] Christopher Capozzola, "A Rough Draft: Selective Service in the Women's History Class-room," *Journal of Women's History* 17.4 (2005): 148–153.

[94] Caroline P. Carney et al., "Women in the Gulf War: combat Experience, Exposures, and Subsequent Health Care Use," *Military Medicine* 168 (2003): 660.

[95] Manning.

[96] Damien Cave, "For Recruiters, A Hard Toll From a Hard Sell," *The New York Times* 27 March 2005, late ed.: 1:1.

[97] Cave.

[98] See Mary Fainsod Katzenstein, *Faithful and Fearless: Moving Feminist Protest Inside the Church and Military* (Princeton, NJ: Princeton University Press, 1998).

Epilogue

An Open Letter from
the Second Wave Mothership

Dear Sisters and Friends:

It's been forty years since we took to the streets to protest the subjugation of women and girls in American society. That second wave of public and political resistance was precipitated, in part, by finding out that our brothers in the struggle for social justice de-valued our concerns as women. Even worse, our brothers actually thought that we would be content making the coffee, running the mimeograph machines and providing sexual and emotional comfort for front-line cultural warriors. "When will they ever learn...when WILL they ever learn?"—we hummed to ourselves. Among other things, our brothers were trying to keep American male bodies out of Vietnam; we were pre-occupied with the terrifying prospects of living as embodied female citizens in a nation that criminalized abortion, limited reproductive control, advanced draconian divorce laws, provided aid and comfort to sexual harassers and predators, and systematically devalued female labor in all areas of the political economy.

We Second Wavers were and are the daughters, granddaughters, and great granddaughters of the American women who worked in war production during World War II—who discovered their aptitude as pipe-fitters and welders and pilots and engineers and draftswomen and chemists and physicists and agricultural experts. Our "mothers" learned that they could do all the tasks for which they had been told they had no "natural" aptitude. When the war was over, our mothers were unceremoniously pushed back into the margins of the political economy. Some were content with business as usual, but the discontent, anger, and yearning of some of our mothers must have rubbed off on us. In the context of the struggle over the Vietnam War and civil rights, we-the-daughters took to the streets and demanded equality and social justice for women.

We learned a great deal from watching our mothers struggle. They were expected to marry, give up their family name, give birth to us, nurture us (instinctively), and find fulfillment in our existence. They were expected to balance housework and childrearing with any activities they engaged outside the home. We watched our mothers hold down day jobs and stay up late doing laundry, cleaning, cooking, and sewing. If they took jobs out of economic necessity, they still were expected to shoulder the domestic burden of running a household. If they took jobs out of boredom with home life, they came under criticism from our fathers, our extended families, and the church. If they had careers, they were expected to subordinate their professional lives to the interests of their husband's careers and to their children. Our mothers were supposed to be content with earning a fraction of what their male co-workers made, even when our mothers were smarter, better educated, and harder working. If our mothers were women of color, their lives were doubly complicated by intersections of race, gender and sexuality.

Our mothers were treated for depression with addictive, debilitating drugs; some of our mothers lived with untreated depression most of their adult lives. Some of our mothers lived in homes with domestic violence where secrecy and shame foreclosed escape or solutions. The reproductive cycle of the female body was shrouded in secrecy and mystery; our mothers sometimes thought they were losing their minds as they lived through the cycles. So did everyone else. In spite of these debilitating conditions, our mothers were smart, tough, and irreverently funny. They dreamed of becoming scientists, artists, and politicians. But their life worlds did not make such dreams plausible. Over the years, some of us watched the lights dim in our mothers' eyes. We whispered to ourselves, fiercely, *this is not going to happen to me.* When we saw that our male peers intended to position us the way our fathers had positioned our mothers, we re-ignited the revolution begun by our nineteenth century foremothers. We made progress, but as we indicated in the introduction of this book, contemporary generations of women face some of the same problems experienced by our mothers. These enduring problems are not evidence of the failures of feminism; rather, they are the consequences of successful resistance to feminism. That is not to say, however, that the Second Wave is without blame.

Looking back, it is so painfully obvious where and how we made mistakes. We did not reach out to our sisters of color, our working class sisters, our lesbian sisters. Worse, it did not even occur to many of us that we should have. Like our foremothers in the First Wave, we did not always acknowledge our own privileged positions. We ignored or participated in racial and heterosexist exclusion. Some of us failed to adequately acknowledge capitalist exploitation of female labor in the working classes. We neglected history: We failed to understand that the political antagonisms between white men and women could not stand in for those who live with racial *and* sexual oppression. We splintered the movement on the issues of capitalism, sex, and labor.

We have paid a heavy price for our mistakes. The solidarity we imagined never coalesced. The purveyors of American capitalism, to whom we represent a potentially incalculable threat, have been very successful in splintering our coalitions, co-opting our goals, undermining our credibility, and weakening our resolve. Sadly, "feminist" has become a dirty word for the hip generations who come after us who gladly embrace their liberties but offer this disclaimer: "I'm not a feminist, but...." We are genuinely troubled when our students, daughters, nieces, granddaughters and mentees tell us that feminism is no longer necessary because female liberation in America is a *fait accompli*. Wow. Our Second Wave knees buckle at the thought of Supreme Court Justices Alito, Scalia, Thomas, and Chief Justice Roberts, working together to protect the Constitution from the pollutions of reproductive freedom and from the "liberal" agenda of human rights. We wonder if we will live to see a female President of the United States or a female Vice-President. We're still waiting for sexual and gender parity in the political economy, the public political sphere, the arts, science and technology, the media, the Congress, the Supreme Court. We are aghast over the FDA's slow approval for the "morning after" pill for over-the-counter purchase and angered that some pharmacists refuse to fill the prescriptions. We are aghast that some citizens in this country would rather risk the lives of their female children than have them vaccinated against cervical cancer. We grieve for the environmental injustices imposed and inflicted on the women in developing countries, as well as at home. We-the-women of the Second Wave wonder, "Did we fail?" Postfeminism proclaims, *No worries—we're there!* We wonder, can generational differences alone account for the chasm between the Second Wave and postfeminism? No! Postfeminism works rhetorically to invent resistance to the goal of feminism—human rights for all.

We began this book, and we end this book, by drawing attention to how postfeminism diminishes our capacity for humane action in the world. Postfeminism is a clever smokescreen that distracts, divides, and diminishes us, using three inter-related strategies: historical disconnection; distortion of desire; and the aestheticizing of political incorrectness.

Let's begin with disconnection—from what, or whom? Strategies of disconnect are crucial to the success of public relations campaigns waged by patriarchal and capitalist interests. Forgetting the past is crucial for maintaining the contradictions between global hegemony and social justice. Forgetting the past is a necessary condition for the celebration of American moral superiority. Forgetting the past is the first step in dismantling legislative and judicial protections for human rights, which are costly and inconvenient for capitalist economies. Rhetorical appeals to collective amnesia, therefore, must be met head-on with the resistance of critical memory: the willfulness of counter-memory. The handing down of feminism from one generation to the next must of necessity be the handing down of a critical history of subjugation, struggle, and mistakes. This history must encompass what Cathy Caruth[1] calls the collisions of history between and among subjugated groups. The history of the subjugation of women must account for racial and sexual difference, for class privilege, and for variation in life experience. Twenty centuries of oppression teach us to be wary of claims that the battles are all won and that the struggle is over. Our experiences as mature women have taught us how challenging it is to bring to the table a diversified, inclusive agenda for women's freedom and empowerment.

Bear with us, sisters of the Third Wave, and all the brothers who support us, while we tell stories of hardship and endurance—of walking to school uphill both ways, in the snow, without shoes. These acts of critical remembrance are grounded in the realities of the contemporary American political economy, where anesthetizing images and messages seek to reassure us that all is well. Remember with us that throughout history, to be a woman was to be figured as the unforgivable body, a body so different that it required perpetual governance, control, scrutiny, and subjugation. To be a woman was to be a transgressor by fiat of existence. As De Beauvoir remarked wryly, almost sixty years ago, "we are exhorted to be women, remain women, become women."[2] Ontological transgressors, such as women and people of color, can seek forgiveness for our difference through redemptive disguises of costume, speech and conduct, living deeply fractured lives for the balance of our days. Or, we can refuse, refuse to cooperate, refuse to merge into or hide within the cultural systems that produce us as unforgivable.

Now, on the face of it, why would any of us agree to spend our lives redeeming ourselves from the original sin of being different? And that question brings us to the distortions of desire, the second element of the postfeminist smokescreen. Distortions of desire says, *let's play!* Postfeminism says, *lighten up— we don't need the seriousness anymore.* From cinematic reincarnations of *Charlie's Angels* I and II, *Bewitched,* and *The Stepford Wives* to television's *Ally McBeal, Buffy the Vampire Slayer* and *Sex and the City,* it does appear that girls just want to have fun. Playfulness is in and seriousness is seriously unfashionable. It would appear that once women can be characterized as international spies, demon killers, high-powered attorneys and sophisticated urbanites, they no longer need to think about the history of oppression. They have been liberated from the burdens of the past, from their mother memory—they are free to disconnect.

Consider the historical disconnect and distortions of desire in some of the recent characterizations of liberated females and their aspirations. The women of *Charlie's Angels* (redux) live independently of men, but they regard as the ultimate achievement giving up everything to settle down with a hunky guy in an ocean-side cottage with Pottery Barn décor. Similarly, happily-ever-after romance resolves the power struggle between a Barbie doll witch and a mortal man in the revisionist cinematic appropriation of *Bewitched*. Gone are the predictable, yet paradoxical, television plot entanglements produced by the actions of a powerful woman who consistently struggles and fails to subjugate herself to the stultifying constraints of suburban American. The remake of *Stepford Wives* blithely reduces the terror of female annihilation in the original story to parody, gender camp, and a battle-of-the-sexes romp. The memory of oppression is out and old-fashioned pleasures are in: romance, marriage, domesticity, and the reassuringly familiar gender wars of comedy.

What do the almost exclusively white, exclusively heterosexual, and economically privileged characterizations of liberated women do with their freedom? They kick butt, they make money, they talk about boys, they buy shoes, they wish for true love, they decorate their homes, and they obsess about food and their weight. Surely there is more to it. Well, yes. They also investigate the putative shortcomings of Second Wave feminism: our tedious binaries, our humorless rejection of conventional feminine drag, our inexplicable anxiety over female sexual power, our insistence on positioning feminism in the public political sphere. From the privileged position of economic empowerment, access to quality education, and professional fulfillment, these Anglophile, heteronormative characterizations question Second Wave rejection of mythic romance, conventional marriage, and queasiness over breeder mentality and motherhood.

Some of these characterizations, such as *Ally McBeal*, charge Second Wave feminism with betrayal, of having robbed generations of young women of their rightful inheritance of romance and mystification. In *Buffy the Vampire Slayer*, the principal character's Second Wave mother represents all that is clueless, uncool, and potentially dangerous about the older generation of women. In one episode, Buffy's mother and her generational cohort fall under a spell and attempt to ritually murder their daughters (burn them as witches). This thinly veiled allegory is perhaps the unkindest cut of all: Second Wave feminism has ruined it for subsequent generations of women.

Postfeminism advances the fraudulent twin claims that the history of female oppression is merely an exaggeration and that feminism is a dangerous social experiment perpetuated by a generation of self-absorbed man-haters. These rhetorical claims epitomize historical disconnect and either complicity with, or ignorance of, capitalist exploitation of women and minorities. Rhetorics of historical disconnection rob us of the ability to see clearly and ethically on pivotal issues of human rights and fundamental equity: women's rights, affirmative action and access to quality education, gay and lesbian rights, access to quality sex education and reliable birth control, access to quality health care, access to safe living conditions, environmental protections, humane labor practices, and racially equitable law enforcement practices.

A third and final element of the postfeminist smokescreen is the aesthetic of political incorrectness. The rhetorical and aesthetic style of postfeminist playfulness is irony, the irony born out of the postmodern fracturing of the grand narratives: the debacle of Vietnam and Watergate, the women's rights movement, the civil rights movement, the gay and lesbian rights movement. In postfeminism, postmodern irony is appropriated as an aesthetic of smirking deconstruction—nudge, nudge, wink, wink. The pleasurable aesthetic of political incorrectness has been popularized through television (e.g., *Beavis and Butthead, Married with Children, In Living Color, Seinfeld, South Park, The Family Guy, The Man Show, Ally McBeal,* and *Will and Grace*), film (e.g., *Pulp Fiction, Big Mamma, American Pie, Barber Shop, Be Cool,* and *The Forty Year Old Virgin*) and comedy (e.g., Jerry Seinfeld, Lewis Black, Chris Rock, Cedric the Entertainer). Without the burden of sexual and racial history, one can participate in ironically framed oppressive cultural practices: Audiences can laugh amiably over racially and sexually disparaging stories about bitches and hoes, niggas with attitude, flaming faggots, and germ phobic Jews. Cunt humor is vogue, cock humor is *de rigor,* and deprecating straight humor about gay men is the norm. The release of *Brokeback Mountain* precipitated a new idiom for straight male humor about male homosexuality, wherein the word "brokeback" has become synonymous with belittling usages of words like "queer," "fag," or "fucked up the ass." The kinder, gentler comedians, such as Jerry Seinfeld and Larry David, qualify their heterosexism with the palliative, "not that there's anything wrong with that."

Because the signifiers have been emptied out, rendered playful and amusing and daring, one can speak political incorrectness as an act of resistance to the alleged oppressiveness of feminism, civil rights, and the gay rights "agenda." Even the cutting-edge liberal critique of American politics within comedy programming such as *The Daily Show* and Rob Corddry's spin-off program relish their adolescent bad-boy sexual humor that shares with *The Man Show* a similar, though more sophisticated, (hetero)sexism. This sort of humor used to be called "snickering," which denoted immaturity, mockery, incivility, and cruelty. Irony, coupled with distorted desire and historical disconnection, constitutes the contemporary practice of snickering. Those not joining in on the joke are branded as humorless, dour, too serious, and/or politically correct. The next move, by the jokesters, is to proclaim that humorlessness, seriousness, and political correctness are oppressive practices, robbing citizens of their right to exercise free speech. As Angela McRobbie puts it, "[o]bjection is pre-empted with irony."[3] And so we come full circle. The benefits of liberation facilitate the move to ahistoricism and unencumbered consumption; complaints about that move are framed as violations of free speech or pettiness. That's pretty slick hegemony.

We note, for the record, that representations of the lives of girls and young women have begun to appear more frequently in television and film. But the limited range of plot and characterization is disappointing and sometimes disturbing. Many of the stories represent, but do not explore or explain, the pathologies produced through conventional gendering and consumerism. *Mean Girls* is a comic update of earlier and darker films such as *Heathers*, *The Craft*, and *Cruel Intentions* where girls and young women prey upon each other and weak boys. *Thirteen* offers up a narrative about scandalous female adolescent self-destructiveness, much like the films *Girl Interrupted* and *The Virgin Suicides*. These films showcase disturbing female behaviors such as self-mutilation, thrill shoplifting, conspicuous consumption, drug abuse, sexual experimentation, cruelty, manipulation, self-loathing, incest, murder, and suicide. However, the films focus far more attention on pathological behaviors than on the cultural contexts from which those behaviors emanate. In that sense, the films offer little more than voyeurism.

We question whether these narratives represent significant improvement over the films that shaped our sense of possibilities as girls and young women. We remember popular narratives about female sexuality and reproduction before *Roe v. Wade* and before oral contraception. The female characters were destroyed, murdered, ostracized, or trapped in loveless marriages. The message was clear: sexual transgression equals death, madness, or despair. Some of these stories have stayed with us our entire adult lives. We can recount the scenes from memory: Jennifer Jones playing the role of a sexually aggressive bi-racial woman in *Duel in the Sun*, doomed from the outset of the narrative by miscegenation and her sexual desire for a rich man's son. Natalie Wood characterizing a confused, virginal teenager who attempts suicide in *Splendor in the Grass* because she is trapped between virtue and desire, surviving only to settle for a conventional marriage to a man for whom she feels no passion. Elizabeth Taylor's Academy Award winning performance in *Butterfield 8* where her character's sexual appetites lead to a life of prostitution, illicit affairs with married men, and ultimately suicide. Our list of cautionary tales about the perils of female sexuality is a long one. The ones we remember best are *Peyton Place*, *A Place in the Sun*, *A Summer Place*, and *Strangers When We Meet*. Even the "fun" films such as *Where the Boys Are* and *Gidget* warned about the dangers of female sexual passion and sex outside of marriage. Doris Day films ritually enacted the norm that devotion to heterosexual marriage and family was the only way to navigate the shoals of female sexual desire.

And don't get us started on the films that appeared *after* the so-called sexual revolution where women were *really* punished for their sexual desires. We name *Looking for Mr. Goodbar* as the apotheosis of gruesome stories where women who transgress (have careers and casual sex, reject marriage and children) are destroyed (in one fashion or another). Many of us were profoundly traumatized by *Goodbar*'s snuff-film *mise-en-scene* and editing. A very young Diane Keaton characterizes an unmarried schoolteacher who smokes pot and picks up men in bars and is stabbed to death by her bi-sexual male lover. We watched in astonishment and horror as her death agony was represented visually through strobe lighting and skip-frame editing. The warning was not lost on us; sexual transgression equals death.

Our choice for the honorable-mention misogyny film is *Dressed to Kill* where Angie Dickenson's sexually transgressive character has her throat slashed by her transgendered male psychiatrist. Little wonder that Laura Mulvey theorized the male gaze in the cultural context of post-sexual revolution cinema. Mind you, these lurid stories merely updated a long history of cinematic representation of transgressive women who were destroyed: tragic mulattos who tried to pass (*Imitation of Life*), lesbians who failed to live lives of celibacy (*The Children's Hour*), business entrepreneurs who abandoned the domestic sphere (*Mildred Pierce*). Third Wave sisters, walk a mile in our cinematic history and you'll better understand why we are more than a little conflicted about representations of female sexuality, heterosexual marriage, femininity, and retribution for transgression. And, you'll understand why Sigourney Weaver's "Ripley," Linda Hamilton's "Sarah," and Jodie Foster's "Clarice" were transformative characterizations of transgressive women—even as we saw the shortcomings of those stories. What a welcome relief to see female characters who thought clearly in the face of danger, fought back against predatory violence, and provided moral leadership in times of trouble.

We recognize, of course, that Ripley, Sarah, and Clarice were embodied by white women, and given the paucity and narrowness of black representation in American popular culture, it matters that icons of positive female transgression were and are whitened. Our sisters of color pointed out the failure of Mulvey and others to include the viewing experiences of black women in the theorizing of the cinematic male gaze. bell hooks, in particular, argues that black women did not and do not necessarily identify with representations of female whiteness, nor with the particular concerns of white feminists working in film studies.[4] Her book addressing these shortcomings, *Black Looks,* is aptly titled.

Have we really come a long way, baby, in current cinematic representations of women's lives? We are told, repeatedly, by our associates and our students that women today have much more powerful roles in cinema. In our classrooms, students proffer a predictable list of "yeah, but what about…" female characterizations to lay waste to our claims that feminism has been subverted through postfeminism: Demi Moore in *Charlie's Angels II*, Halle Berry in *Catwoman*, Angelina Jolie in *Tomb Raider* and Uma Thurman in *Kill Bill I* and *II*. Students who take more than one class from us come to know the questions we will raise about such claims. Based on conversations with our students, we offer our response to the "yes, but" claims that representations of women have come a long way in American popular cinema.

We begin with Demi Moore's body which is itself emblematic of the distortions of desire: well publicized breast implants, aestheticized fecund belly on the cover of *Vanity Fair*, spectacular body building for *G.I. Jane*, and surgical reconstruction for *Charlie's Angels II*. Students (male *and* female) delight to the scene where Demi emerges, Venus-like, from the surf. They admire the "work" (their word) Demi has done re-crafting her body because they celebrate the "body project" culture of American consumerism.[5] At the same time, they sneer at Moore's body of work (pun intended), much as they smirk at Madonna's early videos. Our younger students do not know the history of previous generations of women in Hollywood culture; they have never heard of Jean Harlow, Marilyn Monroe, Dorothy Dandridge, Billie Holliday, or Jane Mansfield—only a handful of the many who did not survive their body projects. They do not know the significance of women having control over their careers, bodies and lives—especially in the popular culture industry. Our younger students take for granted the identity politics popularized by Madonna's provocative playfulness and Demi Moore's appropriation of the Pygmalion myth—iconic women perpetually making and re-making themselves. Lacking historical context for their worldviews, students do not see in Madonna and Moore the pioneering female entertainers who helped fuel the imagination of Third Wave feminism; they see only forty-something female bodies that are always already under reconstruction. They admire the body project even as they disconnect from the historical context that produced the possibilities and constraints for those projects.

We also ask our students to consider the significance of film narrative closure in *Charlie's Angels II*. Moore's character rejected patriarchal control of women's labor, telling "Charlie" that she worked for herself, not him. Predictably, she dies a spectacular death precisely because she has challenged established order. We can name dozens of films where male characters survive and thrive when positioned similarly (e.g., Matt Damon in *The Bourne Supremacy* and *The Bourne Ultimatum*). Moore's aggressive, aging "angel" perishes (literally consumed by flames) because she cannot be domesticated or rehabilitated into a more consumer-friendly femininity characterized through the next generation of angels.

Halle Berry's characterization of Catwoman invites and confronts the male gaze, we admit. Students admire her body project and they read Berry's embodied performance as emblematic of female sexual power and racial progressiveness. Our white students in particular resist and resent our efforts to contextualize Berry through a racial history of representation. Historical connection (rather than disconnection) opens the possibility of reading Berry's embodied performance as a cultural stereotype—the belief that black women are hyper-sexual, aggressive, and wild.[6] If the history lesson is unsuccessful, then we try a direct comparison between Berry and Michelle Pfieffer in *Batman Returns*. We ask our students to compare differences in story arc, *mise-en-scene*, camera framing, and editing of these two characterizations of Catwoman. Jaws drop, minds open, and animated discussion flows.

Some of our students groan when we argue that Angelina Jolie's characterization of Laura Croft is a heterosexual adolescent male wet dream, a comic book dominatrix marked by eroticized violence, phallic weapon play, and gratuitous thigh and ass shots. Killing her male lover near the end of the narrative is the ultimate soft-core "money shot," fulfilling mythic fantasies of the sexually voracious black widow. Similarly, Uma Thurman's characterization of female homicidal violence in *Kill Bill* is Quentin Tarantino's fantasy of eroticized violence. The bitch fight between two aggressive female characters at the end of *Kill Bill II* is a quintessential comic book sexual fantasy.

Are these representations pleasurable? Yes, even for us because it still is so rare in *any* narrative context to see powerful female bodies driving the narrative forward. Do our students understand that these representations of transgressive women are "merely" fantasies? Yes. They explain this to us patiently; *it's just a movie, professor*. So what's the problem? Are we too serious? Humorless? Politically correct? Have we become, in the words of Brian Ott, "like a bad 1970s situation comedy—its outcome simple, banal, predictable"?[7] Worse yet, have we become "boring"?[8]

Ott argues in one of the early issues of *Communication and Critical/Cultural Studies* that critical scholars should embrace what he calls an "erotics of reading" rather than looking for hegemony in all the usual places (which he maintains is like shooting fish in a barrel). Echoing John Fiske, Ott wants critical scholars to approach texts the way he imagines viewers might and the way he believes Barthes recommends: "Barthes is suggesting that all discourses be treated as unfinished and that critics attend to the abrasions and ruptures that readers impose upon their surfaces."[9] Critics should imagine the myriad ways viewers might enact agency in their pleasurable engagement with visual texts. Too often,

Ott argues, the search for hegemony "fixes" a text and "passes judgment on it. In passing such judgments, ideological criticism has replaced one doxa with another, and become the latest (if more fashionable) site of ideological constraint."[10] Ott reads Barthes as proposing more playfulness and less orthodoxy on the part of the critic.

We appreciate Ott's weariness with the production of predictable, formulaic criticism. We agree that critical orthodoxies spring up where we least expect them, especially in what is supposed to be libratory and emancipatory intellectual work. The academy is notorious for producing and policing boundaries and critical and cultural studies is no exception. That said, however, we maintain that the preferred position in most American media texts enables a human agency that supports consumerism and capitalism. Good criticism (which is neither boring nor predictable) maps what Stuart Hall calls the paths of articulation, excavates what Foucault calls discursive formations, and discovers what Barthes (in his early work) called myth.[11] Teaching ourselves and our students to locate and understand the connections between political economies and social constructs is crucial to the possibility of maintaining a democratic society in a consumer culture.

We also find that Ott's reading of theory (of Barthes) is oddly detached from the historical moments and the intellectual politics that produced the theory. As we have argued throughout this book, the death throes of the unified white masculine subject have given rise to postmodern irony and the possibilities for recouping lost masculine privilege. The slick hegemony we see at work in postfeminism exemplifies the point.

In all of the film and television examples provided above, characterized women are imagined within the cultural spaces of postfeminism and postmodern irony: The stories and characterizations are marketed as "liberated," yet women characters desire conventional fulfillment, or they provide erotic titillation for audiences, or both. Constructions of female desire in the narratives suggest that women have all the power they need or want, that all women need and desire romance (with men), and that sexual playfulness has replaced sexual oppression. All of the films participate in an aesthetic of violence that supplants other possibilities for resolving human conflicts. Each film participates in historical disconnect, distortions of desire, and the aesthetics of political incorrectness.

Finally, we question the conflation of *individual* experiences of empowerment (e.g., oppositional reading) with *collective* empowerment (a necessity for the advancement of human rights). Ott builds his arguments on the basis of the imagined subject who constructs his or her worldview through appreciation of "the endless play of the signifier."[12] This notion of play aligns nicely with consumer culture's focus on individuation—choice of product, service, technology, and identity. Identity construction becomes the primary focus of agency; agency is pleasure; pleasure is play. Can such pleasures, such play, support the fight for human (collective) rights? As we have stated elsewhere in the book, we are doubtful, but hopeful. In our lifetimes, play was not an option for achieving legislation and other guarantees for equality and access to full citizenship.

One of the most potent arenas of play in contemporary popular culture is the re-flowering of the princess mythology and the Cinderella fantasy, embraced and nourished by the culture of postfeminism. Since the time when we were girls growing up with the original versions of *Cinderella* and *Sleeping Beauty*, the Disney corporation literally has re-animated the princess mythology of female desire: *Beauty and the Beast*, *The Little Mermaid*, and *Pocahontas*, just to name a few. Touchstone Pictures' *Pretty Woman* combined the Cinderella myth and the Pygmalion story to become a cultural phenomenon for young women and girls in 1990, concurrent with *Thelma and Louise* and *The Silence of the Lambs*. Countless princess films have followed suit, more recently, Anne Hathaway's characterizations in *The Princess Diaries* I and II and *The Devil Wears Prada*.

As our readers are probably well aware, the Second Wave rejected the pedestal (with the crown), as well as the hearth. As Amy Taubin said of Clarice Starling in *The Silence of the Lambs*, we wanted to *rescue* the princess—we didn't want to *be* the princess.[13] We didn't want the tiara; we wanted the mantle of governing authority. We didn't believe in the myth of Prince Charming and we didn't want to be the beauty who tamed the beast. We wanted mature, healthy relationships—with men *and* women. We didn't want the Pygmalion makeover; we wanted the law degree, the political appointment, the science grant.

Embracing your inner princess, we are told by characterized women and girls in *nouveau* princess films, is harmless fun, satisfying play. In the end, the girl gets the career goal she seeks, *and* the hunky boyfriend, *and* loses weight, *and* learns to accessorize. Hathaway's characterizations have come a long way since Julia Roberts's career-making role as a hooker with a heart of gold. Hathaway's updated characterization is socially conscious, college educated, professionally independent, and ultimately, a fashion icon. *So what's wrong with that?* Let's trace the pattern of articulation.

In *The Devil Wears Prada*, the female heroine (Anne Hathaway) takes a job in high fashion only because she cannot get a job as a journalist. Dumpy, dowdy and aesthetically challenged (the ugly duckling), she blunders into a coveted job with the editor of a top fashion magazine. Most viewers anticipate with pleasure that she will be transformed into a swan; they are not disappointed. At the same time, Hathaway's character rejects the culture of high fashion because she is too morally principled to participate in merciless exploitation and betrayal. She abruptly quits her job at the high fashion magazine and takes a job with a legitimate newspaper that will respect her interests in labor unions. She then gains back the weight, goes back to wearing polyester blends, and throws away the fuck-me boots. Well, no. Rather, she has evolved into a svelte, chic, well-accessorized, and confident "serious" journalist. *So? What's wrong with looking stylish whilst writing about the less fortunate?* Let's look at the contradictions that the mythology fails to conceal.

We know early in the story that this young woman is determined to do serious journalism about labor issues. Yet, viewers are never burdened by what she might have to say about the sweatshops that produce the clothing and accessories for high couture (e.g., *Real Women Have Curves*). Rather, we spend two hours reveling in the guilty pleasures of high fashion, which we know we should resist. Moreover, our protagonist smugly rejects high fashion only *after* she has mastered the cultural codes of wardrobe and accessories, skin care, and hair styling. The final scene of the film tracks her walking through the city, much as it might track the runway walk of a newly crowned beauty queen. The unintended paradox in the film epitomizes the culture of postfeminism—lip service to political engagement and steadfast commitment to the pleasures of play and consumption.

The Teflon surface of these communicative practices facilitates powerful resistance to critical efforts to debunk or deconstruct resistance to feminism and critical race consciousness. With our students, we facilitate flexible exploration and discussion of media artifacts in an effort to expose the rhetorical slipperiness of postfeminism, postmodern irony, and ideologically constructed pleasures. We will concede that ideological criticism has fulfilled its mission when our students (and all our colleagues) embrace feminism. Until then, we find purpose and pleasure in living to heckle capitalism another day.

Sisters and brothers who support us, our tasks as teachers, historians, critics, theorists, and political activists are vital to the health of the republic. As beneficiaries of liberation, we ourselves should gladly shoulder the burden of history. We should engage in willful acts of transgressive memory: We occupy bodies that have for centuries been zones of occupation by patriarchal interests. We lived as second-class citizens in Jeffersonian democracy before the Constitution was amended to include us. During much of that time, our black and brown sisters had the legal status of chattel. Our labor has been forced, stolen, uncompensated, and under valued. Our bodies have been objectified, commodified, violated and pathologized. We have been under-represented and misrepresented; we have suffered from image theft. And even so, women have overcome, women have prospered, women have progressed toward equality and achievement.

Feminism *matters*. It matters that we tell stories and write histories about the mothers. It matters that future generations of girls and women have access to a diverse range of stories about female lives. It matters that we safeguard the hard won liberties that women now enjoy: reproductive rights, equal opportunity employment, medical research on female health, access to education (particularly in science and technology), and access to military careers. It matters that women become key players in the American political scene—equal in rank and numbers to their male colleagues. It matters that women see themselves as engaged, responsible citizens.

It matters that we guard the practice of feminism the way powerful men guard the Constitution of the United States: We are a groundswell human rights organization; we go where the women are; we help all people who suffer inequality; we support equality of access to the benefits and privileges of citizenship; we strive to become better citizens of the world; we work for justice and peace; we work to preserve the environment. It matters that even as we enjoy the benefits of a capital economy, we never let the comforts obscure our vision for equity, peace, and a stable environment. It matters that we are *not* taken in by the slick smugness of smirking deconstruction. Feminism? *It matters*.

With affection,

The Second Wave Mothership

Notes

[1] Cathy Caruth, "Unclaimed Experience: Trauma and the Possibility of History," *Yale French Studies* 79 (1991): 181–192.
[2] Simone De Beauvoir, *The Second Sex*, tran. and ed. H.M. Parshley (New York: Vintage Books, 1989; New York: Alfred A. Knopf, Inc., 1952) xix.
[3] Angela McRobbie, "Post-Feminism and Popular Culture," *Feminist Media Studies* 4.3 (2004): 259.
[4] bell hooks, *Black Looks* (Boston: South End Press, 1992).
[5] Joan Jacobs Brumberg, *The Body Project: An Intimate History of American Girls* (New York: Random House, 1997). Brumberg is an historian. She argues convincingly that young women and girls in contemporary American society regard their bodies as "projects" that require continual updating, revision, and transformation. These projects, of course, require full participation in commodity culture.

6 See bell hooks, *Black Looks*; Stuart Hall, *Representation: Cultural Representations and Signifying Practices* (London: Sage Publications, 1997), esp. Chapter 4.

7 Brian Ott, "(Re)Locating Pleasure in Media Studies: Toward an Erotics of Reading," *Communication and Critical/Cultural Studies* 1.2 (2006): 194–212.

8 Ott 195.

9 Ott 204.

10 Ott 206.

11 Stuart Hall, "The Rediscovery of 'ideology': Return of the repressed in Media Studies," *Culture, Society and the Media*, eds. Michael Gurevitch, Tony Bennett, James Curran and Janet Wollacott (New York: Methuen, 1982) 56–90; Michel Foucault, *Discipline and Punish: The Birth of the Prison*, trans. Alan Sheridan (New York: Vintage Books, 1979). Roland Barthes, *Mythologies*, trans. Annette Lavers (New York: Hill and Wang, 1957).

12 Ott 206.

13 This is our paraphrase of Taubin's comment: "Clarice's mission is not to marry the prince but to rescue the maiden…[o]n that reversal her identity rests." Amy Taubin, "Grabbing the Knife: 'The Silence of the Lambs' and the History of the Serial Killer Movie," *Women and Film: A Sight and Sound Reader*, eds. Pam Cook and Philip Dodd (Philadelphia: Temple UP, 1995) 130.

Index

POLITICAL COMMUNICATION

FRONTIERS IN

General Editors
Lynda Lee Kaid and Bruce Gronbeck

At the heart of how citizens, governments, and the media interact is the communication process, a process that is undergoing tremendous changes as we embrace a new millennium. Never has there been a time when confronting the complexity of these evolving relationships been so important to the maintenance of civil society. This series seeks books that advance the understanding of this process from multiple perspectives and as it occurs in both institutionalized and non-institutionalized political settings. While works that provide new perspectives on traditional political communication questions are welcome, the series also encourages the submission of manuscripts that take an innovative approach to political communication, which seek to broaden the frontiers of study to incorporate critical and cultural dimensions of study as well as scientific and theoretical frontiers.

For more information or to submit material for consideration, contact:

BRUCE E. GRONBECK
Obermann Center for Advanced Studies
N134 OH
The University of Iowa
Iowa City, IA 52242-5000

LYNDA LEE KAID
Political Communication Center
Department of Communication
University of Oklahoma
Norman, OK 73109

To order other books in this series, please contact our Customer Service Department:

(800) 770-LANG (within the U.S.)
(212) 647-7706 (outside the U.S.)
(212) 647-7707 FAX

Or browse online by series:
WWW.PETERLANG.COM